Minna; A Novel from the Danish of Karl Gjellerup

C. L. Nielsen

BIBLIOLIFE

Minna

A Novel

From the Danish of

Karl Gjellerup

Author of
"The Pilgrim Kamanita"

Translated by C. L. Nielsen

London
William Heinemann
1913

"HEU ! QUANTO MINUS EST CUM RELIQUIS VERSARI QUAM TUI
MEMINISSE !"   SHENSTONE.

("TO LIVE WITH THEM IS FAR LESS SWEET THAN TO REMEMBER
THEE.")   TH. MOORE.

*As I perused a copy of Thomas Moore's " Irish Melodies,"
bequeathed to me, with some more favourite books (English
and German classics), by my late friend Harald Fenger, I
found this " exquisite inscription " strongly underlined with
pencil. So I thought it fit to place it as a motto at the head of
these recollections of his love-story, the manuscript of which he
confided to my care before he died in London. His death,
I am half-happy, half-sorry to say, took place not many
years after he had lost his beloved Minna. Indeed the fear
which she mentioned in her letter to Stephensen, that Fenger's
chest was not strong, proved to be less unfounded than he
himself supposed. It was also thought probable by his doctor
that the heart-wound, of which these pages tell, added fuel to
the complaint from which he was already suffering.*

KARL GJELLERUP.

DRESDEN, *August* 1912.

BOOK I

CHAPTER I

THE Term at the Polytechnic had been rather tiring. Dresden had begun to grow unbearably hot, and, to make matters worse, I was living at the time in one of the smaller streets of the " old city," which was not exactly airy, though clean and well-kept. I often felt a home-sick longing for the Danish " Sund." The evenings by the Elbe, though beautiful, brought hardly any refreshing coolness, and the thermometer still showed some eighty-eight degrees, even as late as between nine and ten p.m., when I dragged myself, gasping for a breath of air, up the steps of old Brühl's famous terrace. In a way it was consoling, as it proved that I had an undoubted right to feel hot, and that it was an excusable luxury to take an ice-cream outside the Café Torniamenti, while I sat between the columns and listened to snatches of the concert in the " Wienergarten," on the opposite side of the river.

It was on such an evening that I made the bold decision to go into the country during the approaching summer holidays. To myself, at any rate, this decision appeared rather daring, as I was both obliged and accustomed to live very economically. The thought occurred to me that I would go to Saxon-Switzerland, and the last morsel of ice-cream had not melted in my mouth when I had decided upon the little hamlet of Rathen. Dear, tiny nook that it was, it had left upon me the impression of a rarely tender idyll, though, like most travellers, I had only seen it in passing, and then in the twilight, when coming down from the Bastei.

Towards noon, a few days later, I alighted at the little railway station, and walked past the fruit gardens down to the ferry. In this part the Elbe goes winding round cultivated land, which gradually rises into undulating country, dark with pine woods and overhung by rocks, while gently sloping down towards the river. Here lies Upper-Rathen with its substantial, if somewhat scattered farms, and a thin network of fruit trees spreads over the cornfields and green meadows. The opposite side is one long chain of mountains with but a single break in the middle, a small valley disclosing the unimportant village of Lower-Rathen, of which scarcely anything is to be seen but the two inns—the bare new one, and the overgrown old one—lying one on each side of the brook which runs sparkling into the river as it glides swiftly by. To the left of this valley rise the bluish-grey towering rocks of the Bastei, covered down towards the base with woods of pine and beech; these are succeeded by shining sandstone quarries, the most beautiful in the whole country, a series of lofty, yellow walls, some of which rise to a height of several hundred feet. In contrast to these, the quarries on the farther side of the village lie along the base of the hills like one unbroken wall of rock, above which rolls a sea of forests with Lilienstein floating therein—a gigantic man-of-war.

The ferry boat went slantingly, just like a dog, across the current that propelled it forward. It was fixed to a chain, with a barrel midway as float, the farther end of the chain being anchored far up the stream, and in order to obtain the desired motion and direction the ferryman only needed once or twice to tighten the connection chain which ran through a pulley in the little mast. The downward force of the current, acting on the broadside of the boat, did all the work.

Notwithstanding this, the man constantly wiped the perspiration with his shirt sleeve from his face, which was so sunburnt that he seemed to me to be more like a Red Indian than the Sioux-Indians themselves, whom I had seen the evening before in the Zoological Gardens. But here, in the middle of his domain, one could not wonder at his appearance, as the glittering water around seemed rather to shed heat than coolness, and the whole curved bank of the river with its rocky walls opened to the south like a concave mirror, whose point of focus lay in front of Rathen. The ferryman and I agreed that I had not chosen a cool spot. But it was not far to the shaded, well-wooded glens ; besides which I do not easily change my mind when it is once made up. Perchance, on this occasion, the finger of destiny also played a part. The event proved of sufficient importance for Fate to have intervened. At any rate, if I afterwards regretted that I did not allow myself to be frightened away, it was not on account of the heat. And have I ever regretted it ? Even to this very day—it is now five years ago—I am unable to answer this question.

Some author or other—I should even say, were I asked, a very famous one—has said, that in hours of sorrow nothing is so sad as the remembrance of happy days. Of course I have not the courage to dispute the truth of his words, especially as they have been so often repeated that they are almost proverbial, otherwise I should have thought that, in such hours, it would be still sadder if one had no happy moments upon which to look back. And in this frame of mind I will recall, as well as I can, the days of Rathen and those which followed.

To find a lodging was the first difficulty that presented itself. The two inns had only the most inferior rooms left, and these at rather high terms. I was driven from pillar to post, and had many times to cross the little brook and ascend the tiny wooden steps, from the shoemaker's on the one side to the baker's on the other, back again to the watchman, and then again over to the grocer's; but either the lodging was let or else two rooms went together, and to pay for two rooms was more than I could afford. In the end the school-house, which lay far back on the outskirts of the pine woods, remained as my last hope.

As it was not school time, I knocked boldly at the door of the master's private apartments. A small boy answered the knock. He did not know, he said, whether the master was at home, and having vanished for a moment he suddenly flew past me up the stairs, to appear almost instantaneously with a pair of boots in his hand; then again he darted away, to return triumphantly with a coat. Soon afterwards the schoolmaster appeared, equipped in this outfit, with a half-sleepy and half-comical smile on his open, good-natured face. Quite right, he had two rooms to let, but they were only let together and at the rent of two guineas a month. I apologised for having given him useless trouble, and he consoled me with the hope that I might get a single room in the new *Pension-Villa* next door.

The villa, which I now approached, looked very smart; the green shutters were thrown back from the windows, creepers covered the walls, and the verandah was well shaded by foliage. It stood on high ground, and the garden, which I had already entered, consisted of a series of terraces connected by gravelled pathways between flowering shrubs. But notwithstanding that the very attractions of the place made it somewhat alarming to a poor, Polytechnic student, I still determined to accept the smallest of the attics, regardless of cost, if this palace would take me in at all ; for I was heartily disgusted with running about, as I had been doing, and knocking at all doors.

Then, however, a party of ladies and gentlemen appeared on the verandah, and the house looked to me less and less like a *Pension*. Indeed, I felt relieved when a maid, who, at a turn of the path, nearly ran into me, rescued me from my dilemma, though in a very superior and mocking way, by saying—

" No, indeed, we do not let rooms here, the house you are seeking can be seen at the very top of the hill."

So far it had been hidden by the house before me, and I was by no means enchanted when I caught sight of it, for it stood out with a certain bold nakedness against the blue sky, and, as a matter of fact, with hardly so much as a bush to shelter it. Altogether it looked so brand new that I felt convinced that it could never have been inhabited.

I had again to pass down the valley, to cross over the stream, and crawl about a hundred and fifty feet up an arrangement of paths and stone steps to the edge of the hill. The house did not look more habitable on a nearer view ; heaps of gravel, pieces of stone and planks were scattered about, and most of the windows had still to be finished. On entering I encountered a horrible draught, the door banged to, and from the basement I heard a coarse woman's voice hurling forth the many - worded curses and oaths used in vulgar German. A man was hearthstoning the steps, evidently for the first time. A young girl, who was scrubbing the floor in a passage, turned her head at my entrance and showed a pretty pale face with a red spot on one cheek, as if she had just received a smart slap. On my asking for the landlord or landlady, she ran quickly away and disappeared into the basement, leaving the marks of her bare feet upon the sawdust which covered the floor. Soon afterwards she returned, and was followed by a portly-looking woman, whose wide mouth had evidently been the outlet for the oaths I had heard, and whose clumsy palms, which she was wiping in her apron, had, I suspected, been in all too close contact with the girl's cheek. Her turned-up skirt showed her bare bow-legs and flat, sprawling feet.

"You want a room, sir?" she said. "Well, you're just in time, if it has to be a single one. Get along with your scrubbing, you young drab, you, it isn't you who has to show the gentleman about, is it? It's on the second floor, please."

We came into a rather spacious room, light and airy enough, for as yet no glass had been placed in the windows. Even the frames were not painted ; and the walls, though covered with grey paper, still showed patches of damp, and, in spite of the airiness, I thought the place smelt more than a little fusty.

But before I could make any remark about this she began to praise the perfection of the room, speaking of the satisfaction of former lodgers, notwithstanding that both of us knew perfectly well the house had never been inhabited. I asked for the terms, which were ten shillings more than I had intended to give. She protested that it was a bargain, and that her house was both better and

less expensive than any one else's. There was none of the
mist from the river with which the people down by the
Elbe were troubled, and one also avoided the closeness
of the valley. At such a height I should breathe pure
Swiss air and have the best view in the village ; lastly,
there were the shady promenades belonging to the house,
where the lodgers might walk when they did not care to
go farther. She always returned to " them shady promenades," and in so doing spread out her dirty arms to
indicate their extent, always repeating the words " *da'rim
und dort'nim*" (over here and over there).

In the end we split the difference, and she promised
that everything should be quite ready in a week, when
my holidays began. I gave her half a crown as deposit,
and, very happy to have settled matters, I left her.

As I walked away from the house I was bound to admit
that the woman's praise of the view was correct. On the
right one saw a richly wooded stretch of valley surrounded
by mountains ; straight ahead lay a by-path leading from
the town to the cosy saw-mill, at the entrance to the " Blackbirds' Glen," which, with its green fir trees and grey rocks,
soon hid the clear water. To the left, the bend of the Elbe
valley opened out under the sun-scorched stone quarries,
which cast their reflection over the river, where several
rafts and a couple of boats were slowly gliding down with
the current. Below lay all the cottages, either built
entirely of wood or at least timber-framed, with thatched
roofs, and for the most part overgrown with vines. Luckily
there was only one other villa to be seen besides the two
already mentioned, and it was modestly hidden away.
The blue smoke rose from all the chimneys in curling
wreaths, forming a thin veil right across the valley, through
which glittered the brook between silvery willow trees and

sombre alders. How idyllic and how very German it all was! I felt so indescribably happy at the prospect of being able to live for a whole month surrounded by this loveliness, that unconsciously I began to sing—

"Guten Morgen, schöne Müllerin."

With the same lack of consciousness I stopped again so that I might take deep breaths of this fresh and fragrant air—" Swiss air "—as the woman had called it, and then I laughed when I thought of "them wonderful shady promenades," for from the spot on which I was standing, I could only see scattered fruit trees on the high-lying fields, and close to the incline a couple of birch trees, the long trailing branches of which caused the leaves to quiver and glitter in the sunshine.

After taking a small meal at the "Erbgericht" on the terrace overlooking the Elbe, I sought the waiter and discovered him talking to my acquaintance, the schoolmaster. The latter was smoking a pipe ornamented with big tassels and a couple of burrs of a deer's horn, evidently his pride, and of which no student need have been ashamed. The tobacco smelt very good and it was, as he afterwards told me, the real old Alstädter; and he drank Münchener-beer, altogether sure signs of a man with refined tastes and habits. He at once greeted me and congratulated me on having found a lodging. I couldn't, he said, have chosen a better spot in the whole of Saxon-Switzerland; there were plenty of unexplored nooks, and I had only to apply to him for advice. He then asked me to what country I belonged, and when he heard that I was a Dane, he remarked that he also had been in Denmark in 1864, evidently without intending to make himself disagreeable, but only with the object of finding a common subject of interest, in

which he succeeded, as I was well acquainted with the
surroundings of Kolding, where for a long time he had been
quartered. He now became quite excited, questioning
me as to whether I remembered this farm and that house,
this forest and those hills, and with the mouth-piece of his
pipe he pointed out on the coloured table-cloth the position
of the different places. He was most anxious to know
whether the stout Ole Larsen was still in possession of the
farm with the outbuildings of stone and the green fence, or
whether his son Hans had succeeded to the property—for he
and the son had been together in the hospital at Flensburg.

He then talked of the battle in which he had been
wounded.

I cannot say that this conversation was either pleasant
or unpleasant, but there was something both attractive and
straightforward in the way the German spoke of bygone
days. It was agreeable to feel how little personal ani-
mosity such a war had left, though all the same I had a
feeling that everything was not as it ought to be.

I therefore took advantage of a short pause to ask
who owned the smart villa, into the grounds of which I had
wandered.

"It belongs to the Kammerherr von Zedlitz. He lives
here every summer, when he is not with the King at Pill-
nitz. A distinguished family who live in a rather secluded
manner, but who give a considerable amount to the school
fund. But, my word, they have a governess, well, you will
see for yourself, she *is* a pretty girl. Slightly related to
me—not that I know much about her. In fact she is very
retiring, and I only wish she was less so."

Just then the whistle from the river steamer sounded,
and, having said good-bye to the schoolmaster, I hurried
down to the bridge.

CHAPTER II

A WEEK later, at eight o'clock in the morning, I set out.

As usual I came on board at the last minute, and we had already reached the Albert Bridge when, after getting rid of my luggage, I began to look round. The town showed its characteristic profile ; the beautiful towers over Brühls Terrace stood out well against the clear sky, while overhead it was misty, and in front of us rather dark. The air was chilly, so I unfastened my travelling plaid. As we steamed past the three castles the town could scarcely be seen, and on reaching Loschwitz, rain began to fall. That is to say, it did not exactly rain, but . . .

" Well, it is just drizzling a bit," said a stout " Dräsener " to his better half, who put her head out of the cabin door with an inquiring look.

When we stopped nearly opposite, at Blasewitz, the newcomers at once went down into the saloon, and the ladies disappeared from the soaked deck. The men also soon left, one after another. The dismal truth could not be hidden any longer—it was pouring !

I lit a cigar and went to the smoking-saloon, which was filled with people and fumes of tobacco. The weather was the only topic of conversation. A long-haired professor, who was taking his *Frühschoppen*, held forth, saying, that when, after such heat, rain began to fall at this period of the year, it would not be fine again until September. All this time the rain was pattering on the roof, and when it ceased to patter it began to splash. It became so gloomy that one felt almost blinded in the unnatural darkness. Through the cabin windows, over which the water was running, one could scarcely see the vine-terraces and gardens on the banks of the river.

When I had finished my cigar I went to the saloon, in which not a seat was to be found, and it was so stuffy that I did not feel inclined to bring a camp-stool there, but went out into the lobby, where the stairs led up to the deck. A young lady, with two little girls, had seated herself here. I took down a camp-stool from the pile and, well wrapped up in my plaid, placed myself just opposite the stairs.

The fresh, damp air coming down was pleasant, though it often brought a shower-bath, the drops of which remained clinging to the woollen plaid. The upper steps were dripping with water ; a pool had collected in a corner of a black tarpaulin which was spread over some luggage on deck, and a miniature fountain kept spirting up from it.

The young lady, seated on the other side of the saloon door, took a little book from her bag, and was soon lost to all around her.

She did not, however, have much peace, for the smaller child, an overdressed little girl, with flaxen curls, began to cry, and though, in a way, it was appropriate to the situation, the governess had to pacify her. " Lisbeth wants to hear more," the bigger girl said, and the little one confirmed this suggestion by tearfully saying, " More about Peter ! More about Peter ! "

" Oh, for shame, to let the strange gentleman see you like this, Lisbeth ! " the lady whispered. " Do you think *he* cares to hear about Peter ? "

The little one sobbed, sucked her forefinger, and looked

at me with large, discontented eyes. The look, which so clearly said, " Why can't he go away ? " made me very uncomfortable. I felt an intruder, and feared to make matters difficult for the fair young governess, who very likely wished to be alone with her pupils.

I had just made up my mind to move, when she gave me a most humorous look — *how* humorous I suppose she hardly realised herself—a look which clearly said that my company was agreeable to her, though the reason was not a flattering one for me : she did not wish to tell " more about Peter." I smiled back in a way intended to tell her that I had grasped the situation. Then I made myself still more comfortable, and endured with great calmness the angry eyes of the disappointed little one. It was very pleasing to me to be able to do my pretty neighbour a service in so simple a manner.

For pretty, nay, even beautiful, she was, as I had mean-while had opportunity to realise. Her face belonged to the square type ; it was clearly cut, and, as she was a brunette, at first sight she had rather a southern appearance. But the nose was quite German, short, straight, and modest. The lips possessed a rare charm, for the outline and colouring —from nature's hand, of course—were in perfect harmony. It is often the case that lips are either only perfect in colour or in outline, or the two are not in harmony and therefore spoil one another ; here they were perfection itself. As to the little round chin and the curve of the cheek, I had never seen anything so delicately moulded.

She appeared to be of middle height, and rather thin than otherwise. Her dress was not in the latest fashion, which pleased me, but what especially took my fancy was her head-gear. Horribly high-peaked hats, trimmed with artificial flowers, were in vogue that year, and in the saloon

I had just had the opportunity of wondering at the lack of taste shown in this respect. She, however, wore a small, toque-shaped, straw hat, bound with blue velvet, and a silver-grey veil.

To wear a nice veil at a time when veils are out of fashion always shows good taste on the part of the lady, and a pardonable desire to please. I cannot imagine *the* adored one without a veil, this festive streamer on life's billows, always pointing the direction one is to follow, and always making the heart beat, though sometimes leading astray. Well, I am speaking as if I had already fallen in love, which I had not at the time, though when is one not liable to do so? The world of women is for us divided into two classes: the one with whom it is more or less possible to fall in love, and the other in which one feels as if in the society of men. This time I was surely enough in the society of the former class.

We had gone some distance before I had come to this conclusion, for I only now and then dared to glance at her. All the same, I looked perhaps more often than would be considered correct; at any rate I noticed that she blushed deeply, and bent still farther down over the book, which was by no means of a size to shield her.

This little dumpy book began to make me inquisitive, with the real, travelling, rainy-weather inquisitiveness, that may be aroused by any casual circumstance. Old German translations of Cooper and Walter Scott are usually of a similar size, and I had already judged her literature to belong to this respectable type, when a sudden turning of the leaves revealed that it belonged to an even more serious order—it was a pocket dictionary.

This discovery increased still more my interest in the girl, and I looked at her with a certain emotion, picturing how the stress of life must have forced her to accept one of those trying situations as governess, which require more accomplishments than have ever been found in one human being, and perhaps had obliged her to use every spare moment to add to her knowledge in the quickest and driest manner, forcing her daily to swallow a dose of vocabulary *in natura*, a bitter but strengthening mixture on her thorny path.

When so pretty an image of youthful maidenhood has hardship as a sombre background, it can but gain in brightness and relief. Had she been a spoilt young lady of fashion, who passed her time reading the usual library novel, she would not have been half so interesting to me.

Though this interest ought to have been unselfish enough to prevent me from disturbing her, I could not resist doing so in order to start a conversation. I am ashamed to confess that I could not accomplish my purpose any better than by walking twice up the cabin stairs in the hope that she would ask if the weather was clearing—which it was not at all. She never spoke, however, and so I was at my wit's end.

I had thought of and rejected several forms of introduction, when the smaller girl began to complain of the cold. The poor governess had no choice but to wrap her up in her own shawl. As I am myself sensitive to cold, I could sympathise with her in parting with the wrap, especially as I had noticed how contented she had looked when tightening it round her arms and pushing her little chin between the soft folds.

I felt that my time had now come, and courteously offered her my plaid.

As I expected, she politely refused it. " You will need it yourself," she said, " and may catch cold." .

I could not possibly deny this, as I was already troubled with a cold in my head, which had made me sneeze twice so furiously that the little girl had been frightened, and the bigger one had, only with an effort, restrained herself from laughing. So I had no other way out of the difficulty than to say I was going to the smoking-saloon and should not require the plaid.

Then the governess expressed a hope that she was not preventing me from smoking, to which I replied that I would on no account annoy her by doing so. On this point I remained obdurate, and thus affected a consideration that was foreign to me. I added that I wanted to move because the air had become rather chilly; and so I succeeded in retiring, leaving behind me my plaid as—*sans comparaison*—Joseph his coat.

Seated again on the oilcloth-covered bench in the little stuffy smoking-saloon, where I had lit my cigar and ordered a glass of beer, I could not hide from myself the fact that my first attempt at an introduction had not been very successful, inasmuch as it had forced me to retire. Had I been bolder I might have managed so that we had shared the plaid, or, if this was impossible, I might have put the little girl next to me and covered her up with my own plaid. In short, I had acted like a fool, and was the more annoyed as my former place was much more agreeable, and I already began to feel symptoms of a headache.

The boat gave a bump and then came to a standstill. Overhead they were dragging along boxes and trunks. We had reached Pirna. I looked apathetically at the small houses of the town, with the many green trees, and the tent-like roof of the lofty church, but with more interest at its Acropolis, Sonnenstein, which had at one time been a fortress, and was now a large lunatic asylum.

The brush of Canaletto has often glorified this picture, but always in a better light. As if nature wished to relieve the gloom, a gleam of light suddenly fell on the turrets of the castle.

Now when I recall the scene, it appears to me as if a finger from Heaven had pointed out the building in order to attract my attention and to fix in my heart a foreboding of the feelings with which I should afterwards regard it, and with which I, at this moment, see it with my spiritual eye until my bodily eye grows dim with tears, and I am forced to lay down my pen. At that time nothing suggested itself to me but the glad sign of clearing weather. Gradually the light increased and spread, as walls and turrets began apparently to move and slowly glide to the right; I even faintly saw a patch of blue sky, and before the roof of the church down in the town entirely disappeared, I could see a dull, leaden hue on its steep slope. But again the rain washed down the window.

As we gradually came into the sandstone region, the rain abated. The smoking-saloon's puffing inhabitants disappeared, one by one, and were heard tramping overhead.

I went up also. It was raining rather heavily, the drops glittering like pearls in the hazy light, but as the clouds overhead were beginning to disappear, it was difficult to understand why the rain continued.

The stone walls of the old lower quarries, which here are a reddish-brown, seemed to be varnished, and, from the undulating bank on the right, the tree-tops of a pale green forest shone through the rainy mist. The rain, that for a moment had stopped, grew heavier again, though blue sky could be seen through the clouds.

I went down the cabin stairs and found my little party

still in the lobby. The governess was no longer reading, nor was she telling tales, for her little tormentor was sleeping peacefully. This time I did not wait for the question, " Is it clearing ? " but said at once that it was likely to be fine. In reply she smiled cheerfully, and thanked me for the use of the plaid, which she began carefully to fold up, and, as it was a large one, I had to help her, and succeeded in making her laugh at my awkwardness. There was just room enough to put it out to its full length, after which we manœuvred towards each other in the accustomed manner until our hands met. Before I could say a word, she had, with a hurried " thank you," rushed up the stairs, leaving the bigger child to wake up the smaller one.

The moist, shining deck, where one could not yet sit on the benches, was soon overcrowded with passengers. A few drops only glittered through the air, which was quite damp and warm ; above, the sky was blue, the river valley was still filled with a light moisture, and the woods on the rocky terraces steamed, as if each pine-top was a little chimney, from which a blue smoke curled up and dissolved itself in the sunshine.

Ahead the glare of the river was almost blinding. At the foot of the perpendicular rocks of the Bastei, a few houses of Rathen could already be seen, and behind them a strange mass of wildly torn crags—the Gamrig-stone, which I had noticed from my window.

I looked for my small piece of luggage, and found that it had been kept quite dry by a tarpaulin. Being thus occupied, I had not had time to look for my beautiful travelling companion, before I heard the shout—" Rathen, *am steuer absteigen*," and I was busy forcing my way stern-wards with my baggage. But when I had arrived there

2

I saw, to my great delight, the grey veil flying foremost in the row of people, and soon after the governess passed over the gangway with her little pupils.

Before I could engage a porter, both she and the children had disappeared from view.

CHAPTER III

IF I had my wish, a monument to the obloquy of the man who gave this part of the country the name of " Saxon-Switzerland " would be erected in a most prominent spot. Visitors now come here, either with a remembrance of Switzerland, or with a fantastic delusion as to size; comparing, disapproving, and saying, with a sneer, that they had seen or imagined something much grander—a treatment for which the poor little country has never asked.

But if one comes without expectations, and accepts the country as it is, especially not trying to *do* it in tourist fashion, but quietly settling down to live and enjoy— what richness of beautiful nature does it not offer you, and how filled it is with striking contrasts, which are harmonised in its own idyllic, rustic way! Barrenness and prolific growth, wild ruggedness and cultivated land are lying side by side, or one above another; from bright burning heat one suddenly plunges into cool, humid shade. Where do the lungs expand in a fresher and more exhilarating air than in that which sweeps over these heights, and fills the woods and rocky valleys ?

Rightly to understand the peculiar nature of this country, a study must be made of it in order to discover that it is not a mountainous district, but a plateau which, by the action of floods, has been rent, hewn, and washed out, revealing the stone, sometimes as sides of the fissures and sometimes as ruins in them, so that in this way the rocks form more of the excavated than of the elevated part. For this reason one is at first astonished to find a stretch of rich verdure winding up over the uneven, stony surface of a steep rock, as a velvet saddle on an elephant, and still more astonished when, after having passed through waving cornfields, and on looking down a precipice, one suddenly sees a wild tract of rugged rocks with numerous crags and pinnacles, and sandstone columns a hundred feet high.

At first these contrasts are almost irritating, but as time goes on they grow upon one. On the top of this plateau, with the mountainous land beneath, one finds, again, these solitary, towering rocks that give the land its characteristic physiognomy, which is, to tell the truth at the expense of the aesthetic, a rather warty one. For, seen at some distance, these stones, whether called Kingstone, Popestone, Lilystone, or what not, are really more like gigantic warts than anything else, not even excepting the Schneeberg with its two thousand feet and its far-reaching crest. A few, as for instance the Winter Mountains, vary from this type, but they are just on the frontier, and as one comes into Bohemia a more ordinary mountain aspect is to be seen. To be quite correct the Schneeberg is situated in Bohemia, and the boundary is not altogether so sharply defined as is the quality of the coffee, which is so excellent in the first Bohemian hamlets that one might imagine oneself already at Carlsbad ; while, on the Saxonian side, one drinks the famous " Bliemchen-Kaffee," a decoction which has taken its name from the fact that through it one can see the little flower painted at the bottom of the cup.

Only that afternoon I had partaken of the usual quantity

of this beverage, which is by no means dangerous to the heart. The day before I had tasted the Bohemian coffee in Prebischthor, and two days previously——in short, I had moved about a good deal and did not feel fit for any long excursion. I was now sitting dozing in my window, considering whether I had the energy to go down to the Blackbirds' Glen. It was very hot and perfectly calm. The filmy clouds, which seemed to be half-absorbed by the grey-blue sky, had a rosy hue. The grass and foliage did not glitter in the sunlight, but were of a more than usually intensified green colour ; the shadows between the rocks were not transparent, and those cast from one on to another had no sharp outlines. From the Glen the notes of the cuckoo were constantly heard, as they had been for hours, this monotonous sound adding greatly to the drowsy effect which all nature was producing. . . . I certainly did not feel inclined to walk many yards ; I could not sleep, did not care to read, and, as to writing a letter, such an idea was out of the question.

In this state of indecision " them shady promenades " came into my mind. So far I had not thought of them, but now I wished them to serve a better purpose than simply that of a trump-card for the landlady. Just then my eye fell on a small avenue of young birches that faced my window and was about fifty feet from it. This avenue soon made an abrupt turn and disappeared behind the shrub-covered margin of the hill, which sloped down rather steeply towards a little kettle-shaped valley. I had imagined that the birch avenue belonged to the smart neighbouring villa, but it now struck me that it was not in any way separated from the ground on which stood the house I lived in. This ground was used for growing potatoes, lettuces, some rows of peas, and included a grass plot. The plot brought the avenue suddenly to an end, and, farther on, stretched uninterruptedly up to the shrubs at the margin of the hill. It was, therefore, just possible that the beginning of the slope might belong to my landlady, and that the suddenly broken avenue only waited for the finishing touches, which, when the ground had been fully laid out, would join it to the pathway leading to the house ; consequently I thought that " the shady promenade " might be down there.

In my own mind I apologised to the woman for having made fun of her and for having been so unbelieving, and I decided at once to make use of my highly valued privilege as a lodger to walk " *da'rim und dort'nim.*"

I did not go towards the birch avenue, but went across to the coppice of hazel and may. The grass, filled with daisies and buttercups, peeped through all the openings of the scattered bushes, and extended up to a gravelled path. On the other side of this path the grass-covered slope led, rather precipitously, down to the small valley that was covered with fir and birch wood, while to the right the gravelled path was soon transformed into a modest foot-track which lost itself amongst the fir trees. I turned to the left so that I might make myself acquainted with the grounds.

I had hardly walked more than a few steps before I stood in front of a small grotto. Here the underlying stone was apparent, but for the most part one only saw turf and sand on this hill ; the rock was overhanging as if it had run its head through the soil, and the sides were bent forward like two prominent shoulders, in this way forming, nearly all day, a natural shelter from the sun. A table and a couple of garden seats were placed here, and in the middle of the wall was painted " Sophien Ruhe."

For a moment I stood quite impressed ; I could not have believed that Mother Richter held such a trump-card in her hand. I then sat down on one of the comfortable seats, but did not feel quite at home, as I was more and more doubtful whether I had the smallest right to be where I was. While this reflection was troubling me, I caught sight of a little book lying on the seat. I took up the book, and as I turned over the leaves I discovered, to my astonishment, that it was a *German-Danish Dictionary*. I was not aware that any countryman of mine was in the *Pension* which this barrack of a villa was called, in spite of the fact that it was only able to accommodate lodgers. Who, in these parts, could be interested in studying Danish, an interest so rarely found in Germany ? The worn cover was in some way familiar to me.

The gravel crunched under light, quick footsteps. As I raised my head a girl approached along the path, and I saw the beautiful governess of the steamer.

Since my arrival I had been so busy touring about the country, that I had not had time to long for a renewal of our short acquaintance, and during these last few days I had not thought of her at all. Now I suddenly recollected that the schoolmaster had spoken of a pretty little governess living at the smart villa.

She had evidently not expected to find anybody there, for, involuntarily, she gave a tiny scream. I had, of course, scrambled to my feet and blurted out several excuses and apologies, saying that my landlady, having spoken of " the shady promenades," had made me think of coming to the place. I added that I feared I was accidentally trespassing, and regretted it all the more as I seemed to have frightened her.

She smiled shyly.

"Your mistake is quite intelligible, so you really have nothing to apologise for nor anything to regret on my account."

Her glance now fell on the little book, which I, in my confusion, kept twirling between my fingers. The colour mounted to her face.

"Perhaps this is your book?"

"I had just come to fetch it."

"Then I must apologise again for being so bold as to open it. . . . It was a strange surprise to me, for I am a Dane."

"I was quite sure of that," she answered. "I recognised it from the first words you spoke to me on board the steamer."

This remark of hers was not very flattering to me, as I secretly hoped my pronunciation to be so good, that a German might take me for a fellow-countryman living in a distant part.

"I suppose you have associated a good deal with Danes?" I asked.

"I have known a few countrymen of yours," she said, and suddenly her gaiety vanished.

"And these acquaintances have led to your studying a language so little used?"

"Yes," she answered hesitatingly, as if considering how she could bring the conversation to an end.

"Perhaps in some way I might be of help to you . . ."

"No, thank you—unfortunately. That is to say, there was some talk of my going as a governess to a family in Denmark, but the idea has now been given up."

These details about things which were no concern of

mine rather surprised me, and I was expecting her to continue the conversation when she said in a reserved tone—

"I should be very sorry to drive you away from this comfortable seat. It is not at all necessary for you to go. I know the customs of the house, and nobody ever comes in the grounds or the garden at this hour. That is why I was so frightened when I saw somebody sitting here; I am rather nervous. Good-bye!"

I was just going to try and persuade her to remain, as I knew that we should be undisturbed, when I became aware of tears glittering in her eyes, which withdrew their glance from mine. And this, combined with a trembling at the corner of her lips, proved to me that she was on the point of bursting into tears, a discovery which made me utterly confused. I stammered something about her great kindness, of which I should not like to take advantage; at any rate, I had the courage to add, when her society no longer . . .

But she had vanished.

Bewildered by this unexpected meeting, I, however, did not move, but tried to retain the image of the young girl who, on this second occasion, had made a still deeper impression on me. It was now quite clear to me that she was the prettiest girl I had ever seen. She had been wearing a garden hat encircling her face like an old-fashioned hood, which had given me the opportunity to see that her forehead was unusually high and well-shaped. But it was especially the eyes, rather deeply set under this arch, which had struck me. When she opened them wide there was hardly any distance between the lashes and eyebrows, neither of which riveted my attention as much as the clear-cut setting of her eyes. The eyes themselves were striking rather for their brilliance than their size, and were apt to dart quickly from one object to another in a curious way of their own. Their irises, in which yellow and green were blended with brown, made the same impression on one as when, in a shady wooded cleft, one looks down into a stream, at the bottom of which soft sunbeams play; and the expression of them changed as rapidly as that of the rippling water under the movements of the foliage and the clouds.

I felt that they were impressed upon my memory for ever.

This coincidence of the *Danish Dictionary* was very striking. It appeared to me as an omen, the finger of fate, or, in short, something that had a meaning, and could not remain as an isolated fact. I did not quite believe her assertion that she might have gone as a governess to Denmark; but then, why should she have said so ? More than all, why had she been on the point of crying without any apparent reason ?

All this kept on working in my mind, whilst I lost myself in the valley and walked through the big fir wood right across to Polenzgrund, where I took my supper in the Walthersdorfer-Mill. The intense heat had given place to a most pleasant afternoon.

I still enjoyed nature, not, however, with my accustomed calmness, but with a spiritual elation, which resembled the bodily sensation one has after drinking freely of wine. This sensation is by no means disagreeable, for in rendering one's senses readily open to external influences, it at the same time makes things appear less distinct. Therefore it is easier for this " sweet lingering thought " to mingle with other impressions.

If I looked down into the sometimes quickly, sometimes

slowly gliding Polenz, its green and brown shimmer in the golden rays of the afternoon sun reminded me of *her* peculiar eyes. I discovered some beautiful flowers, and at once I thought, " If only I were now on such terms with her, that she would accept a nosegay from me." Then I lay on a steep slope listening to the soughing of the wind in the fir trees, and I said to myself, " Supposing I were a poet, then surely this moment would inspire me to create a poem, which would meet with *her* admiration, and through which my feelings might speak." Yes, I even found a theme. She was a problem that continually puzzled me, and " it seemeth to me "—this expression I found very poetical—that if I could only discover the solution, I might find " Life's Treasure." However, I could not get my words to rhyme, nor could I make any sort of rhythmic connection.

Darkness had fallen before I returned to Rathen. Only a small portion of the moon appeared dimly over the hill on which the villa was situated. Between the bushes and the garden, and in the shrubs near the brook, the fireflies were swarming. The little sparks peacefully floated to and fro, ascending and descending, as if they were tiny lamps carried by invisible elves. Sometimes a few leaves of a bush were lit up by a hidden firefly ; now and again one flew up so high that against the sky it looked like a moving star. No other stars appeared ; it was again sultry and calm.

On the previous evening also I had enjoyed this wonderfully ethereal phenomenon of the erotic of nature, and it was not only because of its being richer on this night that it touched me in quite a different manner, and put me into a most indescribable mood. And to be honest, what meaning is there in these everlasting examinations of

moods, which modern authors feel obliged to make ? As
if, for instance, any one could form an idea of water by being
told that it consists of hydrogen and oxygen in a proportion
of one to two, even if one were well acquainted with both
of them. Surely it would take God Himself to do so,
and then he *eo ipso* has created it, so that would be nothing
to boast of. I can only say this much, that my heart was
beating fast when I came up the hill, and I often stopped
to look down into the valley, in which the little lights
moved about, and where, in some places, a small shining
lattice lit up the surrounding foliage, while around I felt
rather than saw the steep rocks, all of which seemed to
be the same distance from me.

On the stone step, leading up to the door, I saw one more
lonely little spark, spreading its phosphorescent light. I
lit a match and discovered a small grey, hairy insect,
which was again turned into a spark as the match went
out. However, I was afraid to disturb it, as I had a
mysterious feeling for this glow-worm, which now, for
three nights in succession, had been in the same place, in
the inner corner of the step near the cellar window ; and
I had made sure that it was not there during the day.
What was stirring in such a tiny creature, that, night after
night, it found its way to this enchanted spot ? Had it,
perchance, been disappointed each time and still patiently
returned with its erotic lantern of Diogenes, not searching
for what it had found now—a human being—but a mate ?
and did it stay there in the hope that its burning love, in
this conspicuous position, would attract its object ? . . .
Has, perhaps, a secret constant passion, such as this, an
irresistible power in us also, though in our case hidden,
while in the case of the glow-worm one can literally " see
the heart burning through the waistcoat " ?

One would think that I must have been in especial need of such an unusual power, for while I tossed to and fro on my bed (which always felt a little damp), I continually thought of the little light-giver, and, as far as I remember, it also played a prominent part in my rather bewildered dreams.

CHAPTER IV

WHEN I went out on the following morning, I carefully examined not only the stone steps, but also the little recess of the window. But the glow-worm had gone. I made up my mind, that if it was there again in the evening, I would take it as an omen that a closer relationship would be established between me and my beautiful neighbour.

I went straight to the schoolmaster, who had asked me to call for advice with regard to nice excursions, and who was a distant relation of hers.

It was holiday-time, and I found him in the kitchen-garden in front of the house, where he was working with an enormous rush-hat on his head. He was evidently pleased to see me. After having exchanged the usual remarks about the weather, which looked fairly settled, he asked me where I had been, and soon mentioned a walk I did not know of, and that I could not take by myself. I therefore willingly accepted his offer to accompany me directly after midday.

On the way he was—well, there is no other expression for it but the German *kreuzfidel* (wound up). It transpired that he had studied for a considerable time—very likely more in the public-houses than in college—and the re-collections of those days were the pride of his life. He sang one ditty after another from *The Students' Song-book*; many of his songs showing a remarkable lack of sense, as, for instance—

> " On the wall
> In the hall
> Sits an ancient bug ;
> See how well this bug can prance,
> See him gaily lead the dance."

Later on he took the opportunity to sing some ditties from the years of the war. For, when I walked quickly uphill and left him behind, he always blurted out the Saxonian mocking verse from 1813—

> " Be slow in advance,
> Be slow in advance,
> Let the Austrians' attack this time have a chance."

But if I loitered, he said—

> " You Hannemann,
> You go in front ;
> Your boots so high will bear the brunt."

That this souvenir from '64, and especially the name " Hannemann," could not be pleasing to a Danish ear, the thick-skinned German did not take into consideration ; but at the same time he looked so good-natured that, in spite of some patriotic struggles, I could not be offended with him. When we were resting he usually related tales of his student life or of the war, which latter, however, were mostly of a rather peaceful order.

" Yes, there you are perfectly right, it is an excellent tobacco," he said, when he was lighting his pipe after supper. " What do you think of the strange coincidence which happened to me in connection with this tobacco ? But in those days it was of a better quality than at present ; it was famous throughout almost the whole of Germany— the Altstädter-Ziegel tobacco. Well, it was in those days, I think I have already told you, that I was in the Lazaretto at Flensburg after having received a bullet in my shoulder,

and, as I was getting on well, they gave me permission to
smoke just one small pipe. Before proceeding I really
ought also to say that I was born in Altstadt, and that my
mother, who lived there, frequently sent me some good
things; there was no freight to pay, and she always put
a packet of this excellent tobacco in the hamper. To
return to my story, I get the pipe lit, and hardly has the
tobacco begun to burn, before the man next to me (he
was a Dane who had been taken prisoner at Düppel, where
he had come too close to a bayonet), lifts his head a wee
bit from the pillow, and starts sniffing; and I quite understood that the smell was not disagreeable to him, for he
hugged himself with delight. I am puffing with all my
might. He goes on sniffing and inhaling. 'My word,' he
says. 'Why,' I reply, 'does it perhaps smell of sulphur?'
'Nothing of the kind,' he says in fairly good German;
'but I'll be hanged if it isn't Altstäder-Ziegel tobacco you
are smoking.' 'Then you won't be hanged this time,' I
tell him. 'By the way, how do you know Altstäder-
Ziegel tobacco?' 'Well, I should think I ought to know
it,' he answers, 'for I was two years in Altstadt when I
travelled for my trade—I am a watchmaker. Since then I
have not tasted that tobacco, and now, when smelling it
once more, I feel again as if I were with my kind Master
Storch at the corner of Goose Square and Smith Street.'
'Well, I never!' I say, nearly dropping the pipe. 'You
can take my word for what I've told you,' he answers.
'Why, then, you were working under my own father!'—
What do you think of that? And as we came to talk
about it, I was able to recall him, though he had grown
a big beard, a real Hannemann-beard. . . . Finally I gave
him a pipe of tobacco, but it might have chanced that I
had given him a hot bullet instead."

When this story came to an end, I took the opportunity
—if it could be said to exist—of asking him about his
relations, and, after having endured pages of family history,
I was at last rewarded by hearing the name of Minna
Jagemann—"that pretty little governess living with the
von Zedlitzs', whom I suppose you have seen."

At first the information about her was of a very ordinary
and uninteresting character.

Her father had been a teacher in one of the large public
schools, and had died a year ago. Her mother took in
lodgers, and the girl earned a little money by giving
German lessons to foreigners, conversational classes, etc.
She had for the present, contrary to her usual custom,
accepted this situation as governess, which was very well
paid ; otherwise she lived with her mother in one of the
smaller streets of Dresden.

All this sounded very commonplace to me, because I had
conjured up a romantic history for her.

"At any rate, it is not always advisable for such an
innocent girl to associate with these foreigners," he remarked, pushing down the ash in his pipe.

"Why not ? " I asked with interest. "What do you
mean ? "

"Well, one doesn't always know with what kind of
persons one may have to do, and it might lead to things
that are not quite pleasant."

"Has Miss Jagemann had such an experience ? "

"Indeed she has. There was a young painter, a
countryman of yours, an unsteady sort of chap. He
threw her over, and surely she did not deserve that."

"Is that so ? Then they were engaged ? "

"I don't know for certain whether they were really
engaged. I haven't sufficiently inquired into the matter,

but I got my information from Aunt Sophie; perhaps you remember I spoke of her, she was not all she ought to have been. . . . Anyhow, there was some sort of love-affair between them. Every one thought they were going to be married; but he went away, and has not written since. I am not in the least surprised, for he had taken painting lessons in Paris, which is a real Sodom. Not that Dresden is quite . . . well, I suppose you have already noticed it yourself. But Paris, good gracious! It's something awful; and we are so hated that a German can hardly live there. In spite of this, they have to send for our beer; they can't even imitate it, much as they would like to! The other day the French again closed a factory near the frontier, because it belonged to a German. It will never work! Just you see, it won't take many years before we have to go there again. Mark my words, did you notice what Bismarck said the other day?"

He now became immersed in politics.

To tell the truth, I was at the moment much more anxious to hear what happened to the pretty little girl from Dresden, and her Danish painter, than to get the most authentic information of the day and hour on which the Germans were to enter Paris. But I asked in vain if he could remember the name of the painter.

I remained rather silent on our homeward journey, for I was very disturbed by what the schoolmaster had told me. In one way I was content to have satisfied my curiosity, and to have had my suspicions confirmed, but in another I did not like this episode, though it had nothing to do with me, not in the least—and still . . . I now thought of the strange little incident of the pocket dictionary, which seemed to be Miss Jagemann's favourite literature, accompanying her both travelling and walking. I surmised that it was a *Postillon d'amour* which drove this little linguistic omnibus, where the noblest and simplest words are to be found side by side.   Did she faithfully cling to a dear remembrance when learning words of the language which was this painter's mother-tongue, or had she not yet given up the hope that it also might become hers by adoption ?   Perhaps she did not know herself.

I thought of the little glow-worm keeping its faithful watch evening after evening on the same spot, and throwing its light out into the night for companionship.

As I came close to the stairs its spark met me from the corner of the stone steps.

CHAPTER V

To one who loves German music—and who does not love it ?—these shady and well-watered valleys possess a wealth of suggestion which can only be described by music. Men's choruses by Schumann seem to pour forth and meet one from the fir-trunk columns, when evening peacefully falls over the mountain woods; the clear mill-stream, in which trout glide swiftly by, trills out a Schubert melody, and the hunting-horn of Weber echoes in the wild labyrinth of rocks from its "Wolf-pits" to its "Hawk-pinnacles," which seem to be ideal scenery for *Der Freischütz*. But Wagner requires the grander scenery of the Rhine country.

Notwithstanding this, I stopped one fine day outside a small cave in which was placed a primitive bench, consisting of a plank, a hand's-breadth in width, supported on a couple of thin poles; and on the uneven stone-wall I found that the imposing name "Wotans Ruhe" was painted.

Had this inscription been put by a too naïve Wagnerian, or, perhaps, by a malicious anti-Wagnerian ?

This question I addressed to no less a person than Miss Jagemann.

She was not seated on the bench, on which, in fact, no human being could sit, though maybe a god might, for I suppose they are made of a lighter material. She had chosen a more solid seat, a large block of stone, which

36

projected far over the turbulent brook on the other side of the path.

There was a narrow fissure between this block and the path, so it almost formed a little island, and as a shrub was growing in front of it, I might easily have passed without seeing her, especially as I had been turning my back towards her while looking at the " Wotans Ruhe."

But she revealed herself, whether intentionally or not, by mingling her fresh youthful laughter with my involuntary outburst.

" Never mind," she said, " anyway he deserves to be laughed at ! "

She sat on the grass, resting on one arm with the other lying in her lap, and in her hand she held a bunch of the lovely flowers that are so plentiful in these parts.

The sleeves of her pink morning dress were tucked up over the elbows, either for the sake of comfort or coolness. The arm in her lap looked milk-white, while the other one against the rich green grass showed a brownish outer side, and was overspread by a fine down which shone in the rays of the sun, its plump soft form giving the impression of childishness which is so touching in a woman.

The two little girls sat next her, making chains of straw ; the juice of the bilberries, which they had been enjoying on the way, was smeared all over their faces. Miss Jagemann's lips also showed traces of the bilberries, and when she laughed her teeth did not shine as usual.

" It is rather incautious of you to speak in that way, Miss Jagemann," I answered, " as you cannot be sure that *I* am not an anti-Wagnerian."

" In that case you would not mind being laughed at by a girl. But, besides, you are from Denmark, and there they do not know much about Wagner, or so I was told."

As she spoke her gay expression disappeared, and I fancied that I was able to trace the thought which was passing through her mind, and casting a shadow over her face.

This secret thought, which she of course could not guess that I had fathomed, gave me a feeling of depression, and I became as silent as she was.

Suddenly I noticed that she was looking at me with an astonished glance which clearly said : " Why has he also nothing to talk about, and why does he look so sulky and disagreeable ? " And at the same time I felt that my lips showed annoyance or mockery. It was indeed that tell-tale look of hers that made me conscious of my own mood ; and this mood greatly surprised me, for I could not disguise from myself that it was caused by jealousy. And could anything be more foolish, than to be jealous for the sake of a girl with whom I had hardly spoken, and should very likely never become well acquainted ?

During these meditations I had begun to be talkative. I told her I had been long enough in Dresden to gain some knowledge of the works of Wagner, and that they had a special interest for a Dane, as, in the *Niebelungen-Ring* he had used a subject from our own sagas.

Then I passed on to Danish literature, and hastened to ask if she had been getting on well enough with the language to read any of our authors.

" Yes, I have read *Aladdin*, by Oehlenschläger," she answered. " I spelt my way through it when I only knew a few words and a little grammar."

" Then, I suppose, you did not enjoy it much ? "

" Indeed I did ; I read it over several times, especially

parts of it, which I found quite beautiful. But in the end I was rather annoyed because I could not feel any interest in this loafer who is always favoured by good luck."

I made some remarks about the Aladdin and Faust types, and about the Danish and German national characteristics—a part of which I borrowed from something I had read years before in a magazine ; but the other part consisted of ideas which came to me on the spur of the moment, and which could not have been of any value.

" What you have just said," she remarked, " is not very flattering to your countrymen."

I looked at her in surprise, for it had not occurred to me that my words could bear such a meaning.

" Well, to be perfectly candid, do you really find that Faust is so much to be admired ? I mean, if one looks at him with the sober eye of a moralist ? To give up one's soul to the devil, to seduce a young, innocent girl, to kill her brother in a very doubtful duel . . ."

" I know that, but all the same . . . You are a Protestant, aren't you ? " she suddenly asked with a triumphant smile, as if she had thought of something very much to the point.

" Yes ? "

" Then you know that human beings are not judged by their actions only."

" By what, then ? I really do not consider Faust an orthodox saint, in spite of the fact that he translated the Bible."

" Perhaps you are right, but Faust is anyhow worth more than this Mr. Aladdin," she said, evidently pleased at having used this mocking " Mister " instead of an argument—though no argument was really needed, as, at the bottom of my heart, I shared her opinion.

" In the same way as Marguerite is worth more than Gulnare," I remarked.

Naturally, in speaking of Marguerite, I thought of *her*, though in appearance, anyhow, she did not answer to the traditional notion of this German maiden, much less to a foreigner's conception of her. I could not help smiling as my thoughts reverted to a little Frenchman at the Polytechnic, who, whenever we passed a fair girl, used to nudge me and say, " Gretchen ! " without troubling to notice whether she was nearly a dwarf or a giantess, a bold minx or an overdressed girl with a self-assertive air. Always, " Voilà Gretchen," with the impossible *ch* !

If *she* did not resemble Marguerite, neither could I in the least be compared with Faust—a fact which I at once made evident, by lacking the courage to offer myself as her escort.

For her part she seemed quite content to remain where she was. But I was in a difficulty, for although to converse across a chasm on such elevated topics appeared to be absurd, yet I could not persuade myself that I had the right to join her. Indeed, to propose such a thing was quickly made impossible by the smaller child exclaiming—

" Why doesn't he come over here, when he so much wants to speak to you ? "

After this remark there seemed nothing else to do but to pretend that it was time for me to go home. So I wished her a pleasant walk, and consoled myself with a hope that I should soon have another chance to meet her.

This hope, however, was not realised. Day after day I wandered about, looking and listening like a hunter—

coming again and again to " Wotans Ruhe." But all in vain.

I also fruitlessly taxed my poor brain to find an excuse, a way, any means—it did not matter what—to establish a communication between us. Impossible !—I might as well have tried to write a novel.

CHAPTER VI

WHEN I was not going for a long expedition, I took my dinner every day about one o'clock at the " Erbgericht," on a beautiful terrace by the river, shaded by glorious maples ; the lower parts of these trees were clipped straight, forming a pretty green shelter, which gave a pleasant light and allowed the sun spots to play on the table-cloth, and sparkle on the lids of the glasses.

One day, when I arrived a little later than usual, every place seemed to be occupied. I was looking around inquiringly, when, to my surprise, I heard some one calling me by name. An old couple, who had a table to themselves, were beckoning to me. They were two of my Dresden acquaintances, and, in addition to that, favourite ones. I was very pleased to have escaped from my difficulty in such an agreeable manner, and was soon seated with, so far, only a glass of beer in front of me, beside the homely pair.

At first glance one saw that the old man was a Jew. The shape of the very hooked nose was unmistakable, and the sparse, rather bristly moustache and beard did not hide the thick lips, the lower one of which was underhung, and, when he was talking, gave the impression that he was sucking something in. It seemed also to affect his speech, which was slow and lisping. The eyes were overshadowed by strongly marked grey brows, and under them hung big wrinkled bags. Their expression was lively, clear, and quite unusually good-natured. His wife was a stately old lady, of a more Southern than Jewish type ; her fresh face, which was constantly smiling—with the smile that one sees in paintings of the Empire period— was decked on both sides by a bunch of grey curls, in the old-fashioned style, and so tight were they that they looked as if they were made of wire.

I had been introduced to this venerable pair by their son, to whom I had become attached at the Polytechnic, though he was my senior by several years. He now had an appointment in a factory at Leipzig. I had at once won the favour of the old man by my unfeigned interest in his hobby. He was a bibliophile, but his greatest passion was for the autographs of famous men, of which he had a large collection, from Luther to our time—I should think that if Hermann the Cherusk had left any writings he would surely have got hold of them. The documents were arranged in portfolios, each of which was numbered, and to each portfolio was added a protocol of hand-made paper, (written with goose-quill and specially prepared ink for the sake of eternity), containing proofs of authenticity, as well as reference to biographical works and letter collections, and to these were added his own notes. This precise man was not content to collect only, but when he had got hold of a little manuscript he had no peace until he had found out to what period it belonged ; and in cases in which this problem had already been solved, there were still commentaries to be written regarding the persons named, the circumstances referred to in the manuscript, and finally all the conclusions which he had drawn from his research had to be tabulated.

In this way his passion flowed back and contributed, as it were, to the source from which it had sprung, namely, the history of literature. To gratify this passion, it was necessary to acquire a great fund of knowledge, but this fund, having been acquired, paid an excellent rate of interest. With him it was far from being an unprofitable hobby—as hobbies so often are—it was rather a living expression of his inner self, satisfying at the same time his highest spiritual aims and his orderly business instincts.

Old Hertz had retired from business some ten years or more, and at this time was living in Dresden, in the " Rentier Corner," as it was, not without reason, called. He had been a merchant in Königsberg, where he was born, and had belonged, so to speak, to the merchant nobility. This home had left a lasting impression on his nature and development.

Königsberg is a commercial town which has obtained its peculiar character from the master-mind of one great man—a fortunate circumstance which sometimes happens in small towns that do not produce many celebrities ; for people whose interests might be given to some less worthy object can cling with pride to the memory of the man who made their town famous. What Erasmus is for Rotterdam, this, and still more, is Kant for Königsberg ; partly because he is a greater personality, and partly because, being of later date, the present older generation in Königsberg are the children of those whom he used to visit.

This was the case with Hertz. The great philosopher had willingly associated with members of the large commercial firms of his native town. These formed a powerful stock which guarded as a precious legacy the spiritual and literary interests he had grafted upon it. As a class they possessed the breadth of mind and versatility characteristic of business men, and they afforded him welcome shelter from the dripping sky which masked the darker days of pietism. It followed naturally that Kant, more than any one else, was the old man's hero. How deeply he had penetrated the philosophy of Kant, of course, I could not judge; but an almost touching tone of profound reverence was noticeable whenever he uttered the name of his great fellow-citizen.

He had chosen Dresden as the spot in which to spend his old age, partly on account of his relations and acquaintances, partly for the sake of the well-known Polytechnic, where his son studied, and lastly, I suppose, because it is the most beautiful town in Germany. But its spiritual atmosphere did not please him. Both from a commercial and literary point of view he looked down on this unscientific and unenterprising residential city, where an unimportant aristocracy ruled. He often remarked that Schiller had already called Dresden a spiritual desert, and in those days Körner resided there—but now? Therefore the old Königsberger lived in great isolation, and associated mostly with the already infirm Gustav Kühne, a veteran from " the young Germany " of which Hertz had known almost all the Coryphæuses. This was nearly all I knew of this quaint old man, who now saluted me as with the kindness of a friend. It was a nice trait in this couple that they were very fond of young people. I also noticed that the youth of both sexes almost involuntarily showed them more respect than the younger generation of our day are in the habit of showing to elderly people. Perhaps they gained this respect by their own very modest manners, which even had the appearance of a certain fear lest they might be a trouble or an inconvenience to others.

They were not at Rathen upon a trip, as I imagined, but had taken a small house by the Elbe for six weeks, where they had already spent three days.

It so happened that I had been out on excursions, or taken my meal at a different hour, so had not met them before; but now I had to promise to look them up and take coffee with them on that same day.

"And you shall not feel the hour hang heavily upon you with no other society than that of two old people."

"No, you shall not feel the time long at all."

"But you must not speak like that."

"Indeed, we should not like to encroach on your time, especially when there is so much for your young legs to do. But a young lady is coming, and it would please us very much to give her more youthful companionship than we ourselves can offer."

"You will not regret making her acquaintance—at least I hope not." These last words the old lady added with an arch glance.

"From this place?" escaped my lips.

Mrs. Hertz misunderstood my question, and laughed.

"No, you need not be afraid of a too rustic naïveté. She is not a Rathener."

"Nor is she a Königsberger."

"Perhaps she knows but little of Kant? Tell me, Mr. Hertz, do you really think that all ladies from Königsberg have read *The Critique of Pure Reason*?"

"Unfortunately, my young friend, they have not even read *The Critique of Judgment*, which they need so much. As we are on the subject, I have in my day given lectures for women. . . ."

I had put my rather satirical question in order to affect a great indifference to the present topic, and also to gain time; as in a way I feared to be robbed too quickly of the hope which I had suddenly begun to cherish. But the old lady had read my thoughts.

" Be honest, Mr. Fenger, and admit that you are burning with curiosity, and would much prefer to know something about the young lady, than about my husband's lecture."

The old gentleman laughed.

" Look at him; see how he is blushing! Yes, my wife knows something of human nature; she is quite a Lavater."

To hide my confusion I drained my glass of beer.

" Well; is she pretty ? " I asked.

" Pretty ? My dear fellow, she is quite a beauty! Yes, but not exactly what one ordinarily means by a beauty. Don't misunderstand me, she is a Thekla from the bourgeoisie, a Lotte, a Fredericka Brion, though perhaps not quite that ; she is not a clergyman's daughter from the country either, however idyllic that may be. She is a Kätchen, more than anything a Kätchen ! "

" But, dear husband, do you need the whole range of German poetry to aid you ? In this way you will raise too great expectations."

" On the contrary ! Not even German poetry is sufficient ! There is only one thing that is better than German poetry——"

" Kant's *Critique*, I suppose you mean ? "

" No, I mean German women—when they are charming. But, joking apart, she is an excellent girl."

" Well, you will see for yourself. She is a relation of mine, rather a distant one. I think I told you that I am from Dresden."

These last words made me lose all my interest. Then, after all, it was not Miss Jagemann of whom they had been speaking. In the first place, she did not look like a Jewess; and secondly, from what the schoolmaster had told me, I was convinced that she was not one. I listened with a polite smile, but without attention to Mrs. Hertz's recital of the family pedigree.

Suddenly, as if in a dream, I heard her say, " But I quite forgot that you may have already seen her, for after what you have told me, she must be your neighbour. She is at present a governess——"

A cold shudder ran down my back. Strangely enough, at that moment I was not so much conscious of joy as of a certain conviction. Then, after all, it must be the finger of Fate ! In my confusion I answered that I did not think I had seen her, supposing this to be the best diplomacy. But hardly had the words escaped my lips, when I realised that this untruth was sure to be found out, and would put me in a ridiculous and rather doubtful position. I wished to take back my words, but could not make up my mind to do so, which made me so distrait that I quite misunderstood a question of Mr. Hertz's.

Luckily, the waiter just then brought me the bill, and in my bewilderment I gave him twenty-five pfennig as a tip, which gained for me a polite bow from the man, and a fatherly reproach from Mr. Hertz, who advised me to be more economical in my dealings with such people.

CHAPTER VII

WHAT was to be done ?   Would it be wiser to confide the circumstances of the case to Miss Jagemann, and ask her to pretend not to know me at all ?   At first this idea seemed quite impossible, but as time went on it grew upon me, until finally it seemed to be so attractive that I no longer regretted my foolishness.

It was quite an easy matter to meet her on the way, and, when greeting her, I added that I believed we were bound for the same destination.   On hearing that I was invited to the Hertzs', she said gaily—

" Well, then at last we are going to be introduced to one another."

" Yes," I answered, " it is just for that reason that I have a rather queer favour to ask of you.   Will you pretend not to know me ?   I mean, will you appear as if we had not met before."

" I can easily do that, but why ? "

I told her what had happened, and my explanation was received with laughter.

" Are you always so absent-minded ? "

" Not always.   But I got so confused when suddenly it became clear to me that I was going to meet *you*."

She looked at me in a naïve inquiring way, then suddenly blushed and withdrew her eyes, with all of which I was more than satisfied.

" *Au revoir*, then.   I must go up the hill again to fetch

4

my keys, it would not do for us to arrive together," I said.

The old couple had taken the middle house of the three small ones which had been built close to the rock by the Elbe. As I went up the many little stone steps leading up from the bank, I saw the party sitting in the summer-house, the top of which, like the greater part of the white-washed, timber-built house, was covered by a vine. The afternoon sun was blazing upon it, but over this corner the fruit trees cast a deep shadow, in which the white table-cloth and the shining kettle formed a bright centre to the little company. Minna was busily making the coffee.

We went through the ceremony of introduction with the usual stiffness; but, in offering me a cup of coffee, her half-hidden smile told me that she, as well as I, enjoyed the harmless way in which we had deceived our host and hostess. This slight confidence between us appeared to me, and possibly also to her, of exaggerated importance; it seemed to whisper the promise that we should also be able to keep a greater and sweeter secret than this acquaint-anceship from those around us, and the hope that it would be so.

" By the way, you, too, know some Danish. Why not practise now ? " Mrs. Hertz said.

I received this surprising news with as much astonish-ment as, at the moment, I could muster.

Minna told again the tale about the Danish family in which " there had been an idea " of her being the governess. But her gaiety was suddenly mingled with nervousness, and this confirmed my suspicion that she was concealing something. At the same time I guessed that Mrs. Hertz knew the true state of affairs.

" Then perhaps, Miss Jagemann, you have made yourself
acquainted with our literature ? " I asked.

To this opening she replied very readily, and we then
—almost word for word—reproduced the whole of our
conversation at " Wotans Ruhe " about Faust and Aladdin.
Only it ran more fluently, as a well-studied scene, and
was urged on by an undercurrent of youthful hilarity
which now and then brought forth a new and happy idea.
Such an improvisation in the rôle on the part of one speaker,
gave at once an incentive to the other, who did not care to
be surpassed, but also, with a smile expressive of " I'll
give you tit for tat," showed a new side to the question.
And in this way the discussion got fuller and deeper, though
the subject now was indifferent to us, and only a means for
coquetry. We, however, made such an impression upon
our audience, that Mr. Hertz said to me : " How talkative
you have made the little Minna ; she is not generally so
communicative." And, later on, Minna herself confided
in me that Mrs. Hertz had said to her : " There, now you
have found one with whom you can talk."

These remarks seemed to breathe a real satisfaction,
and I think that the old people, after this meeting, came
to the rather hurried conclusion that we were well-matched.
As they had taken us both to their hearts, it was easy to
understand that they wished us to become better acquainted,
and so much the more because they thought that Minna
needed to have some sweet, though only too painful,
remembrance banished by the awakening of another and
fresh interest. This idea, even in those days, I had already
grasped, and afterwards it was still further proved to me.
And so it came to pass that several times a week we met
each other at the little house by the Elbe. Minna could,
without difficulty, get off from her duties in the evening,

and, with regard to myself, I, of course, never had anything better to do than to be in the place where I could meet her.

Apart from the fact that Minna and I were daily becoming more intimate, each of these meetings was almost the same as the first one, the only variation being that the heat sometimes drew us to one of " the cool glens." As a rule we remained near the river, this being most convenient for Mr. and Mrs. Hertz. When the sun began to steal into the summer-house, it was the signal to take a walk. The shadows from the plateau of Lilienstein gradually grew deeper, and the edges of the stones stood out in high relief, throwing long quivering streaks over the river. Underneath, in the long yellow slates of the quarries, all the cracks and crevices showed violet and purple, like a cuneiform writing relating to industrial achievements. The reflection in the river grew clearer and more distinct. In the middle of it a long raft might be gliding, winding in and out, following the bend of the river, while its oars, four or five in a row, both fore and aft, moved glitteringly. Or a couple of " Ziller," heavily laden barges about the size of a schooner, would come down the stream with the current, their coal-blackened hulls looking like enormous beetles, or with large outspread sails, which shone far away over the fields long after the boat itself was out of sight. Then a chain steamer might come puffing and blowing, and tugging half a dozen of these barges up against the current; while the submarine chain would wind itself round its flat bows with a deafening rattle, which made, however, in the distance an agreeable tinkling sound.

When dusk came the rafts carried small blazing fires, which seemed to float on the water and would light up a couple of hairy faces, or would silhouette a strong figure which bent forward and thrust the slanting pole against its shoulder. Afterwards the tug flotilla would appear like a grand illumination, winding round the point, close under the dark Bastei rock, like a procession of perpendicular staves with large golden knobs on the top led by a ruby and an emerald one.

Nor did life stand still on the other bank of the river, as a train now and then passed from one side or the other, stopping and whistling at the little station. This would continue until about half-past nine, when the express for Prague and Vienna flew by like lightning among the trees, without so much as slackening speed, and always reminded us that it was time to go home. We needed this reminder, because " in the house of the happy the clock does not strike," as Schiller has it.

Moreover, I was not the only one who was happy. The sadness, which had at first overshadowed Minna, gradually wore off and gave place to a youthful gaiety. That some sorrow still remained in the depths of her soul one could only guess from the strange shadows which, now and again, would fall upon her brightest moods. I might, without being too conceited, ascribe to my own influence some part of this change in her. The kindness of the benevolent old couple towards both of us did Minna good ; it took the character of the caressing sympathy with which one encourages the convalescent to enjoy life. To me it was rather irritating, but she seemed only to feel comfort in it.

Thus we watched the big stream, with its quaint life passing by, in the same manner that one allows life to drift along in happy days without desiring anything more.

It also gave a topic for our talk. She told me all about the raftsmen's life, especially up in the mountain rivers, where the men have such a constant fight with the currents that until they land in the evening they have no time to snatch a meal. In return I had, as well as I could, to give her a description of the big ships, of the busy traffic in the sea-ports, or the peaceful life of the fishing villages on the coast. Then the quarries, which on both sides were reflected in the river, and sent their blocks down stream in shiploads, made us talk about what the sandstone town of Dresden owed to this little stone region. It struck me that the cut stone used in its beautiful edifices seemed to impart to them some characteristics of their own rock life, so that the rococo town suited the sandstone land, in the same way as the Greek architecture goes with the noble gable-shaped marble mountains, and Egypt's colossal temples with the vast plains and heavily-terraced rocks. Such reflections were of course new to her, for her knowledge of architecture was rather primitive, while I have always been specially attracted by this art, to which, probably, I should have devoted myself, if circumstances had permitted.

CHAPTER VIII

ONE day as we were sitting in the summer-house after coffee, Minna handed me a note-book and asked me to draw the capitals of the Doric and Ionic columns with the entablature appertaining, and add the names, all of which she thought most peculiar. While I was sharpening a pencil, the wind turned over a page, and I saw an unsuccessful attempt at the same thing on the page before me.

" No, you must not," she said, her face quite flushed and imploring, as she tore the book from my hands; " you will only laugh at me ! I will see myself if it is rightly done. Of course it isn't, and the names I could not remember at all."

I promised not to look at her attempt, and started on my own, which, I assured her, would seem very poor in the eyes of an architect. It did not indeed take long before I began to get muddled ; for it is simple enough to know what architrave, triglyph, and metope mean ; but when one has, for the first time, to express oneself on paper, many minor difficulties arise which are not easily overcome. It was therefore a welcome suggestion when Mrs. Hertz asked Minna to help her to clear away and to wash up the cups. She was sitting near me, evidently to watch, and had not anticipated being called away before the drawing was finished. Hesitatingly she responded to this summons, and before she went she seemed more than once to have something on her lips, which she could not bring herself to say ; her anxious glance also clearly told me not to examine this mysterious book, on the homely linen cover of which was printed, in very clumsy golden letters, "Poesy," and I reassured her with a smile.

I sat alone gnawing my pencil, wondering whether the architrave in the Doric order was parted or not, when the draught again turned the leaves, and on this occasion to written pages farther back. Both prose and poetry revealed themselves. I did not imagine for a moment that Minna was the author of these compositions, but that made me wish all the more to see what favourite sentences and extracts she had liked to preserve, and in this way to gain an insight into her character and knowledge. Twice I resisted the temptation ; but a longer piece of prose remained open before me until, half against my will, I caught sight of a few words which whetted my curiosity too much.

I made sure that I was not watched, and read in German the following extracts, written in a fine, rather sloping Gothic handwriting :—

" Between a young couple, who by nature are in harmony with one another, nothing can add more to a pleasant intercourse than for the girl to be anxious to learn, and the young man willing to teach. It produces a profound and agreeable relationship between them. She sees in him the creator of her spiritual existence, and he in her a creation, which owes its perfection not to nature, accident, or a single will, but to a union of wills ; and the interchange of thought is so beautiful, that from such a meeting of two natures, the strongest passions, bringing as much happiness as misfortune, have sprung, at which we cannot wonder. So it has been since the old and the new Abelard."

In reading these last words I heard a door being closed

upstairs and quick steps coming down. I hastily turned the leaves, and resolutely drew an architrave with one division with the triglyph over ; the lines were not very clear, for my hand was shaky, and the guttae I forgot altogether. But whether the palpitation of my heart came from what I had read, or from fear of having been discovered, I cannot tell.

Minna sat down next to me with her needlework, and seemed very satisfied to find me so engrossed in my drawing. The air had been sultry all day, and clouds had gathered. Hardly had I finished my two sketches before we heard loud thunder, and big dark spots soon appeared on the stone steps. I helped to take off the table-cloth, and then we went up to the old people. We but seldom occupied their sitting-room before tea-time, for being a corner one, facing south and west with two windows on each side, it was, on sunny days, unbearable during the afternoon.

Between two of the windows stood a small, hard, up-holstered sofa, and between the other two windows, a table. Over this hung a common oleograph of the Kaiser and the Crown Prince, and under them Hertz had hung one of his special treasures, which followed him after the fashion of the Penates ; it was a small portrait of Kant, a Königsberger-print, faintly coloured, and from his own time. The whole figure of the philosopher was shown standing near a long-legged writing desk, and so stooping and humpbacked, that one would say an invisible hand was pushing his face down to the paper ; while from the little grey wig protruded a bit of pigtail, over the high coffee-coloured coat collar. This quaint and old-fashioned picture, with its mildew, spots that came from old age, and flat mahogany frame, gave a certain cosiness to the low room, which was increased by the small window panes, and by an enormous fire-clay stove that occupied, I should think, an eighth part of the room.

Near this latter Minna soon seated herself, with her back turned towards the window so that she could not see the lightning, which constantly lit up the reddish brown bend of the river. When the blinding reflection came into the room, or the thunder roared so furiously that the house shook and the window-panes rattled, she gave a start, and sometimes even a little scream, though she evidently tried her utmost to control herself. Mrs. Hertz got up from the sofa and calmed her with motherly kindness, and Minna smiled as courageously as she could, though with the fear of the next shock always written on her pale face. Old Hertz looked sympathetically up from his newspaper, which the constant flashes nearly prevented him from reading.

As for myself, I sat near the little window, down which the rain was washing like a shower-bath. My thoughts were constantly occupied by what I had read in *The Poesy-Book*. I did not know the extract, but the style reminded me of Goethe. When recently I read his autobiography and, in the lovely episode with Gretchen, suddenly came across these well-known words, what a storm of feelings overwhelmed my soul! In *Wahrheit und Dichtung* I did not get further, but tried to calm my painfully sweet emotion by writing down these memories, which can only lay claim to the first word of this famous title.

The question as to the authorship did not trouble me much in those days, but the application of it distressed me considerably. I had noticed that Minna, in our conversations, sometimes betrayed artistic knowledge which she could not have gained in school or college, nor by herself. Besides, knew quite well from whom I suspected that she had obtained her information. Were those reflections written now, or then? There was no date to them, and they were separated, by a considerable interval, from the leaf upon which I had been asked to draw, but it had not escaped my notice that this piece of prose was written with fresher ink than the preceding extract, dated a couple of years before. This, I thought, might be in my favour, but on the other hand my hopes might be built upon the sand.

It was nearly tea-time before the storm was over. Then Minna, who in the reaction from her nervousness had become quite jubilant, took a grey stone jar and went down to fetch water, and I followed her. The way of obtaining water at this spot was very romantic; there was neither well nor pump, but all the water had to be fetched from the spring close to the banks of the Elbe below the house. Just where the meadow-grass ended, and only separated from the running stream by three or four yards of stone and gravel, lay the little basin with clear water, that constantly bubbled up from the small stones and sand, which latter moved as if it was full of small living animalcules. We jokingly called it the spring of youth, after a fairy tale that old Hertz had told us one evening.

The breeze which met us was fresh and pure, with a healthy smell of wet earth mingled with the odour of moist foliage and grass, and spiced with the scent of flowers, especially of honeysuckle; an air which the lungs drink in deep draughts, in the same way that one enjoys a pure wine. The heavy clouds had parted; here they were rolling away in murky, smoke-like masses; there dissolving into fleecy vapour or vanishing like thin mist. Overhead, the sky shone a lilac blue; farther on there were patches of pale green, and golden rays were appearing in the west. Between the low-hanging clouds with their deep leaden or reddish stone colour, high ones, standing out with glowing tops, could be seen. On the side of Lilienstein appeared a broad rainbow column which rapidly grew more vivid. At the very top of the longish plateau of this isolated mountain lay a small detached cloud which remained suspended in the fir wood, in the same way as tobacco smoke might remain when blown into a child's curly hair. Only a dull light from the sun lit up the hills over the long quarries ; and all the steep crags around lay in a cool bluish haze. The river was still an opaque reddish brown in the curve, but farther on it again resumed its mirror-like appearance. Now and then faint flashes of lightning were to be seen over the open country, and long drawn-out rolls of thunder were heard echoing in the mountains.

"Look," Minna exclaimed, "what colouring ! It is quite a Poussin ! "

These words of hers stabbed me to the heart. My God ! what young girl knows Poussin, and still more has him ready to hand to quote ? All the same, the resemblance was quite striking. Now, if she had only said : " It looks like a picture of Poussin in the gallery." But this : " It is quite a Poussin," made me furious ! I longed to seize her, as " Carl Moor " seizes " Roller," and cry out : " Who inspired thee with that *word* ? That human soul of thine did not produce it, but that of a *painter* did."

But she had already run down the long row of shiny wet stones. Whether my face had betrayed my feelings, or whether she was ashamed of having borrowed another's phrase, I do not know, but evidently she had run away from her Poussin.

She did not at once start baling out the water, but placed the stone jar on the lower step near the spring, and turned to a pretty little twelve-year-old boy who sat close by.

He was the son of the landlord, who had a partnership in one of the big quarries, the rows of which start under the Bastei rocks. The farthest and largest of the quarries stood out against the bright sky-line like a promontory split up to its summit, where a thin line of weather-beaten pines seemed to touch the copper-coloured edge of the low-hanging clouds. The boy pointed out to us the quarry which was his father's property.

He was very busy over an ingenious toy: a water-mill, which he had constructed at the outlet of the spring. Through a little unripe apple he had stuck a stick as an axle, and round it he had fixed, in a circle of incisions, large wings cut out of wood. He had dammed up the water-course, so that a tiny mill-pond was formed from which there was sufficient fall; and there the wheel whirled and whirled, without, however, accomplishing any work. From the summer-house, and also from the window, I had seen this funny little thing continually turning round and round. The powerful storm of rain had broken through the dam, and the boy was occupied in trying to repair it, but he found it difficult to get the axle to rest in such a way that it could not get stuck.

" I should so much like to make it go by the time father comes home from work," said the boy, looking earnestly at Minna. " For father is always amused when I find out a thing like that, and I should like him to be in a good temper to-night, for then I will ask him if I may go to see the blasting to-morrow."

" Are they going to blast in the quarry ? "

" Oh yes ! A whole wall."

" Do you think we might be allowed to see it ? " Minna asked.

" You might ask my father."

" To-morrow would suit me admirably; my pupils
are going with their mother to see an aunt at Pirna.
Wouldn't you also like to see this performance ? "

Naturally I had nothing whatever to say against such a
proposal.

A long " Oh," into which the little boy suddenly burst,
made us look away from the quarries and turn round.
The rainbow column had grown to a perfect arch, a reflection of which was just forming, but the lower part only
stood clear, while the arch itself was very faint and broken
in places. Soon afterwards this also became perfect, and
the two bows formed the outer and inner brilliant edge
of a broad violet band. Under this bridge the encircled
sky-ground was darker than that above it, where the blue
soon shone through ; in the middle of this dark ground,
under the glorious arch, and lit up by the sun, which shed
its rays under the clouds through the whole valley, stood
Lilienstein, like a smoking stone altar, with the little
cloud still resting on its surface. This image had also formed
itself in the little boy's imagination, for quite lost in
wonder he said : " It's just like in master's picture-bible,
where Noah makes his offering."

In perfect harmony with this patriarchal impression,
Minna took her stone jar, the plain homely shape of which
no old German painter would have hesitated to put into a
Rebecca's hand ; but her blue skirt, which she lifted with
her left hand, might perhaps have been scarcely suitable
as a dress for that nomadic lady, though it was neither
draped nor trimmed. Bending down over the spring, in
order to press the obstinate jar into the water, her one shoe
with its non-nomadic heel slipped on the wet stones, and
she would have got a cold bath, if I had not caught her
round the waist and kept her steady. She let go the jar,

which floated upon the water; the mirror on the surface
of the pool reflected a smile on her face, which seemed more
arch than displeased, but in the same moment the jar
had filled, and, in going to the bottom, produced a whirlpool
that obliterated the image in the water. She had now
recovered her balance, but I was far too careful of her, as
if the little pool was a precipice, to hasten to release her;
yes, I even felt that in this favourable moment I might
have permitted myself more than this lingering pressure,
which was excusable, had the surroundings only been more
secluded. But a few yards away we had the youthful
observer, and the windows were not far off.

"Thank you, I shan't fall any more now," she said,
and jumped up to the path. "By the way, the water?"

I took the full jar out of the spring, and carried it after
her.

When, after tea, we heard the landlord's voice, we went
down to ask about the blasting. It was to take place
the next day, surely enough, and we should be welcome
to see it. Accordingly we arranged that little Hans, whose
request had been granted, should show us the way to the
quarries.

The moon had risen over the wood-covered heights on
the other side of the river. It reflected itself in the middle
of the stream, and between the stones close to the bank.
The sky was almost clear, save that behind Lilienstein,
which was but dimly visible, a dark mist was hanging.
On the other side the contour of the rocks was clearly
defined against the pale sky, but presently their masses
also assumed life; the projections stood out, while the
fissures were in deep shadow, and the surface of the quarries
was but faintly lighted. On the terrace of " Erbgericht "
many lamps shone amongst the foliage; and on the top

of the Bastei a bonfire burned in changing colours, and scattered notes from a waltz tune came down from the heights.

The beautiful evening soon tempted Mr. and Mrs. Hertz to come down, though it was too wet to walk on the grass. We remained on the steps in front of the house, and entertained ourselves with the landlord and landlady. The handsome, rather square-built woman rocked a baby on her arm ; Hans sat on one of the steps and cut new wings for his water-mill ; the landlord, meanwhile, perched himself astride on the railing and puffed at his pipe, delighted over the storm and the coolness it had brought. Well might they need coolness up in the stone quarries, where, although the sun at midday sent the temperature up to a hundred and thirty degrees, hard work had still to continue. Old Hertz inquired about the profit and the prices. The landlady told him of the difficulties during high water in the spring, and of some years when the river had come up almost to the foot of the steps.

A sudden whistle, which rang through the valley, and a passing light between the trees on the other bank, gave the signal for dispersing. As usual I accompanied Minna to her home.

To tell the truth, during the whole evening I had looked forward to this little moonlight walk with a certain nervous expectation. It seemed as if, from the moment near the spring, something was due to me, but if so the vital hour had evidently not come. In spite of the moon, the brook with the alder shrubs, the mountain valley, the loneliness, all undoubted sentimental ingredients, nothing would bring Minna into a sentimental mood. Had she only been silent ! But she chattered in the sweetest way about many things that were not in the least connected with love.

She would not understand anything : I delicately alluded to the well, but this only caused her to discuss the difficulties of the inhabitants when the river overflowed in spring, and to wonder what would then be the nearest spot from which to fetch water. " Very likely ' Erb-gericht ' ; but perhaps there would be a well on higher ground in the old inn ' Zum Rosengarten,'—surely there must be ! "

In short, we talked as sensibly, and parted as formally, as if no such things as slippery steps nor springs of youth had ever existed.

CHAPTER IX

AFTER many warnings to be careful, we set out on the following afternoon with the jubilant Hans, who both acted as our guide and carried our basket of provisions.

Our path, which followed the Elbe, soon ran on the right-hand side, by long slopes of stone, rubble, and gravel which, like a bastion, rose fifty feet or more up to the plateau of the quarries, and downwards was bordered by a wall of more than a man's height. Here and there, in front of each quarry, this gave place to wooden rails, leading from the high-lying works to the bank, where the cut stones are sent down on a species of sledge. Near one of these loading places lay a barge, already half-filled with its heavy cargo ; and close by, some very muscular navvies were unloading a trolley, while the next in order stood ready to follow on the top of the rails near the winch.

I suppose we had walked more than a mile, when Hans stopped near a ladder leaning against the wall. We climbed up to the foot of the slope without difficulty. Here, however, we halted, examining, with distrustful eyes, the path which was to lead us up, and which could only be dimly perceived, like a pale zigzag line on the steep greyish surface. On closer examination we discovered steps of a sort, formed by projecting stones, or simply dug out with a single stroke of the spade, but these looked as if they might give way under one. Hans, who had already climbed a good way up, turned round in astonishment, wondering why we were not following him.

"But you must go first," Minna said, turning red.

"No, Miss Jagemann, it won't do. If you slip in such a place there is nothing for you to catch hold of. I can manage to steady myself and support you if you stumble; you need not be afraid of pulling me down, and any-how——"

"If only you would go on now," she interrupted.

"Dear me, do let us give up being so ridiculously particular. Would you, for the sake of such trifles, risk breaking your neck? Bother it all, there must be another way up. These stupid people! But in any case there is no danger if only you will do as I tell you. Please do not be so squeamish!"

In saying these words I pretended to be much more impatient and irritable than I really was, and I did it designedly. It gave me a delicious satisfaction to play the part of mentor, and to tyrannise over her for the sake of her welfare.

"I know you mean well, and so I won't be offended at your peremptory tone," she said, and looked at me earnestly. "In a way you are right. Indeed you would be quite so, if it were pretence or affectation on my part. But, unfortunately, I have this feeling, and to such an extent, that my movements would be like those of the dolls which used to be fashionable and whose boots were attached to one another by chains; and we should both, in the end, turn somersaults down the slope, which seems admirably adapted for such a performance. If, however, you go in front and allow me to help myself, and climb as ungracefully as I like, then, I promise you, the worst misfortune which can happen will be that I may scrape my knees a little, and if you find that I am an obstinate person now, then console yourself with the idea that I shall certainly not be otherwise when I reach the top."

The decided manner, mixed with pleasant humour, with which she said this, suddenly dragged me down from my pedestal, and, to tell the truth, made me feel so small, that I might have crept into a mouse-hole. In default of such, I crept up the slope, and bore the deadly fear that something might happen to my companion, as a just punishment.

Both of us, however, reached the summit in safety.

The white surface, which stretched in front of us right up to the blasted rock, suggested to me the ruins of a temple. Mill-stones were lying about in long rows, like enormous portions of fallen columns. We also saw regularly cut stone blocks and curb-stones, which together gave the idea of partial foundations. Heaps of sand, rubble, and larger broken stones had here and there formed banks intersecting the ground, some of which were covered with miniature woods, consisting of the American elder, the scarlet-coloured berries of which stood flaring against the shiny white masses of stone. On one side appeared a tiled roof with a smoking chimney ; it was a smithy, a thing which each quarry possessed.

After having passed over one of the banks we found ourselves in the hindermost part of the quarry, just in front of the rock itself. Here stood the owner and two workmen. Our landlord took his wooden pipe from his mouth, and welcomed us by saying that we had just come in the nick of time ; they were quite ready. A big man, in neat check trousers and a fairly clean shirt, stood with his back bent towards the stone surface, where he seemed to be examining something ; he turned his red-bearded face for a moment with a familiar nod, while a smaller man of a gnome-like appearance, and covered with dirty rags, scowled furtively at us as he moved away some tools. A few yards away a couple of workmen were hammering small wedge-shaped iron poles into a big stone which was to be split. Farther away one heard the sound of pick-axes and crow-bars.

The man in the check trousers stepped back from the stone ; then we noticed a thick cord, hanging like the tail of an animal which had crept into a hole. It hung hardly four feet from the ground on a projecting part of the blasting surface, some twenty feet in height. The projection had already, by a narrow rent, loosened itself from the rock wall. This ascended bare and yellow-tinted for some hundred feet or so, until dark, rough shapes of rock appeared with shrubs and fir trees on all prominent points and in every fissure, giving the mountain the appearance of an enormous moss-grown tree which had been stripped of its bark and split at the base.

The landlord recommended us to go up the nearest stone bank, which lay on the side of the blasting operations. He waved away a man, who came from the smithy with a couple of pick-axes on his shoulder, and having put his hands to his mouth, he shouted : " Beware ! " After this he knocked some ashes out of his pipe, puffing vigorously as he went towards the stone, where he put the end of the slow-match into the bowl of his pipe, which he did not take out of his mouth, and then sauntered quietly towards us, still smoking, and with his hands tucked under his leather apron. The spark of the slow-match that for one moment had been visible, disappeared ; a thin smoke oozed out of the stone. Minna and I looked at each other with a strange smile of nervous anxiety, expecting a terrific explosion. At last we heard a rather faint muffled report; pieces of stone were thrown out, a small cloud of dust and smoke spread; the solid mass still stood, though very much undermined. The owner swore, the man with the check trousers scraped some loosened bits out with his pick-axe. In the gash of the stone wound I could see the black trace of the mine.

"We shall have to bore again," he shouted to the owner.

While we were inspecting the spot at close quarters, and the men were looking for the best place to bore, I had taken a pick-axe and chipped one of the pieces, which had come off by blasting, and which easily broke into regular flat bits under my tool. Suddenly I found myself caught and tied up with a piece of the fibre which they used as a wad, while a roar of laughter burst upon my ears, and a red-bearded face bent over my shoulder. I also laughed, of course, but in the unnatural way which is always a clear proof that one does not altogether appreciate the joke. The gay captor, it is true, did give some sort of explanation, evidently under the impression that I understood the whole thing, but he spoke in such broad Saxonian dialect that I was none the wiser.

Minna laughed heartily at seeing me in the arms of the giant, and still more, I suppose, at the funny expression on my face, which said clearly that "I was not in it," but should like to be. At last she controlled her merriment, which, against my will, had annoyed me a good deal.

"He expects you to pay a ransom for your liberty, and he has the right to do so," she said. "It is one of our traditions that if any one trespasses on a workman's preserves, the latter has the right to handcuff him just as you have been."

She had said this in Danish, slowly and with faltering accents, sometimes using a German expression. It was the first time I had heard her speak my mother tongue, and it both surprised and flattered me, because we Danes are always pleasantly astonished when a stranger can make himself understood in a language so little known. And besides, I suspected her of having recently made a special study of it, though she had not said anything to me about it.

I willingly paid my ransom with interest, so that besides the toll exacted by the red-bearded man, there was a tip for the others, but it is not unlikely that the presence of Minna had something to do with my generosity. Then my humorous captor, having pocketed the money with a polite " Thank you," released me, and, after this encouragement, he started with the fresh boring, while the poor gnome, whose rags might, one feared, at any moment fall off completely, drove his iron pole into the stone with the help of a heavy hammer.

As it seemed to be a long business, we went round the quarry to look at the traces of former blastings, and to enjoy the sight of these brittle and gritty stones being so easily shaped by such clever workmen. After this we took to the less serious pastime of gathering some of the beautiful flowers which grew between the blocks ; but when Minna came upon some coloured, almost transparent, pebbles, she turned her attention to them, and in her enthusiasm lay down on the ground, thinking she had found a mine of wealth. I lit a cigar, and took a seat on a stone close by in the scanty shade of some bushes.

" Are they not sweet ? " said Minna, holding towards me a sea-green and lilac pebble, and, blinded by the white glare of the quarry, she looked at me with blinking eyes.

" Indeed, awfully pretty. But what are you going to do with them ? "

" Oh, I shall give them to little Amelia. Though, to be quite honest, I should like to keep them myself. . . . You think me rather childish ? Well, it is just because they remind me of my childhood, though there is not much worth remembering in it. And yet I like to recall it. It is strange how it is ; but time softens everything, even what lies but a short distance off seems glorified. Isn't it always a comfort that the hour will come when a halo will be shed over all memories and make them beautiful ? "

" Yes," I replied, " you are right. And this present time, this very day, perhaps a time will come when one will find it almost painfully beautiful, and reproach oneself for not having appreciated it enough at the moment ; still, as far as I am concerned, that would be unjust."

Minna bent her head lower, and added some fresh stones to the collection in her handkerchief.

" As a child I adored these clear stones, I had plenty of them, and imagined myself to be a Princess, and that they were my jewels. I said that I would give them to little Amelia, but it is quite likely she might be offended by such a present, and her father silly enough to give her real ones instead of them."

" It cannot be an easy task for you to be a governess to such spoilt children. I daresay you have had a more sensible bringing up."

" Honour to whom honour is due," she said a little bitterly, and shook the stray hairs away from her eyes. " Sense ! There was not much of that."

" Was your home very simple ? "

" Had it been simple only, I should not have minded,

but it lacked joy and homeliness. Certainly we were poor, but that alone was not the cause of the discomfort. Can you imagine, I was fourteen years old before I had ever been to Loschwitz ? Of course we came now and then on to the terrace. It was a gala day for my brother and me when father took us to Plauen, where he sometimes had his glass of beer. In those days most of the factories had not been built; it was lovely in the small valley by Weisseritz, and we so enjoyed clambering about the rocks. It was there I found just such beautiful pebbles as these. In the evenings he also sometimes took mother with him to the beer-house ; it was a reminiscence of the early days of their married life, when she used to accompany him every evening. And if you, when you go back to town, look in at ' Zur Katze ' in Castle Street about eight o'clock you will see, in the inner room, an old woman, who is supposed to be like me, sitting with her glass of beer ; and if she has a friend with her, she will spin a long sentimental yarn about the many cosy hours she has spent in this very room with her late dear husband. When the remembrance of home-comfort lodges in ' Zur Katze,' you can imagine what remained for my brother and myself ! We attended a good school, but that was our whole education. Father never troubled about us, and that was a great pity, for he was not only a well-educated man, but also right-minded and very honourable. This, however, I only recognised as I grew older ; it was quite in a frag-mentary way that I got to understand anything about him, for he was most reserved. He never spoke to mother about anything but the weather, and sometimes after reading the newspaper they quarrelled a little about politics. Father was an Imperialist, but mother was on the Saxonian side and hated the Prussians ; she could not understand the good of the great Union, and insisted that it only brought heavy taxation. In that respect I am my mother's daughter ; I can never forgive the Prussians, because in sixty-six they cut down all the trees in Ostra Avenue ; and I can never see those stiff-backed military figures strutting along our streets without feeling irritated. Otherwise they had no subject for discussion, as I have already told you. As time went on I understood better how they felt towards each other, and I am convinced that with another wife he would have been a different man, and also a better father ; and that, in a way, it was just his best qualities which, during the years he lived with mother, caused him to grow more and more reserved, and which finally turned him into an oddity. Odd, he really was beyond all description, and his peculiarities especially recoiled upon us children. Most annoying was his fury if he encountered any strangers in the house. It was an impossibility for me to have a friend with me if he was at home. Once, it was my birthday—I was eleven years old—my mother had given me permission to have a small party down in the garden, at an hour when we knew that my father was giving lessons. For some reason or another the school closed that day. Mother, who saw him coming down the street, flew out to us with a terrified face, and the whole party had to take to their heels through the next garden. You will understand that in this way he became quite an ogre to us, and that we took the part of mother, who really showed more feeling for us. Unfortunately this state of affairs led to our hating everything about him, and we hid much from him, with mother's knowledge and at her instigation, which his disapprobation might have stopped us from doing ; while, as it was, his disapproval only seemed to us another proof of his bad temper, from which we had to escape. But why do I tire you with these reminiscences?"

"Surely you are telling me this because you know that it does not tire me at all, and that at the present moment nothing has more interest for me. I am very grateful to you. I have had a happy childhood myself, and can possibly, for that reason, sympathise with you all the more fully in what you have missed. But you will have to make up for it by enjoying the brighter side of life, and I am sure you will not miss the opportunity."

Minna did not answer, but examined carefully a new heap of pebbles which she had scraped together.

"You spoke of a brother. I have never heard him mentioned before. Has he, perhaps, left Dresden?"

"He died two years ago."

"Poor you, to have had that sorrow also. It must have been a very bitter one."

Minna shook her head.

"No, I did not care much for him. While only a boy he was not kind to me, and made my childhood still worse; and later on, when he was grown up—well, I suppose he was eager 'to make up for what he had missed of the lighter side of life.' I am afraid he would never have given us anything but sorrow."

She looked at me with a defiant expression as much as to say, "I can quite imagine that you think me hard-hearted. Well, do as you like! Should I love him only because he was my brother, when he did not otherwise deserve it? . . . For the rest, do not imagine that I am so good and kind."

"Were there no other relations who might have helped you?" I asked, in order to change the painful subject.

"I had a great-aunt who was my godmother, and who for that reason felt a sort of call to look after me. She even cared for me in her way, but I am sorry to say it was a very disagreeable way, which repelled me. She always grumbled and complained of everything, even to the dressing of my hair. In those days I wore heaps of curls, so she was right in that as in most other things. It was with her the same as with father, except that she really did take trouble with me. It was only much later that I understood the value of their intentions, which in her was hidden under severity, and in him under indifference. She was an oddity, as well as he, and was very fond of him ; but she looked down upon my mother, and therefore regarded with suspicion everything in me which might possibly be inherited from her. When she gave me a present it was as a rule with a threat ; for instance, she allowed me to subscribe to a classical periodical, and gave me, in advance, the money for binding—she never did anything by halves. It is quite a small library, containing about a hundred volumes, and when she gave me the money she said : ' If you ever, even in the greatest need, part with your classics, though I am dead, my spirit will return and torment you,' and I am perfectly certain that she would keep her word. I have, however, no cause for fear, and I have not allowed the books to stand idle on the shelf ; if only for this gift I have great reason to be thankful to her. I had always good literature to my hand, and as I didn't have so much recreation as other young girls, or rather none at all, to take up my time, I was enabled to read a good deal, an opportunity which most young girls do not get. Indeed, I read some things which would have been better deferred. Funnily enough, it never struck my otherwise pedagogic aunt that the good classics contain some things that are not fit for a fourteen-year-old girl to read. I was not older when the subscription started ; but either her literary memory was rather faulty, or the immaculate 'German Classics ' were for her something so elevated that such an idea could not enter her mind. At that age I read *Oberon*. Well, probably you have not read it. After all, I don't think there was much harm done. And these evenings, when I sat and read the great authors, long after mother had gone to sleep, were the first happy hours I experienced. They were more than happy, but also thereby less so, for while they opened out many beautiful visions, they at the same time brought with them the dark shadow of self-recognition. I understood that there existed quite a different world. I do not mean the world of outer circumstances, but of thoughts and feelings, quite different methods of judgment as to what has value and what has not, which had been obscured by the web mother had spun around me of doubtful and elastic rules of life, and to these were added many specious and sentimental phrases which, apparently, only served to cast a sort of veil over them.

" Perhaps you wonder that I had to gain this experience from the authors, as I had received Christian teaching. It was indeed not precepts I needed, but life itself, which in our little circle had nothing which might be called, I will not say elevated, but noble and pure. Of course we saw only mother's relations, sisters, aunts, and cousins, and of them she was the best ; they were scarcely tolerated by father, and only came when he was out, or they crept into the kitchen and held a gossiping conclave. Oh, how it disgusts me to think of all this ! The fact that the clergyman who confirmed me, and over whose sermons mother cried, had not the best of reputations socially, must also, I suppose, have been a bad influence. Goethe and Schiller had to preach for me, and they were not the worst of prophets. But this brought, of course, a violent revolution in me, with many struggles and doubts, which greatly affected me. As I had to get up early in order to help with the household duties, this evening-reading, which often developed into night-reading, was very exhausting. To this was added the fact that we always lived too frugally, and, still worse, unwholesomely; so that without knowing it I had, in a way, been starving all through the years of my growing up. I suffered from anæmia and nervousness, and these circumstances combined had the result that, in those days, I was never really well. I would suddenly turn giddy when walking in the street, and I used to be overcome by unreasonable fears. At times it seemed as if I was no good to anyone, and I was terrified lest my reason should go. With regard to my spiritual development, I felt that I might have had some help from my father, but reserve had then become his second nature, and, at the time, in-firmity was added to this barrier. He died about a year ago, without my coming nearer to him ; and some of the blame was mine, I suppose. That he never troubled about my inner life made me haughty, and I felt that I shut myself off from him. I frequently made up my mind to approach him with confidence and affection, but when it came to the point, it annoyed me to think that there should be any difficulty, and that such an effort was necessary between father and daughter, and I remained silent at the critical moment. The last time I went in to see him he kissed me and said : 'Always continue to be a brave girl.' Giving way to the feelings of the moment I nearly burst out crying, but the old voice within me whispered : ' What have *you* done to help me to be so ? And how do you know that I am one at all ?' It ended with a formal promise and a cold embrace. When a few hours later I returned from giving some lessons, my father was dead."

Minna remained quiet for a long time, with downcast eyes ; the corners of her mouth twitched, and I expected every moment that she would burst into tears. Suddenly she lifted her eyes and looked at me with a tearless, but singularly earnest and piercing look, as if wondering what effect her narrative had produced on me. Surely she was saying to herself : " No doubt you now think me very nasty ! I sincerely wish I was better, but anyhow I will not make myself out to be better than I am." Her face was very sorrowful, and I was convinced that it was more this thought than the painful recollections that caused her troubled expression.

I myself was strangely moved, and would willingly have pressed her hand ; but we were seated a few paces apart, and the workmen were close to us. A pressure of my hand would have made her understand the whole depth of my feelings for her better than any words, which on such an occasion are enshrouded in shame at their own feebleness. I told her I had long suspected that something sad in her past lay heavily upon her, but that I had no idea it was so deeply rooted in the whole of her childhood and development.

At this remark her face assumed a peculiar, suspicious and almost ironical expression, which I well knew.

" But you have only dwelt on the dark side of your life," I said, to change the subject. " How is it you have not mentioned Mr. and Mrs. Hertz ? They were already in Dresden in those days, I suppose ? "

" Yes, but I only made their acquaintance at that time, just at my father's funeral. . . . The relationship with Aunt Thea was so distant, really none at all . . . so

much the better, perhaps! . . . Their house became
another home to me: no, I ought not to call it 'Home,'
something much better, but that you know. . . . And after
what I have told you, you can realise better what these
excellent people have been to me. . . ."

She said this slowly, and as if she was distrait, perhaps
tired of talking, and maybe regretting that she had been
so confiding.

Our landlord now interrupted us with a request that we
should go back to our former safe seats, as everything was
ready for the fresh blasting.

I had almost forgotten where we were, and why. Some
of her words, with their melancholy and often bitter tone,
kept sounding in my ear, as they do even now. Regarding
the account, it has, of course, formed itself in my memory
into a more continuous whole than at the time when it
came from her lips, and it is very likely that, in reality,
some of the incidents were only told during the following
days; but such small inaccuracies cannot affect the main
impression. What especially struck me was the clear
reflective way in which she spoke of and judged her life;
it was evident that she had frequently thought over all the
details and their connection with one another, examining
both cause and effect. I saw in this the proof that she was
of a more melancholy nature than I had thought. For
I had lately been misled by the youthful gaiety that so
often broke forth.

The fresh blasting passed off just like the first; the stone
mass still stood, though now it was almost entirely undermined, and hung free like a shelf. The red-bearded
workman approached carefully, and scraped out with his
axe the loose bits which the explosion had not removed.
At the corners in the background some half-split blocks

still gave a little support. While the owner and the ragged workman kept an eye on the mass of stone in order to give the alarm at the smallest movement, the courageous man struck heavy blows on those places. In the beginning he paused between each blow, ready to jump away, but little by little he became too excited to be cautious. The pickaxe made its way, blow followed blow, and small bits flew about him; he seemed enraged at the stubborn resistance. It looked terribly dangerous; the eyes, which were tired of gazing on this blinding surface and hardly dared to blink, seemed each moment to see movement in the edge of the colossal block. Twice was the alarm given, and after each disappointing pause the attack commenced afresh, more furiously and with growing danger.

Minna was quite pale, and pressed her lips together. I, for my part, my feelings blunted by the long suspense, went a few steps nearer, the better to see the effect of these giant strokes; then she jumped after me, and with an impetuous grip on my arm dragged me back. Simultaneously a shout was heard; I saw a huge glare moving overhead and on the side, and heard a heavy thud. The whole stone mass lay some distance off, and loose blocks fell a few yards from us. My first thought was for the clever workman; he stood safe and sound on the side of the stone monster which he had overcome, and nodded to us with a smile as if to say, " It was a near shave." I supported Minna, who was trembling violently, and made her sit down on a stone.

CHAPTER X

THE afternoon sun shed its full glare on the rocks, but over them dark clouds were hanging, and the rain suddenly began to fall in such big drops that its stormy character could not be mistaken. We were obliged to hurry over the shrub-covered bank to the smithy of the quarry. This effort gave Minna back her strength, and she, who a minute before had hardly been able to support herself, now ran the last few steps through the pouring rain, as if her nerves had not been in the least shaken.

It was a great change to come from the vast, bright space, with its white, sunlit rocks, into a small room over-crowded with workmen, and enveloped in a sooty and black obscurity which was only relieved by red-glowing flames. A strikingly handsome young man stood by the forge ; he stretched up his muscular arm, caught a rope, and pulled the long bent pole which worked the bellows. The heap of coal flared brightly, he poked it, threw on another shovelful, put a pickaxe with a blunt end into it, and took out another one with a red-hot point ; then he spat on one of his fingers, with which he skimmed the hot metal, and dipped it into a trough of water, causing it to frizzle and send up a white steam.

Minna laughed.

" Just now we saw Siegfried fighting with the dragon, and here we have him alive in the forest smithy."

She had again been speaking Danish to me, and the

workmen looked at us wonderingly, astonished at this gibberish. The smith did not seem to pay any attention to it ; just at that moment he laid the smouldering pick, which was beginning to turn grey, on to the anvil, and worked it with his hammer, so that the sparks flew about, and we stepped back a few yards out of the way. Minna looked at him with an admiration which did not please me.

" Don't you think him handsome ? " she asked. " As he stands there at his work, one cannot imagine anything more picturesque. If only Gudehus [1] looked like that ! "

" Of course he is good-looking, but you will spoil him by admiring him so openly. He will be so conceited, that the poor little village maidens will never be able to please him again."

" He is occupied with his work, surely he does not notice it."

" Then the others will tell him."

" But, really it is so delightful to see something absolutely perfect ! "

However justifiable this might have been, I did not like it.

" I wonder if he is a Saxon ? " she said, a little while after.

" No, miss, I am from Schleswig," the workman answered quite calmly in Danish, throwing the pick aside, and occupying himself by blowing the bellows.

One would have thought that he blew the flush on to her cheek, so red did she turn. The workmen about chuckled a little, and seemed to have understood the situation. At first I enjoyed her confusion, as a fitting punishment, but soon I began to pity her, for she did not seem to have the courage to lift her eyes from the ground.

[1] Famous Wagner singer (Siegfried) in Dresden.

Fortunately the rain had nearly ceased. We bade good-bye to our kind landlord and the red-bearded giant ; the gnome scowled from a corner, and the Adonis of the smithy sent a gay " Farvel " after us.

We were, of course, not inclined to risk going down the same way up which we had crawled. So the little Hans was ordered to show us the way through the neighbouring quarries, but I soon told our youthful guide that I could manage for myself, and eventually succeeded in escaping from him.

Most of the quarries were deserted by the workmen. One saw everywhere the same white ground and walls, shrub-covered banks, rows of hewn stone, gigantic masses of rough blocks, which had the appearance of ruins, and here and there parts of rocks that had fallen over, remains of the much more extensive winter-blasting by which, at times, the river gets blocked. By keeping as close as possible to the rock-wall, we had little difficulty in finding a fairly good pathway. The quarries were separated from one another by waste ground covered with chips of stone, that moved and gave way under one's feet, for which reason there was often an opportunity to support Minna, who screamed and laughed on the unsafe ground, stretching out her arms to me either to find support, or when she thought that I was slipping. The sad recollections on which she had dwelt, the nervous excitement while the blasting was going on, and, lastly, her confusion in the smithy, seemed but to have dammed her stream of gaiety, which now burst forth with still greater force. Once we both fell, she on the top of me—fortunately I was the only one at all hurt ; Minna got up laughing, and helped me without any sign of shyness. Perhaps at this moment she would even have forgotten to send me on in front if we had been obliged to climb up the mountain ; really she appeared to have no thought for anything but her exuberant mood, and perhaps also for mine, and for Nature's, which with scent and twitter met us from the mountain wood we now entered.

The strong, incense-like perfume, which the sun had drawn out from the slope, was refreshed by the rain ; and, intoxicated by the sweetness, the birds sang as if it were spring-time. The evening sun cast its rays between the firs, the bent, fringed branches of which glittered as if hung with stars. Underneath, between the trunks, one saw the river as a gliding light, and above, the gently nodding tree-tops were surmounted by a bark-coloured, grooved and cleft rock, bounded by a bluish rim of weatherbeaten firs mounting upwards towards the cloudless sky.

Now and then the soughing of the wind, like a wave approaching us, was heard from above, big drops fell on us, and Minna's skirt fluttered aside. It was of a soft pale chamois-coloured material, which hung in loose folds from her leather belt. She walked cautiously on the sloping ground, which, wherever it had remained dry, was made very slippery by the fir needles and the cone shells ; she often slid, stretching out her right arm with a little scream, so that the wide sleeve was caught up over the dimple of the elbow, while the other one, with its ungloved and sunburnt hand, seized hold of the moss.

Suddenly I burst out laughing, and as she turned with a questioning smile, I pointed to her shadow, which, in a stout unshapely form, showed itself on the perpendicular stone surface next to her ; she answered with an even heartier laugh, and pointed out mine, which, longer legged than a stork, stretched up a height. For a long while we could not get away from this place, as by the smallest movement the two shadows cut a more and more ridiculous figure. When at last we moved on, and came to a place where the incline grew less steep and the wood had been allowed to spread, the shadows again began to play their funny tricks ; now lying over the green turf, then jumping from trunk to trunk, and bounding directly from a tree close to us to one lit up far away in the density.

" Do you know ? " said Minna, " what a good thing it is that you are not Peter Schlemihl, for in that case you would now be discovered ! "

" Without doubt I should be, and what then ? "

" Well, then—? Anyhow, I should not like it at all."

Her little ear had turned quite red, and this could not have been due to transparency, as the sun was behind us. My heart danced with joy, for I could not doubt that she thought of the place in the immortal book, where the poor shadowless man, Schlemihl, walks at night in the garden with his beloved, and suddenly comes to a spot where the moon shines, and where only *her* shadow is to be seen stretching out before their feet. She had also instantly understood that my—apparently—very simple " and what then ? " was more bold than stupid, for she herself had lately lent me the book—a volume of those classical periodicals of which she had spoken.

Yes, suppose my shadow had not been visible, then she would have fallen into a faint, and I should have been obliged to leave her for ever ; but now, being perfectly alive and playing hide-and-seek with her shadow in the forest, suffused by the evening glow, what obstacle was there in my way ? Sure enough, I had no inexhaustible purse in my pocket, but my shadow was complete enough. Did it not stand just now on the sloping stone surface, black and white, as an indisputable proof that I was an honest

fellow with no devilry about me ? And the little lobe of
the ear in front, which was so rosy red, did it not say that
it belonged to a woman who loved me just a little ? Why
then should not my heart jump for joy ?

"Do tell me, are you as thirsty as I am ? " Minna
suddenly asked.

"That's a question I cannot answer, but I am *very*
thirsty."

"Well, over there I see lots of bilberries, and I do not
know why we should let them dry up and be of no
use."

I was quite of her opinion, and we began to plunder the
small bushes as quickly as we could. As it was too uncomfortable to stand for long in a bending position, we went
down on our knees and crept from bush to bush on all-fours.
Soon it became too much trouble to pluck off the berries one
by one, so we tore off stalks and pulled them through our
mouths, and in thus satisfying our thirst we for the first time
realised how great it had been. Minna almost hugged
herself, and even began to make a purring sound like a
contented little animal. Seeing that this amused me, she
carried the joke further, and snapped the berries from the
bushes with her lips, not using her hands, which were
spread out, like paws, upon the ground. Then she glanced
up at me with a very humorous expression, at the same time
purring and shaking her head, with some little curls dancing
round her brow. Her lips were dark blue, and her smile
showed a row of bluish teeth. Whether it was this rustic
négligé which rendered her mouth less unapproachable than
my respect had previously found it, or whether this colour,
as a sign of our childish mood, aided my natural diffidence,
I know not ; but it is certain that it gave me an irresistible
desire to kiss her. At this moment we both discovered a

berry as big as a small cherry, and our heads collided;
while I still laughed and rubbed mine, she snatched the
berry, and, immediately afterwards, my lips pressed a long
kiss on hers, and my glance pierced her eyes, which grew
quite small and in their depths had a gleam of the last
golden sunbeam. Only our lips met, our arms rested on
the ground like fore-legs; and just as I wanted to make
a more human use of them, and place them round her
shoulders, half unconscious and intoxicated as I was by
the heavenliness of the first kiss, she jumped to her feet
and ran down the path. Before I could overtake her, she
had already reached a spot where I could not walk by her
side, as the path was only a foot in breadth, and the slope
was steep. Aware of this, she walked quietly.

" Minna ! " I called softly and diffidently.

She did not seem to hear me.

" Were you unable to find my shadow ? " I asked, trying
to make a joke of it, " since you so suddenly ran away from
me. Just look behind, and you will see that I still have it,
though it has turned much paler, but so has yours."

Still no answer.

" Are you angry with me ? "

She shook her head, but neither stopped nor looked
back. The manner of her answer had, however, calmed
me; I did not know what to say, nor did I wish to bother
her, though this silent march, one behind the other, was
dreadfully painful to me. At last we came near the place
where the tiny mountain-path, between the outer firs, sloped
down to the meadow near the river, only a few minutes'
walk from Rathen. There I should, at any rate, be able
to see the expression on her face.

Like a deer which is brought to bay, she turned to face
me.

" I will now say good-bye. We are near home, and you are not to come any farther with me."

" But why not ? What do you mean ? "

" Let me alone ! Do let me go by myself this time, it is the only thing I ask of you, because I let you, because you . . ."

" But, any way, tell me . . ."

" Good-bye, good-bye ! "

She ran rather than walked down the stones, and over the meadow, where her steps grew noiseless ; only the leather belt round her waist creaked with her quick movement, just like the girth of a horse's saddle. It had creaked like that whilst she crept amongst the bilberries. I grew quite sad when I could not hear it any longer.

There I remained on the same spot, gazing after her as long as I could see her light dress.

BOOK II

CHAPTER I

MORE in a dream than awake I wandered near the river bank for a long time. One reflection alone continually recurred to my mind with ever-increasing joy: she was not only free now, but had apparently always been so, and perhaps knew no more of heartache than I did. It was absurd of me to have been jealous of the good-looking workman in the smithy, but still more absurd to have indulged in the same feeling towards the visionary person called " The Danish Painter." No doubt the whole of this story was only family gossip gathered from an old aunt who, according to the schoolmaster, " was not quite what she ought to have been." In addition to which Minna herself had spoken often about these aunts and their foolish tittle-tattle.

She was to be mine. Was she not mine already? I still felt her kiss on my lips. But why had she left me so suddenly? Why did she not allow me to take her home? Girlish fancies! Who can comprehend them, and who would be without them?

It was already growing dusk. The after-glow of the evening sky dazzled the eye to such an extent that one could hardly judge the distances in the sombre foreground. A faint gleam of light still fell on the edges of the rocks above, and a grey cobweb seemed to stretch over the green meadows on the other side of the water.

I heard voices ahead, and saw a man and a boy coming towards me. The landlord and his son were returning from the quarry. When we were close to each other the boy ran towards me with something white in his hand.

" Here is your letter," he called out.

" My letter ? "

" Yes, I suppose it is one you wanted to post," said the owner of the quarry, " for it is addressed to Denmark."

" I found it where you sat so long while the boring was going on," said Hans.

With an uncomfortable feeling I took the letter, which was quite moist.

In the fading twilight I had some difficulty in discovering that the blurred address on the letter was to " Axel Stephensen, Esq., Artist." I wanted to see once more if my suspicions of the handwriting were correct, but the light dazzled my eyes.

" Yes, it is all right, thank you. Good-bye."

There stood the name of " The Danish Painter." If I had suddenly seen a ghost my back could not have felt more icily cold.

Axel Stephensen, indeed ! Of course I knew him. Who does not know our young artists, even the least famous of the celebrities ! It was some small consolation to me that, at any rate, I had not to cope with a genius. I knew him, that is to say, I had met him once at a café; I also remembered a rather nice landscape of his in the academy ; and I had from time to time heard him mentioned, though not always in the most flattering terms, for he was considered rather fast. But what struck me as a most remarkable coincidence was the fact that on this very day I had received a letter, in which a cousin of mine had made some slangy insinuations about Axel Stephensen himself, to the effect that this Paris dandy was persistently carrying on with a young lady of our acquaintance, whose purse was more attractive than her looks, and whose portrait he had painted in so flattering a manner, that both the object of his attentions and her family were quite delighted. Unfortunately for the painter, the one to whom the portrait gave especial pleasure was its destined owner—a fully-fledged naval officer whose successful examination was now to be rewarded by the announcement of the engagement.

So Stephensen was the man who had played a not unimportant part in Minna's life! From what the schoolmaster had said, I understood that a couple of years must have passed since Minna had known him in Dresden, and yet they still wrote to each other. What could it mean but a kind of love, a secret understanding, or something of that sort? But on the other hand her confidence in me, her innocent coquetry, this kiss, which she willingly enough had allowed me to steal; how could one reconcile this with such an intimacy, except in a girl of a frivolous nature? The more I thought of these contradictions the more incomprehensible they appeared.

My reverie was at last interrupted by the bell-like sound of a chain-worked steamer.

It was quite dark.

The moon was indistinctly seen behind the fir-tops on a height on the other side of the river; its light did not yet reach down upon the water, and one could not see the ships, but the line of lanterns with their long reflections in the water moved on slowly, again reminding me of a procession of golden staves with big knobs, led by a ruby and emerald one.

This sight, which recalled so vividly our happy life by the river, made me still more depressed.

I went slowly home with the fatal letter in my hand.

As soon as I had lighted the lamp I began to look at it more closely. The moisture had loosened the gum so much that the envelope was only fastened in one single spot.

It would be the easiest thing in the world to open and to close it without being discovered.

This thought made me turn hot and cold ; I threw it on the table in terror, and kept on walking round the room and glancing at it as I walked.

Suddenly I had the letter in my hand and was picking with my nail at the closed spot ; but, as if it had only been done in a fit of abstraction, I quickly turned the letter over and eagerly examined the address.

If I had so far been able to doubt whether the handwriting was Minna's, my uncertainty quickly vanished.

But a certain circumstance occurred to me ; both the address and the piece of prose by Goethe in the poetry-book had been written in the same reddish and rather muddy ink which I thought was very probably to be obtained from the Rathen grocer. If this was the case I was, without doubt, the cause of the insertion of that lovely fragment, and this thought made me regard the tiresome letter with greater equanimity.

I took a piece of notepaper and wrote to Minna that this letter, which evidently she had lost, had been found and brought to me, but that I did not like to post it without her consent, as the address seemed to have suffered a good deal from the damp, and was so illegible that I thought she might prefer to have the letter returned to her.

I then put a big wrapper round the whole thing, addressed it, and went out at once to take it to the post-box at " Erbgericht." Thus I got rid of both temptation and annoyance.

Clear moonlight lay on the heights over the sleeping hamlet, of which only the roofs of a few houses were high enough for the moonbeams to shed their rays over the small window-panes. Far above these stood the crown of steep rocks, appearing closer and more than usually blended together in vague, shadowy shapes. The quarries shone in the distance, away over the bend of the river, and I could distinguish the spot where we had spent the day together.

This quiet, cool beauty calmed me, and its effect was soon enhanced by a deadly weariness which suddenly overtook me as I again began to climb up to my mountain-home.

More quickly than I had thought to be possible I went to sleep in expectation of " the things which were to come."

CHAPTER II

THE next morning I ran down at once to the grocer, and brought back a bottle of the only sort of ink that he had in stock, as likely to be the presumed *corpus delicti*. My investigation gave the wished-for result : both the letter and the transcription in the poetry book had been written with this *instrumento*, and I quickly began to look at things in a more cheerful light.

I began to consider " the things which were to come." She would by now have received what I had forwarded, and I did not doubt that an explanation on her part would follow. It seemed to me that most likely she would choose to answer in writing. Would she send me a letter by hand ? But that might easily give rise to gossip. Perhaps, however, she might not have time to write early enough in the day to make this mode of despatch of any avail, and the post might bring the letter as quickly. This day would have to be dedicated to the exercise of patience.

How was I to wile away the dreadful time ? First I thought of taking a long trip, but I shivered at the idea of letting my own thoughts have sway, and being doomed to turn and twist the same question over and over again in my mind. I preferred, therefore, to give myself up to the perusal of a German novel of the domestic type, with the purest aims, and with contents which mercifully time has blotted from my memory. I then ordered my dinner to be sent for.

By and by it grew dreadfully hot and no air came through the open window. I threw off one garment after another until I lay on the bed in my shirt, which was hardly considerate to the figures depicted in the novel, who were the essence of propriety. I did not think there was any risk of other visitors, the old Hertzes could not possibly venture so far up. Suddenly an idea dawned upon me : Suppose she herself came to see me! It seemed impossible, but in such cases one must be prepared for any emergency.

At once I began to dress with the greatest care. Yes, I would even have shaved had not the sun been so blinding. As my eye caught sight of the little birch avenue, I was possessed by a new idea—the grotto " Sophien-Ruhe "! She had said that at this time the people of the house never came there ; what if, trusting to my memory and shrewdness, she expected to see me there! Surely she would do so. It was like a revelation! And off I darted.

A few yards from the place I paused in order to gain control over my feelings, and at the same moment a tall gentleman, with moustache and beard *à la Kaiser Wilhelm*, came out of the grotto with an aggrieved air.

" I beg your pardon," I stuttered ; " I am afraid . . . perhaps this is private ground——"

" Strictly private, sir," answered the Kaiser-bearded gentleman in a most majestic tone, and I disappeared from his lordly and offended gaze.

Not in the best of humours, I returned to the house and plunged into the second volume of the novel. Just at the most critical point, another idea occurred to me. Might she be with the Hertzes, why had I not thought of that before ? No—she had said yesterday that she would be unable to be there. Again the wave from the waters of Lethe was borne upon my bewildered brain by the sentimentality of the novel, until the candle had burnt down in the socket and sleep wafted me away from noble Counts and still more noble clergymen's daughters.

The hour of the post next morning came and passed by.

> "The post for thee no letter brings,
> My heart, my heart." [1]

I attacked the third volume of the novel, which, like the others, contained five hundred pages. When that was finished and I noticed that the sun had already passed the one window frame, I hurried my preparations for shaving, taking into consideration that it is advisable to be well-shaved when a scene of a delicate description is imminent. The time for the second and last postal delivery approached rapidly ; I did not care to contemplate what I should do in case of disappointment, and still I was almost sure that it awaited me. I had cleared the stubbly field of the right cheek, when my hand shook so much that I had to put down the razor, the reason being that I saw, coming up the zigzag path of the hill, the long, thin postman, who, in his uniform jacket and military cap, resembled badly-drawn pictures of Moltke. I remained at the window in breathless expectation and, as I saw him disappear round the corner of the house, I listened for the steps on the staircase, and was still listening in vain when his figure became visible marching down the steep slope.

A dreadful disappointment overcame me and, exasperated beyond endurance, I threw myself upon the bed. Clattering steps of bare feet were then heard on the landing,

[1] Schubert, *Die Post.*

and there was a knock at my door, that was locked on account of the *négligé* attire which I had assumed during the reading of the novel. As soon as I had opened the door a big, wet hand thrust a thick letter into the room.

CHAPTER III

IT really was from her! I tore open the envelope and pulled out several closely-written pages of note-paper, from which fell a smaller letter—the one to Mr. Stephensen—in an open envelope. This confidence astonished me, but seemed to be a good omen; naturally I did not at first stay to examine it more closely.

Her letter, which, woman-like, was undated, read as follows :—

"DEAR MR. FENGER,—I wonder what you really think of me, though, I am sure, that you positively do not know what to think. I quite understood that the reason why you did not post my letter was not because it was wet, but because you wished to ask me 'What does it mean?' Such an explanation I think you have a right to demand or, at all events, to expect. Even without this incident I should have taken the first suitable opportunity to let you know, at any rate, most of the contents of this letter. I have been in doubt whether it would not be better to speak to you—there are plenty of lonely walks and the children could always be with us—but, after all, I thought writing would be best, for really I am going to make a sort of confession. When it is over, you will not think so well of me as you do now. But just for that reason it is a necessity to me that you should come to know me, however sad it may be to destroy pleasant illusions.

"It was a lucky coincidence that I had given you a rather detailed account of my home and my bringing up. Not altogether a coincidence, however, as I had previously decided to let you know what I had experienced, and my former confidences had to be the introduction. I therefore ask you to call to mind as much as you can remember ; the main points will, I suppose, have given you a distinct impression, even if my description was rather confused, and without it you might judge me much more harshly than I perhaps deserve.

"But let me begin. Ah! I wish you were sitting opposite to me, it is so difficult to write about it.

"I do not know if I told you that my mother had six sisters. They were daughters of a wealthy inn-keeper, whose hostel was chiefly patronised by country people. They all had to take their part in the household duties, and consequently did not get much education. Of family life there was hardly any, as the mother was occupied in the housekeeping, and the father in the business. He sometimes flogged his daughters with the stick, it was nearly their whole education, and it did not bear good fruit. (I am thankful I am *writing* now.) Five of them had children before they were married, my mother and her younger sister alone being of the opinion that everything was permitted so long as one did not commit that error.

"By such a mother I was brought up, and I clung to her with a great love ; for while only a little child I was made her confidante and shared her sorrows, while father never spoke to me. When quite a little girl, I heard her tell her love stories, and I grew up with the idea that one rose in the eyes of other people in proportion to the number of admirers one had.

"Shortly after my confirmation, I renewed acquaintance

with a former school-friend, who was some years older than I. Our gardens joined and she often called me over to her. I soon remarked that, when we walked out, Emily sent many covert glances towards the house in the neighbouring garden, and she soon confided in me that 'her darling' lived there, but I was not to tell her mother. One day two young men looked out of the window, the 'darling' and a friend of his, and I could hardly believe my eyes when the friend nodded to me. I told it all to mother, who was very much amused. How it happened I don't remember now, but a meeting was arranged to which my mother accompanied me, and I can still distinctly call to mind the mingled feelings of disgust and pride which filled my mind as I walked with this stranger. After this he came to see us ; I was then not more than fourteen years old. He sat beside me and also kissed me, and we took walks together. Oh, dear friend, it was dreadful! Imagine, I believed that this was quite correct, and yet this individual was so unsympathetic to me. He went away, and we wrote occasionally to each other—God knows what about! I always lived with a vague feeling that things were not as they ought to be, especially as this introduction was deceitfully hidden from my father.

"It must have been shortly after this that a young musician came to live with us. I had to wait on him as I did on the other lodgers. He was more intimate with us than any of the others had been, and, unfortunately, I grew very fond of him, but quite—I must now ask you, dear Mr. Fenger, to give me your absolute trust—in an innocent way. When, through the door, I could hear that he was preparing to go out, I quickly put on my hat and jacket, pretending I had a commission to do for my mother, but really with the hope that I could walk down the

street with him. One day a picnic was arranged by my
cousins, and I asked if the musician could be of the party,
but as the others objected to a stranger, I stayed at home.
He then invited me to go alone with him to Loschwitz,
which my mother did not object to, and, as usual, an untruth
was told to my father.

"After this we one evening played a game of forfeits,
and he was deputed to kiss me, which I distinctly refused
to allow. He went into his room, and my mother, by some
ruse or another, sent me to him. He repeatedly asked me
for the kiss, and got it, and from that day I really loved
him so much that, according to my fifteen-year-old ideas, I
thought that I could never love another so well. The
previous intimacy now began to worry me dreadfully,
but I did not see any way out of it. However, the correspondence soon came to an end.

"The young musician asked my mother for my hand,
but she told him I was far too young to think of a serious
engagement. Soon afterwards I heard that he was on the
point of being engaged to some one else—which report,
however, turned out eventually to be untrue—and my
despair was beyond everything. Anyhow he left us, and, a
fortnight later, Mr. Stephensen took the room. The day
the musician departed, I knelt on the floor and tore off some
dead twigs of a garland which he had won at a shooting
competition, and kept it as a souvenir.

"Mr. Stephensen then came. Later on he assured me
that he had only engaged the lodging for my sake, as in
reality he did not care for it. He was thus already attracted
by me, and, as he afterwards told me, looked upon me as
a superior and unapproachable being. For the sake of
both these men's honour, I must remark that they were
never unduly familiar towards me. Therefore I could

afterwards understand the passion of Mignon, which is also so perfectly innocent.

"When Mr. Stephensen had lived with us a fortnight, the musician came one evening to say good-bye. I went with him to the door. There he asked me to kiss him at parting, which I did, Stephensen "—(a commenced "Axel" was here crossed out)—" in his jealousy, listening at the door. Since then he has told me that from that minute he looked upon me as in no way different to others, and began to want me to be his according to his own ' views.'

"Oh, dear friend, it was hard to learn that in a moment, when I was so little conscious of doing anything wrong, I had lost a man's respect and love, and in his eyes lowered myself to the level of a worthless woman. Never shall I forget the feelings which overwhelmed me when I came to realise how low I had fallen in the eyes of one who, though he had known me so little, thought so highly of me, and whom I afterwards came to love! Thousands of times I cried bitter, despairing tears. My only consolation was that I knew myself to be innocent. Often, when I have pondered over it, it has appeared to me that when a man has formed so pure and beautiful an impression, which after all must be intuitive, he ought not, through an accidental circumstance, to change his opinion so that it becomes entirely different, but should wait until he is calm again and is able to judge dispassionately. I think that a real lover ought not to have thrust me away, but have made allowances for a childish indiscretion, considering that, after all, my faults were those of my bringing up and surroundings, and that he would be able to shield me from harm and raise me to the ideal he had formed. But perhaps this was too much to expect, and very likely it is only ignorance of feelings which makes me reason thus. Maybe that in reading this you will understand Mr. Stephensen better than you do me, and feel that in his place you would have reasoned in the same way.

"It was this recollection which so strongly overcame me after I had allowed you to kiss me. If you had known whom you had kissed, and that it was far from—oh, so far, from being my first kiss! And did not even this kiss prove that he had been right in considering me flighty? Perhaps you also had discovered it, and therefore took advantage of the knowledge. But no, I could not think *that* of you after our innocent intercourse. Such a kiss would not have been in accordance with it; perhaps it was a childish, thought-less, or playful kiss, but certainly it was not one of love's Judas kisses. However, I understood neither you nor myself, and I was afraid for both of us. When I came home, I cried as if my heart would break, without really knowing why I was crying.

"But I must return to the old days. Mr. Stephensen spoke much to me about what I have told you, pointing out how wrong it all was, and correcting the objectionable views in which my mother had brought me up, and gradually he opened my eyes to many things to which I had previously been blind. He also discussed his art with me, and found that I had a good deal of natural taste for it (the painter Jagemann from the Weimar-period, a friend of Schiller, about whom perhaps you have read, was one of my an-cestors, and my father had, as a young man, painted a little himself). I often went with Mr. Stephensen round our glorious gallery, where he was copying two pictures. During this time he grew more and more demonstrative, to which I strongly objected, and I only put up with it because I was so fond of him. Besides, I had the hope that he would marry me, but he always tried to talk me out of it. He had no means, and his art, he said, would suffer under domestic troubles, and when I promised to be so good a housewife that it would not cost him more than when he was single, he replied that such a tie was not good for an artist, who had to travel about and give himself up completely to his work and ideas. He kept on trying to convince me that the suggestion of a closer bond was mere Philistinism and selfishness on my part, and that free intercourse between man and woman, under such circumstances, was a quite worthy, nay, even, ideal relation. I have never been able to agree with this, and while he, with good reason, had begun to find my moral education very unsatisfactory, I ended by finding his own morals rather loose—perhaps it was prejudice on my part, but, anyhow, I could not adopt his views. So much I know, that it was not calculation or worldly wisdom in me, but an unconquerable feeling, accompanied by the painful knowledge that his love for me was far from being so tender as mine for him ; of course he also had his art, while I only had my love.

" When his time in Dresden was over, we parted with the understanding that we should remain good friends and write to one another. I was to try and marry well and be sure to tell him all my experiences, so that I might not again take a false step.

" This was my position. Can you imagine how very lonely I was ? For my mother I felt an aversion. The dearest in this world, the only one with whom I could converse, had left me, and I had not even the right to long for him. I tried to take up my piano-playing again, but every beautiful melody made me so indescribably sad that I had to give it up.

" It was at this time that my father died (about which I think I told you) and I came to know Mr. and Mrs. Hertz,

with whom I found an atmosphere as totally different from
the one in my home as—on the other hand—from the
artistic one which I came to know through your countryman; and this helped, more than I can say, to bring me peace.
But I can never forget that it was Mr. Stephensen who by
his sympathy and interest for me, first of all awoke my
feeling of pride and prevented me from being ruined by
the unhealthy atmosphere which surely bid fair to destroy
me.

" With regard to our correspondence, it has continued
ever since, with longer or shorter intervals, for a year
and a half. He has always answered my letters rather
quickly and asked me to write again soon ; sometimes he
has sent a leaf of his sketch-book, and last Christmas a
beautiful painting. In order to make you understand this
kind of correspondence, I beg you to read the enclosed letter,
which has already been through your hands. Not that I
think you have any suspicion from which I could, by this
means, clear myself ; but you will not misunderstand my
fancy, even if you do not understand it. Perhaps I do not
understand it myself, but only feel that I want you to know
it ; it even seems to me as if the circumstances have given
you a sort of right to do so, and as if by simply tearing the
letter up I should deprive you of it. Send it off I will not,
for, as you will see by the date, it will soon be a fortnight
old ; I was sure that I had posted it, and rather expected
the case to be reversed, and that the post would bring me a
letter from him.

" And now, good-bye ! I have been writing half the
night and am dreadfully tired. My hope is that you will
not judge me too harshly after this communication, but,
anyhow, you must tell me quite candidly what impression
this letter has made on you, and not out of kindness be too

lenient. Unless this confidence is frankly answered, how shall I benefit by it? That I value your judgment you know beforehand, and you will also see it by my letter to Mr. Stephensen.—Your friend,

"MINNA JAGEMANN."

Confused though I was by the many conflicting emotions caused by the reading of this letter, I did not at first try to come to any clear comprehension of it, but at once opened the letter with which two days before I had been tempted to tamper. I did not doubt that it would contain observations about myself.

I quickly ran through the opening sentences, with the usual excuses for not having written for so long, and the remarks about the weather and the country. A little more attention was bestowed upon a short, not very complimentary, description of the honourable family with whom she was living, and I noticed that she did not try to play the novelist, a part which young letter-writing ladies—especially in the governess line—are apt to indulge in on such occasions. After this I read with a palpitating heart the following lines—

" I have made acquaintance with a young student by the name of Fenger, a countryman of yours. It was, as you will understand, this fact which first recommended him to me, and made us more quickly acquainted than is usually the case. I very often meet him at the Hertzes. He is not exactly handsome, but has one of those frank fair faces which please one, especially when he smiles. He is very tall, but stoops a little, and sometimes it seems to me that his chest is not very strong. I should be very grieved if such was the case. He shows me so much attention that

I cannot hide from myself that he appreciates me. Time will show, however, if this is anything more than a fleeting summer-holiday fancy. He is still very young, his age is only twenty-four, but really he seems much younger, as if he was still untouched by life. With regard to myself, I hardly know what position I should take in case things took a serious turn, and I cannot make myself reflect over this and take up a position accordingly ; such a course being against my nature. Of course, when one can be accused of having 'encouraged' a young man—I think that is the expression—or even of having 'flirted' with him, which often only means having been gay, natural, and having given way to moods, and then when it comes to the point drawing back, which means not being willing to follow him to the ends of the earth ; well, then, of course, one is a horror, or, at any rate, a rather contemptible person. For my part, I think it would be extremely foolish and stupid if two people dare not so much as look at each other because their acquaintance might culminate in love, which, after all, is not bound to be unhappy. Then again, mere friendship can exist between man and woman, and the greatest possible advantages may result from such companionship. No, if I started such calculating considerations I should always feel both conceited and foolish. In short, I very much like this Mr. Fenger, and to talk with him is both pleasant and in many ways instructive. But perhaps you now think that I am, if not actually taking a false step, nevertheless upon a dangerous path ? "

After this followed the finishing remarks, and the signature, " Your friend."

CHAPTER IV

I ONCE more took up Minna's letter, in order to read it carefully word by word. On the first reading I had been overwhelmed by a dreadful fear that, in truth, as she had warned me, something would be revealed that would lower her in my estimation, a terror which restlessly haunted me from line to line, my eyes always running on in advance. This fear diminished as I proceeded; her almost exaggerated repentance because of these innocent entanglements made me smile half pitifully, and when my brows were knitted it was with indignation against this Stephensen ; and yet I could not help feeling a sort of gratitude towards him for not having bound her.

An exultant joy at the same time grew upon me : the consciousness that with this letter she laid her fate in my hands. Throughout it was instinct with the feeling that we stood in front of a decisive step, and with the honest resolution that nothing in the past was to be left un-cleared. She wanted to be able to say to herself : " I have told him everything, before I allowed things to go further."

And if I now said—and how deeply I felt that I could and had to say so !—" Well, after having heard all this, I think as before, only that you are more precious to me, because I know and understand you better," how could she then draw back ? Was not this confidence a per-mission to speak the language of love ?

The letter to Stephensen showed that she herself had thought of a union between us, though her expressions on this point were not quite satisfactory. But it was only during the last two weeks that we had been growing daily more intimate, and by her pointing out that the letter was a fortnight old, I saw a hint that these remarks were no longer to be considered valid.

I wanted to write to her at once.

I had, however, the self-control to take time to shave the left cheek, on which the dried-up lather was still visible, for the sun was already striking the window-post and would soon have made this necessary operation quite impossible. During this performance I collected my thoughts, and managed with flying pen to write the following letter—

"RATHEN, 14*th August* 188 .

"DEAREST FRIEND,—To what extent your sweet letter has moved me, and how far it is from having by its confidence revealed anything save that which but finishes and deepens the beautiful picture I had already formed, I have only one means of convincing you.

"You say you will send Mr. Stephensen a new letter. Now I propose that you should copy the old one up to the remark where you fear my chest is weak, which I can assure you is quite without foundation.

"After this you should then—according to my idea—continue—

"'He has already shown me so much attention that I could not very well doubt his feelings for me. It therefore did not come as a surprise, when he to-day asked for my hand. He has no private means of his own, but will certainly in a year or so have a respectable income, very likely in England, where he has a well-to-do uncle who will help him. I do not doubt for a moment that I ought to link my fate with his,' etc. etc.

" If you are able to send off such a letter then come to the Hertzes to-day at the usual hour. If I do not see you there when I come, I shall look upon it as a sign that I shall miss you for ever, and that my friendship, instead of being the beginning of an everlasting happiness, was only a passing but blessed dream.

" In that case, farewell, and may you be happy !—Yours affectionately, HARALD FENGER."

I put this letter, together with the one to Mr. Stephensen, in an envelope and sent it down to the villa by a little boy.

CHAPTER V

THE afternoon was beautifully still and warm when the time came for me to go down the hill. I ran rather than walked along the path, which passed cottages and hedges, and through the little lane between the garden walls that opened to the glorious, bright Elbe valley. But as every stride brought me nearer to my fate, and altogether I had only a short distance to go, my pace slackened, and I came to a complete standstill when I saw the lower stone-step leading from the narrow meadow up to the cottage. The smallest movement would now have enabled me to see its corner, with the projecting summer-house appearing behind the foliage of a fruit tree in the neighbouring garden. It was as if somebody had caught hold of my throat, and my legs seemed to have disappeared from under me.

There was the sunlit lime wall under the shining tiles, the vine creeper, the shadow projected by the tree, enveloping the summer-house, where the grey-green table-cloth had a crooked sun-streak of yellow—I looked for a long time at this streak so that the critical moment might be delayed ; some leaves of the fruit tree hid the corner of the table-cloth, and over them came the steam of the coffee-machine. A white-bearded man I had already discovered, now also the old lady, but no one else was there.

I continued to stare, hoping that I might after all be able to see *her*. In spite of the intense heat of the sun I shivered as if I was standing in an evening mist, but I

8

was again master of myself, which, until then, I had hardly been. My first idea was to creep away, for I did not doubt that, if she had wanted to come, she would already have been there. But perhaps she had gone up to fetch something for the coffee-table, or she had been prevented from coming, and a message was waiting for me. This explanation of her absence I offered to myself, and then refused it as a weakness of my poor soul, which dared not look matters straight in the face.

A rattling stone, or an indistinct vision of something which moved, made me look in the opposite direction, down towards the river. There, at the little well, hardly fifty yards from me, a figure rose into view. . . .

It was Minna.

I wanted to run to meet her, but Hertz had already discovered me and called out, " Mr. Fenger, do hurry up, do hurry up ! " I also saw that he waved his hand, and though I did not understand the meaning of all this excitement, I obeyed willingly. When running at top speed, I had reached the verandah, I nearly knocked over a long, bony woman, who rushed out of the door with a bag and a plaid in her hands.

" At last ! What a good thing that you came ! " Mr. Hertz said.

" We nearly sent for you, but Minna insisted that you were sure to come."

" Just imagine, we are off to Prague this evening ! Yes, in a minute."

" But we are not going to drive you away for that reason. On the contrary, we hope you will accompany us for a little way. The express does not stop here, so we are obliged to go on to Schandau, and we will do that by boat. The weather is beautiful now, so you might as well take that trip with us. There is a train back at nine o'clock. Minna has already promised to come."

Of course I hastened to do the same.

My fertile, self-tortured brain had for a minute whispered to me the possibility that my letter had not been delivered, and that Minna's presence was without meaning, and that everything might still end in disappointment. But Mr. Hertz's remark that Minna had insisted that I was sure to come calmed me.

She herself now came up the steps, dressed in the same light chamois-coloured frock which she had worn during our expedition to the quarry. In giving me an unusually long and firm shake of the hand—her way of shaking hands was individual and sincere—she smiled, but only with her eyes, that looked straight into my soul, with a glance as different from all former ones as "my love" is from "my friend." All the blood flew to my head; and when she let go my hand, it trembled, and my knees shook. Now, for the first time, when I had certainty and felt quite calm and happy, I could physically feel how much the dreadful strain and fear had affected me.

Minna had felt it, and could not help smiling secretly with a rather flattered air, while she poured out the glass of cold-well water for Mr. Hertz, which he always appreciated so much with his coffee—it was just as if we were in a café. And while he was sipping first the coffee and then the water, he talked in his excited way—

"For you must know, yes, it is sure to interest you, perhaps it will tempt you to follow us to Prague. Well, you will not? But indeed it is better so, for then Minna will have company on her return, and to you we dare trust her. Well, in Prague a manuscript has been found of Faust, OF FAUST, my dear boy, that is to say, a part of the first scenes—which differs, of course, only in details,

but, all the same, *there* lies the interest.   It is supposed
to be stronger in expressions, and is very likely one of the
first sketches.   A queer old man, he is a pensioned colonel,
inherited it, God knows how long ago, from a great-aunt or
some one like that, who, at the Court in Weimar, was—
well, how intimate with Goethe I really cannot say !   And
it doesn't very much matter.   By the way, there you have
our modern military Germany !   He inherits a chest with
letters and papers in which, if he had not been an ignoramus,
he might have guessed there were things from Goethe ;
but contempt for everything literary prevents him from
even opening the chest.   He is in want of money, a spend-
thrift of course, and must throw himself into the arms of
the moneylender, though all the time he has a treasure in
his loft, with which he could buy a castle.   And it is not
as though no hint had been given him, for we had an idea
that something might be there, perhaps not a manuscript,
but letters and information—I have written to him myself.
But no, family papers, defamatory secrets perhaps, and he
would see that they were not given into the hands of those
damned literary fellows, of course he reasoned like this.
So he contents himself with Johannisberger-Dorf in his
cellar, it is notorious that he was a skilled connoisseur of
wine.   And all the time a castle in his loft.   That is Nemesis !
Oh, how this fellow has annoyed us !   Well, he is dead
now, thank goodness, and the manuscript has been found.
That I should not be there !   But to-day, dear friend, I
received a letter calling me in, so to speak, as an authority,
and you can imagine . . ."

Just as no smile of Minna's escaped me, nor any of
her movements, so no word of his account was lost upon
me.   I felt a vastness and elasticity of mind, as if at the
same time it could hold all sorts of impressions, so long as

they were pleasing and pure.   The old man had never had
a more sympathetic and attentive listener, indeed some of
his exaltation even communicated itself to me.   My condition was like a slight opium intoxication, which makes
music sound still more wonderful.   While I congratulated
him on this interesting journey, which conferred so much
honour upon him, and questioned him and answered his
lively outbursts, I drank my cup of coffee which Minna
had poured out and given me.   But far from finding the
" brown nectar," prepared by my beloved's hands, incom-
parable, I decided in my own mind that Minna, true to
her Saxonian origin, made " Bliemchen-Kaffee," and that
the time would come when she would have to grow
accustomed to be less economical with the coffee-beans.

I do not think, however, that I should have had the heart
to refuse another cup, if I had not heard from the river
the dull sound of the steamer's propeller.   The others
insisted that it was too early, but soon afterwards we saw
the funnel of the ship over the green fields, like a black line
coming forward on the white background of the waste
slope under the quarries.

We were soon seated on the deck under the awning, and
saw the house gliding by, the greenish table-cloth still
shining in the shadow of the summer-house.   We sailed
towards Lilienstein and its twin brother Königstein, which
now appeared opposite the former, with sunlight on the
margin of its wall and on the small watch-towers.   The glare
of the yellow quarries flickered over the water, in which
each red spot, or violet-shaded line above, here grew into
a long, quivering streak.   Along the banks, the fields, bushes,
and fruit trees dipped their green reflections in the river.
From the ploughing prow long mussel-shaped waves slid out
to the sides, and as they came towards the bank the reflect-

ing colours flowed into their blue, shining valleys just like
a fluid which suddenly finds a canal and draws out the
picture in an elongated distortion, until everything was
jumbled up in a vibrating mixture of tongue-shaped and
twisted spiral colours, all light and clear as glass.

Old Hertz was very lively, and talked untiringly about
the wonders of Prague ; about the peculiar Teyn Church,
where my famous countryman Tycho Brahe was buried,
about the dirty Jewish quarter with its gloomy Synagogue,
and the overgrown churchyard, where the plain Oriental
grave-stones stood slanting and leaning, and crowded so
closely together that they looked as if they would push
one another out of the ground.   About Hradschin, the
Bohemian Acropolis, and its terrace-shaped Palace-gardens
climbing up the side of the rock.   Of all those wonders
which I should be able to admire the next day, if I allowed
myself to be persuaded to go on with them to-night.   For
he pretended all the time to hope that I would eventually
give way, and good-naturedly enjoyed listening to the
many feeble excuses I made to his reiterated invitations.

But he always wound up by saying, " Yes, yes, it is
also a good thing that Minna gets company, though I am
quite sure that she would not be afraid to return alone."
Then of course she began to assure us how willing she was
to do this daring act, and that I was " on no account to
give up this enjoyable trip for her sake, when there was
such a good chance to take it with pleasant companions."
While teasing me in this way she laughed with her half-
closed blinking eyes, so that in the end I did not know
what to answer. We, in our turn, amused ourselves
heartily over the fact that the good-natured man, while
meaning to make fun of us, was in reality himself deceived,
as he could not have any notion of how on this, of all

evenings, it was really impossible for me to leave her. Mrs. Hertz, however, who sat on the bench opposite us, sometimes shook her grey curls and smiled while she looked at us, as if this talk tired her, but at the same time with a questioning look, as if searching a secret under this play of words.

In Schandau we scarcely had time for anything except to have supper in the garden of an hotel near the river. Dusk closed in quickly. Hertz reminded us about the home-journey. But Minna assured us that the steamboat, in connection with the train service, started regularly a quarter of an hour before the departure of the train, a fact which we must surely know from the time-table. As the station is situated on the other side of the river and a good half-mile from the centre of the town and the landing-place, the communication is kept up by means of a little steamboat. This combination made old Hertz feel uneasy ; he began to get travelling fever, and every minute pulled out his gold watch with its face cover.

Minna admitted at last that it was now time for us to be moving.

There was no boat visible at the little bridge. The black water, which had a shimmer over it from the light of the lanterns that collected in the whirlpools, flowed freely past its empty planks, where there was not so much as a portmanteau or handbag to be seen.

" Surely we have come to the wrong bridge, it must be the steamer bridge," Mrs. Hertz said.

" Not at all, we are only too early," Minna answered, and she seemed to be a little hurt at this want of confidence.

We dawdled up and down for a few minutes, without seeing anybody or anything. Hertz went into the open shed, which served as a waiting-room, and sat down. In one corner there was a working man sleeping, with the brim of his hat pulled down over his forehead, for the smoking oil-lamp gave just sufficient light to dazzle one's eyes. Hertz stood up after having consulted his watch two or three times, approached the stranger, sauntered round him, coughed, and at last cautiously asked whether the gentleman also waited for the steam-launch going to meet the Dresden train.

"Nach Brag!" the stranger muttered mechanically, without looking up, and almost without waking.

A faint hope began to break upon me. When I saw a porter slouching down to the bridge I went up to him and asked for information. "The steam-launch for the Dresden train left ten minutes ago," he replied. Inwardly beaming with joy, and outwardly as annoyed as possible, I went up to the ladies with my news. They stood close to the little lamp, and I could see that Minna's annoyance at being disgraced over her assurance was struggling with a joy which, fortunately, was not imcomprehensible to me. She seemed purposely to avoid meeting my eyes.

"There is plenty of time, it is sure to come, he has not had proper information. . . . Look, is it not the one out there?"

A red lantern approached from the other side of the river, near the spot where the station was. A couple of ropes were soon faintly to be seen, and the steam, driven ahead by the wind over the launch, which slowly came up against the current, floated above like a little rosy cloud. The stroke of the propeller could be heard.

I felt rather mortified, and looked impatiently at old Hertz, who uttered a heart-felt "Thank goodness," and hurried down the bridge, as if there was no time to be wasted, and as if he himself was going to Dresden.

The boat came out of the darkness, the whistle sounded, a shout from the launch was answered by the porter, and past the bridge-lantern flew a lasso, that nearly caught the good Hertz, and landed a few yards behind him. The little steamboat lay beside the bridge with its coal-smeared hull still quivering; on the low, dirty cabin wall fell the glare from the machine-room, where the slow puff-puff still continued; and nauseating fumes of burnt oil, mixed with coal smoke, streamed into the fresh night air.

" For Dresden train ? "

" No, the express for Vienna. There's plenty of time, for we stay here nearly half an hour."

" Yes, but the train for Dresden ? "

" We have just taken the people across for that."

" But there's still time enough. Can't we get a boat to take us across ? "

" I don't think you will get any boat at this time of night. I say, Heinrich, is there any boat to be got ? "

" No, of course there's no boat to be got," answered the porter, and spat in the water. " People ought to be here in time for the launch."

A load fell from my heart, and it seemed to me that Minna also breathed more freely. But Hertz looked quite terrified; evidently he felt that he was solely responsible for having put us in this predicament, and for being compelled to leave us in it.

" But it was also your fault, Minna ! Why were you so positive ? One ought never to rely upon one's memory in such a case, and the time-table may be altered from one year to another. I ought to have thought of that myself. It really is very annoying."

" Oh dear me ! " said Mrs. Hertz soothingly, " after all, it is nothing so very dreadful. You will be obliged to remain here for the night, but anyhow there are plenty of hotels in Schandau; the town contains hardly anything else."

This practical remark quieted him down.

" Luckily there is an early train to-morrow. But perhaps you will be missed," Hertz said to Minna.

" Oh, I shall be back before anybody is up," she replied.

We walked up and down for a few minutes, and then Hertz took me aside.

" Tell me, dear Mr. Fenger, you came on this expedition so unprepared, and besides you did not think of staying the night here—I mean have you, by accident, not enough money with you ? "

I hastily reassured him, as I, really " by accident," had more than sufficient with me.

The old man looked at me in astonishment and hesitatingly put his purse, which he had already taken out, back into his enormous deep pocket, while he moved his lower lip as if he was going to speak.

" The ladies and gentlemen will be obliged to stay overnight," shouted the mate of the steamboat; " there are no more trains northwards."

" No, but we are going southwards. We are bound for Prague."

" But you were asking for the Dresden train."

Hertz began to explain the situation.

A steam whistle sounded on the other side of the river, and like a shining centipede the train glided past hissing and squeaking. It was the one that was to have taken us back to Rathen. I stood alone next to Minna and, as I thought nobody noticed us, I gave way to my gaiety and made a face at the passing train. Minna burst out laughing, and a rather coarse bass, a little to the side of us, joined in. I turned round, almost alarmed, and discovered the porter, who seemed to understand the situation.

"But what in the world are you laughing at ?" asked Mrs. Hertz.

Hertz now busied himself with getting on board, as if there was danger of the launch leaving them behind. They remained near the railing, and for a quarter of an hour we kept up a spasmodic conversation, searching for something to say, all of us tired of waiting. Hertz recommended an hotel which was good and "moderate." At last the signal bell rang. Hertz remembered the man in the waiting-room.

"Let him come if he cares to," said the mate.

But the old man got excited. I ran and woke up the phlegmatic stranger, who followed me grumpily. As soon as he had passed over the gangway, it was hauled in, and the steamer glided away, turned slowly, and disappeared in the darkness. Minna kept on waving her handkerchief.

I was on the point of embracing her, when I remembered that perhaps we might still be visible from the boat. Besides, the porter was sitting a few yards away, astride on the railing.

CHAPTER VI

WE walked slowly back. At the corner of the shed was a big, blue letter-box. Minna smiled, pulled a letter out of her pocket, and held it in front of me so that I might read the address, which was, as I had guessed, Stephensen's. Then, having looked at me with a questioning glance, which said, " Shall I ? " she stretched out her hand and put it under the flap. The letter fell with a dull sound into the empty box. Though this sound gave me the answer I longed for, it, at the same time, raised in me a faint feeling of uneasiness, as of a bad omen. This passing and apparently quite uncalled-for feeling I remember most distinctly, though not for a moment did I yield to it. For I had already drawn her to me, and soon felt my embrace returned with a fervour which had not so much the character of passion as of deep tenderness. Her strong maiden-arms in thus clinging to me seemed to seek to bind us so closely together that nothing could part us. When she noticed that I gasped for breath, she suddenly let me go.

" Have I hurt you ? I am so violent."

She looked so terrified, as if I really might have broken to pieces in her arms, that involuntarily I burst out laughing, and covered her face with kisses, until she hushed me with a still startled, yet roguish, look peeping out of wide-open eyes, and whispered from half-parted lips on which she laid her finger. But nobody was near, and the corner of the shed hid us in a three-cornered shadow.

We left it at last. I wanted to take her farther out along the river, but she did not like the darkness, and wanted to go towards the town. " We can be reasonable," she said. But our words were not so much talk as translated caresses.

We walked slowly arm-in-arm on the broad quay towards the lights of the town, which, like scattered sparks, mounted towards the stars, and some distance ahead of us, against the bend of the river, culminated in a golden border inlaid with the green enamel of the hotel gardens. On the opposite bank nothing was to be seen but two coloured signal lamps, and the dark mass of rock only showed as a starless part of the sky.

The express tore past on the other side of the river, and reminded us of the time. But just now the light in front of us began to brighten with a mother-of-pearl-like shade, and under the clearing the dark bend of a mountain appeared. The masts of a couple of Elbe rafts showed against the sky. The glare quickly became redder, as if from a fire ; had one been near the Rhine, one would have imagined it to be Brünhilde's rock ablaze, mounting like a glowing dome over Winterberg's even wood-stretches, just where the depression midway silhouetted itself. A few minutes afterwards the moon floated free, growing ever less golden and more crystalline over the mountain landscape with its river band, a scene which it seemed to create out of the chaos of the night and gradually bring to perfection.

It was too beautiful for us to think of parting. We kept on going backwards and forwards along the river, from the little lonely waiting-shed until we came so close to the garden of the first hotel that we could see the black coats and the many-coloured hats of the ladies moving under the foliage.

Alone in this strange spot we seemed to be a newly-married couple on their honeymoon, and I blessed the happy incident which had forced us to stay overnight.

"I was in reality also pleased at first," said Minna, " but soon afterwards I felt anxious, for in a way I had it on my conscience. I ought not to have been so positive. I myself had only a few marks in my pocket. If you had not had any more, my recklessness would have brought us into a nice dilemma. I *did* feel relieved when I saw you talking to Hertz and understood that you did not need to borrow anything from him. I was already quite alarmed. . . . Oh, the money, Harald ! Perhaps it was a reminder how one always has to think of it when planning out anything."

We soon lost ourselves in plans for the future and calculations as to how little, with the help of economy, would be enough ; apparently a very prosaic subject, but one that for a young couple (just as poor as loving) in reality possesses a greater attraction than even the most elevated romance. Notwithstanding our enthusiasm, I doubt whether the gold that the moon shed over the darkness of the river appeared to us more poetical than that with which our houschold needs were to be paid in due time. And I must admit that the one was just as unreal and fantastic as the other.

CHAPTER VII

WE had, at last, to make up our minds to look for our
hotel. It was not one of those which faced the river, but
lay with its front towards the same square on which their
nobler brothers turned their backs, an oblong place,
half overshadowed by the church on the short eastward
side. Twelve strokes had just boomed from its tower, the
small tiles of which shone like wet scales.

The porch was lighted by a dim lantern, and the stairs
were in darkness. A waiter, whose ears projected and
whose face was covered with pimples, scowled at us, and
seemed to be looking both for a tip and for our luggage, the
latter of which was, of course, entirely lacking. Then he
scratched his carrot-coloured hair and answered, while he
winked one of his pig-eyes in an especially impertinent
way—

" Two rooms ? And I suppose they must join ? Well,
I'm not quite sure——"

" Then make sure, on different floors, it does not matter ;
but be quick, there are plenty of other hotels in Schandau,"
I said roughly, controlling a violent desire to pull one of his
ears. Minna had turned quite crimson at his rudeness, and
looked terrified.

A woman's face, in Rembrandt light, peered over the
second landing. We heard the woman on the landing
calling out various numbers to the waiter ; and then
the man suddenly took up a diplomatic position and

invited us, with a gracious wave of the hand, to go up the stairs which were covered with well-worn cocoa-matting. Then he handed us over to the woman-genius with the light, who dropped big streaks of candle grease down upon the somewhat red-grey shoulder of his tail-coat, while in a deep guttural voice he announced the numbers of the rooms which had been chosen for us. And, after peremptory orders to wake us in time to catch the first train in the morning, we obeyed his summons.

The rooms were next to each other, and even communicated, and though I had so promptly declared that they might be on different floors, I must admit that I was well pleased to be Minna's immediate neighbour. I do not know if it was by accident that we at the same moment put our shoes out into the corridor, which was empty and dark, and only lighted by a distant lamp. Silently we crept out to the neutral ground, and gave each other a long good-night kiss.

When I was again in my room, and was pulling off my coat and waistcoat, I noticed that the key was in the door on her side. This discovery put me at once into a pleasantly agitated state, but brought at the same time annoyance and anger when I recollected the nasty leer of the waiter with the winking pig-eye. And then I called to remembrance how crimson Minna had turned at the time, and saw quite distinctly her dignified and alarmed air, and this picture gave me intense delight. I fell into a reverie, with my waistcoat hanging over one arm, and continued to stare at the important keyhole. Was the key turned or not ? Creeping towards the door I touched the handle, but dared not turn it, for fear of frightening her.

Then I went back into the room and continued to undress; still, however, peeping at the key in the same way that I had peeped at her letter two evenings before. But

I had left that untouched, and this very day I had received it with the right to read it. Such a clear proof of the reward of virtue strengthened my conscience. " This barrier also will some day fall away, if only I have patience, and we shall have nothing with which to reproach ourselves."

Just as I had put out the light and laid my head on the pillow, a gentle rapping startled me. I was on the point of jumping out of bed, when it struck me that the tapping was on the wall just by my head, and I remembered that her bed stood by the same wall. I quickly answered, and she responded, alternately in softer and stronger tones, with the knuckles and the palms. Through all tempos and in different rhythms the telegraph was continued, as if two " rapping spirits " were communicating with one another ; and this conversation without words, which expressed clearer than any words could have done our separated nearness, our longing and our hope, left me in a quiet, happy frame of mind.

I knew that on both sides of this wall, which was under no conventual scrutiny, had moved the same moods, feelings, and thoughts,—even if they had not in her taken such a tempting and decided form. This hour seemed to me in a mysterious way to have brought us closer to each other ; and while my joy so far had been the consciousness of being allowed to love, I now was overcome by the blessed feeling of being loved, of being myself the object of another's longing and secret wishes.

9

CHAPTER VIII

I FOUND Minna waiting for me in the little sitting-room of the hotel. She poured out the coffee from a tarnished pot, and we sat down at the table just like a newly married couple, as if, indeed, the bowl of honey on the tray was a symbol of honeymoon days. The room was rather gloomy, for the mist, like a blind, obscured the windows. The unusually early hour at which I had been obliged to rise affected my head, and also made me feel rather nervous.

As we stepped outside we could not see the church, and the houses on the other side of the square appeared but dimly, as an indistinct mass. The pavement was greasy ; Minna slipped and took my arm. Two street-sweepers moved grotesquely in the milk-white atmosphere. Under the barber's signboard, which seemed to be a free floating moon, a glass door clinked, and was opened with a kick. Near the grocer's, at the corner, a variously mingled and rather spicy smell impregnated the air for a certain distance ; we suddenly stepped into it, and just as suddenly out of it.

We arrived in good time for the steam launch.

Hardly had it left the bridge before the bank had disappeared, and we might easily have imagined ourselves at sea. We only saw the little waves shining like scales close to us, with the mist passing over them like steam. The sooty coal-smoke from the funnel struck down over the deck. The whistle sounded continually, sometimes with long hissing sounds, sometimes in short staccato shrieks and sighs. At times another whistle or a long shout replied to our warnings, and a big dark shape glided by like a phantom.

Minna drew closer to me and pressed my arm.

" I hope a collision will not take place."

" Surely not ! " I assured her.

But why, I asked myself, should this little steamer not be run down ? One drowns as easily in the middle of the Elbe as in the Atlantic.

This feeling of danger united us more closely than all the dreams of the future. But the same mist that had created the danger soon dispelled it by chilling us through and through. Fear of colds and coughs drowned the romantic terror, and with it the hope of being united in a sudden death.

So confusing was this journey in the bewildering mist that when a bump announced that we had landed, we were in such a state of perplexity that we thought that we had returned to Schandau. When we stood on the platform and the Dresden train puffed in, we imagined that it was the one going to Bodenbach.

We quickly, however, discovered that it was really our train, and, thanks to a well-invested tip, we were soon by ourselves in a second-class compartment. Over the misty white pane of the window flew grey shadows of leaves, branches, and bushes, and one drop after another rolled slowly down it.

The train shook so much that our shoulders constantly met, but Minna hardly responded to the pressure of my hand, and she spoke very little. I wanted to draw her to me, but she moved away and pointed with a shy look to the window, which was darkened by the figure of the conductor.

When our tickets had been collected and I, after having closed the window, turned round, pleased by the idea that we were now to be undisturbed, Minna got up. A sudden jerk of the train threw me down on the soft cushion, and immediately Minna was kneeling at my feet. I laughingly wanted to lift her up, but was stopped by a frightened and imploring expression in her face.

"Harald! I have something I must tell you. But promise me not to be angry. . . . No, no, you must not promise anything; perhaps you won't be able to help it."

"But, Minna, what does all this mean? Do get up, my dear!"

"No, no, you must first listen. I was so nasty yesterday. . . . I have deceived you all, and also told lies to you."

"But what do you mean? When?"

"Have you no idea? Can't you guess?"

"No, I assure you."

"Just think of it!" she continued, with a heart-broken expression upon her face, "you cannot imagine that I can be so false. . . . And when you hear it you will perhaps fear that I am always so."

"But what is it, then? So far you have told me nothing."

"Well, it was yesterday evening. It was my fault that we were too late for the ferry steamer. I knew quite well that the steamer for the train went earlier than I said it did, and I pretended——"

"But is that all?" I interrupted laughingly.

"You are making fun of me! It would be much better if you would beat me! Is it nice to get a wife who can tell lies and deceive you like that ? . . . Don't you think that it was at all wrong ? "

I made some kind of explanation, but she continued rapidly—

" And the good old Hertz who was so troubled, evidently he felt the responsibility of having drawn us into the adventure. I also forgot that I, without permission, must make use of your purse, and that perhaps you had not money enough, and might be put into a most awkward position. All this was very wrong. But the worst of all was, when you yourself began to talk about the fortunate mistake and I had not the courage to confess, but continued telling lies to my own dear friend. Then I was quite disgusted with myself."

" But why did you not dare ' to confess,' as you call it ? "

" At that time I could not possibly dare to do so, but now I cannot do anything else. Though I had really made up my mind never to tell, or at any rate not until much, much later. . . . Oh, perhaps you cannot understand it at all ! But isn't it true that we enjoyed being alone together—for so far we really had not been able to speak in private—more than being ferried in a boat filled with people, and stuffed into a nasty train. That train is always overcrowded, horrid, you know ! And then "— her voice sank to a whisper, and she rested her face on my knees—" was it not also a little—just a little—sweet to be so near to each other in the night ? "

I bent over her.

" And when you tapped the wall."

" Hush ! " she exclaimed, putting her forefinger to her lips, and looking at me with a queer and somewhat terrified face. But suddenly her expression became almost sulky.

"But you calmly said that it did not matter whether the rooms were on the same floor or not."

"Before the waiter, dearest."

"Yes, yes, I understand."

She jumped to her feet and suddenly gave me an eager kiss; it was as if I had been hit in the face by a soft ball.

"Then you are not angry any longer?"

I lifted her to the seat by my side.

"Any longer? But I assure you, Minna, I have not been angry at all."

"But you really might have been; yes, you ought to have been."

"Oh, nonsense! I only think it much sweeter now that I know that it was not an accident but your wish."

"There is nothing to be done with you; you will absolutely spoil me, and I can't imagine what the end of it will be!" Minna exclaimed, and pressed me tenderly to her. "But look how the weather is clearing. We shall have a fine day after all."

Outside, on the white sheet of mist which was stretched in front of the window, appeared dusky crowns of fruit trees, pointed fir-tops, and the margin of a roof with a tiny shining skylight, everything becoming indistinct as it approached the ground, just like the pictures of a magic-lantern that are beginning to take shape.

And above all this appeared a dark mass; it was the rock plateau of Lilienstein, floating like an island in the air with the mist stream gliding round its rough stone sides, with long dark purple clefts, and with myriads of little fir-tops pointing up towards the sky, which shone through with the bluish tint of an opal.

"And what shall we do to-day?" I asked. "To-morrow afternoon we are going to meet at the Hertzes', but I really must see you before then."

" Yes, indeed, we must use the time—' Our pleasant sojourn in Aranjuez is coming to an end.' [1] So you really go away the day after to-morrow ? "

" Yes, my sweet Minna ; it is after all for the best. The holidays are over, and my landlady has let my room."

" Well, in a week I am also as free as a bird. . . . Let me see, I will take the children out for a walk. If your many engagements do not prevent, you can expect me on the forest path, the one turning off to the left, you know, just beyond the school-house. I will walk on until I meet you."

The train whistled and stopped. We had already reached Rathen.

As we went down to the ferry, the mist only fluttered, like torn bits of cobweb, over the wet grass which was glittering in the sun.

[1] Schiller, " Don Carlos."

CHAPTER IX

NEEDLESS to say that I was on the appointed path in more than good time.

It was my first tryst. I do not know whether my delight was greater than my wonder when I thought of how, hardly four weeks ago, I had strolled about here and on other pathways in the vain hope of meeting Minna. And now! Even in those days the sun had laughed and smiled through the air, the shadows had refreshed me, the woods had been filled with perfume, the song of the birds had made everything joyous, and the fresh, light breeze had rustled through the high crowns of the trees. But now, with how much more intensity did the same nature, that was as radiant and summerlike as ever, fascinate my overwrought senses! I threw my hat into the air; I meant it to have flown up into the sky as a salute, but it scarcely reached the lower branch of one of the gigantic pine trees. I boldly cried out to a little robin redbreast which twittered on a dry twig of one of the trunks: "Ah, ah! you little one, are you also waiting for some one? I am waiting for my beloved one, for my darling, my little Minna."

Thereupon I peeped round, frightened that some one might have witnessed my childishness. At the same moment Minna appeared at the turn of the path with her little pupils, and with as much calmness as I could muster I hurried to meet her.

"Here I am with my chaperones," said Minna. And

she quickly added : " Remember to call me Miss Jagemann, and if you feel tempted to say something which they
are not to hear, then speak Danish ; I shall manage to
understand it."

" Little pitchers have long ears," I remarked.

Minna laughed heartily, and pointed in front to the
eldest of the little girls, who happened to be endowed with
large projecting ears which glowed transparently in the
sunshine.

How gay and full of spirits Minna was ! Though
generally she looked older than her age, now she seemed
so childlike that I involuntarily said to myself : " Is it
possible that this is the girl who loves me as a woman loves,
and who, unfortunately, has even loved before ? " She
wore the hood-shaped garden hat made of black straw,
which I knew from ' Sophien Ruhe,' a practical head-gear,
as it shaded her face down to the middle of the cheek.
From this calm shadow, which caught a green light from
the wood, the clear, deep-set eyes looked without a cloud,
at nature and at me. Her dress was of some light material,
in blue and white stripes, falling in long pleats from the
waist, which was tightened by a light blue silk ribbon,
instead of the usual belt.

I had already, for several minutes, expressed myself
in Danish upon rather indifferent topics, when the catas-
trophe foreseen by her occurred. I became so overwhelmed
by my feelings that I exclaimed : " But, Minna, how well
that dress suits you, how sweet you look in it ! " As I
had already accustomed myself to express my love in
German, this little Cupid, on leaving my lips, put on
that becoming linguistic garment. Of this I first became
aware when Minna violently caught hold of my arm,
and I saw that one of the projecting ears in front

had disappeared, while the other one was turned towards us.

Minna bit her lip. At the same time the smallest girl turned round and held her doll towards her.

" Miss Jagemann, shall we soon be in the shade? Otherwise Caroline will get freckles."

We were only too glad of the chance to laugh, but the child was very much insulted by our outburst.

" Then I will say it is your fault, and mother will have to give Caroline some of her toilet water."

" Good-day, Cousin Minna," suddenly sounded behind us. " I say, how jolly ! Good-day, Mr.—Mr. Fenger !" The schoolmaster, marching along in shirt-sleeves, with his jacket hanging on a stick over his shoulder, had come up behind us, and Minna replied a little stiffly to his greeting.

" Ah, is it you, Mr. Storch," I exclaimed, feeling as if he had caught me in a trap.

" Yes, indeed," he answered, with a wink which clearly said : " Well, so you have discovered her, the little governess, my beautiful Cousin Minna ! Now, did I not say so ? "

" Nice weather, but warm—pouf ! It is the last day of my holiday," he added with a sigh.

" Where are you going ? "

" I am bound for Hohenstein ; will you come with me ? "

" Thanks, not this time."

" Do not mind for my sake, Mr. Fenger——" Minna began.

" My goodness ! An engagement is an engagement, and what is best is best. In your case, neither would I go— ' Why gaze into the distance, look here—the good lies near.' Thank goodness one knows one's classics. As long as one can quote Goethe, drink München beer, smoke

Altstädter Ziegel-tobacco, climb up and down the mountains, and one more thing, which I dare not mention before Cousin Minna, so long Poland is not lost, even if one has to ram knowledge into the heads of stupid youngsters six hours a day ; or, to use a more stylish expression, to work in the noble service of the education of the people. Well, good-morning ! "

He disappeared quickly, humming a gay ditty—

> " We make a night of it,
> We make a day of it,
> We make a whole life of it. . . ."

" What a funny fellow ! " exclaimed the smallest of the girls ; " and he called you cousin ! "

" The baker's Tinka says that he gives them so many slaps," the eldest one added. " A nice cousin ! What a dirty shirt he was wearing ! "

" Mother always tells us to say ' chemise.' "

" Not about that sort, Sophy ! "

Minna threw a look, not of the kindest, after the sleeves of the garment mentioned, which shone between the trunks of the trees, and asked with a little annoyance—

" How is it that you are on such intimate terms with my honoured relation ? "

I told her about our acquaintance, the reason why I had taken a walk with him, and how my expectations had been rewarded.

" So already in those days you made inquiries about me," she said, shaking her finger, and at the same time smiling quite gaily. " If only I had known that ! "

" What then ? "

Minna laughed, and having put down her parasol she pointed with it to a shady road which almost seemed to breathe out coolness in the heat of the sun.

" Let us go down here, then Caroline will avoid freckles, and we, very likely, tourists."

The road was so overgrown with long grass that the wheel tracks were obliterated. A fine moss of tiny green stars, in which drops of the morning dew were still sparkling, covered the ditches, and a whole hedge of different kinds of ferns bent over the olive-brown moss-cushions, which swelled out on the margin of the other side.

" Just look how pretty ! " Minna exclaimed, and pointed to some ferns that only consisted of one single stem with lancet-shaped fronds. As a rule they were not higher than a span's length, but some of these were quite a foot high. " I wish I could have one or two of those, roots and all. I have already got several ferns. Here, too, is a beautiful one."

She pulled off her silk gloves and knelt down. In the meantime I succeeded in jumping over to the other side.

" If only we can get them properly ! Have you got a knife ? "

" No, but we say in Danish : ' Five fingers are just as good as a boat hook.' "

She laughed and shook the loose hair from her face ; then we began to dig and scratch away the earth. At last we got the plants out of the ground, and as I recrossed the ditch I succeeded in wetting one of my feet. Minna carefully bound her handkerchief round the ferns, so that she should not lose any of the mould that was hanging to the roots. We showed our earth-begrimed hands to each other and laughed like a couple of children as we hurried after the little girls, who had nearly gone out of sight and were now beginning to call for us.

Above the tops of the dark fir-trees the arched sky was of a reddish blue. Into the deep brown shadows between the grey trunks, keen slanting rays of the sun penetrated like golden spears, while dim lights quivered, glittering like silver, on the huge ferns that resembled the outstretched wings of an enormous bird ; and bright yellow flames of the sulphur-like saxifrage shone along the edge of a bit of rock, which lay between the trees, like a little house with a garden of ferns and young beeches on its flat and slightly sloping roof. The air was fragrant with the scent of firs and the fresh smell of fungi.

I do not remember what the subject was on which I began to talk, but even if the theme had been interesting, I at any rate wasted my breath, for I noticed that Minna constantly stared at me with a peculiar, inattentive smile which had something almost teasing in it, and increased just like a spreading light.

" Why do you smile ? " I asked, a little mortified. " Do you not think so ? "

" What ? "

" Oh—of course——"

" I do not know. I have not heard anything. I have not the faintest idea what you have been speaking about, and I do not care about it at all "—(the words came hurriedly) —" but continue, please do. I am listening to your voice, to your voice alone. I have no mind to understand with ; I look at your mouth and your profile. Do you know, Harald, you have a nice profile ? And your mouth is so funny when you speak. Your lower lip protrudes—like this—with every pause. But it suits you, and the dimple in the chin gets deeper, and the nose bends right at the point, and that is the best of all. It is a Schiller nose, and you are an idealist like him—you are indeed, darling."

Quickly glancing ahead to see whether the children were out of sight she kissed me impetuously.

" But, Minna, you cannot mean what you say ! "

I was quite intoxicated by this sweet flattery. It was the first time in my life that my physical vanity had been tickled. Formerly, on the contrary, I had always had to hear about my " beak of a nose," and about being a little underhung—really not much, it seemed to me—and now ! That this pretty girl should find something attractive in me, and just in these peculiarities—it was like a fairy tale. I felt myself in the seventh heaven, and God only knows how foolishly I should have behaved, had not the children come running to tell us that beautiful ripe raspberries were to be found—in this seventh heaven !

The wood became less dense, with low shrubs between big moss-covered stones. The road we had followed now narrowed down to a path, at the side of which we stopped beneath the shadow of a baby rock, while the little girls crawled about between the bushes. Minna took off her hat, lay down on her back, and looked up into the deep sky. Suddenly she burst out into brief laughter.

" What is it ? "

She half got up, and, supporting herself on one arm, said—

" Do you remember, Harald, there are on the Zwinger some tiny children—fauns I think they are called—with goat-legs, quite plump, you know; they also have a small tail ? "

" Well ? "

" It struck me if such a little chap came jumping along how sweet it would be. I would take him on my lap and pet him."

" Yes, I should like to see that. How funny you are ! "

" Am *I* ? " she asked with a comical little stress on the " I."

At the same instant something living moved with big bounds within the bushes. The smallest girl began to shriek, and the good-natured head of a pointer appeared, his long tongue hanging out on one side of his dry mouth. The next moment a bearded forester with a gun over his shoulder stood on the path a few yards from us, and scrutinised us with a most sullen look. Surely this man could have no human feeling in that broad breast of his since he could scowl at Minna in such a way, as she sat there with her bodice tightened by the uplifted half-bare arms, which she had raised to put straight her hair and hat. A veritable forest ogre !

"What are you doing here ?" he asked sternly. "This is not a road for tourists."

"Well, you must excuse us, but there was no notice-board with 'Trespassers will be prosecuted' at the entrance."

"As if you couldn't see that it was only a wood-road ! . . . Hang it all, there are pathways enough made for the public."

"So one is not allowed to take a step beyond the laid-out pathways ? Upon my word, it is too bad !" I shouted, and began to lose my temper.

"No, damn it, you are not allowed !" he yelled, his face extremely red and angry.

"We really did not know, otherwise we should not have come here," Minna said politely but firmly. "But I do not think we have done any harm."

"Then it's not your fault," he mumbled, a little less irritably. "A few yards farther on there are plenty of fir trees about the size of a nail, and anyhow the kids don't think where they are stepping. You too, I suppose, have also something else to think of." And annoyed at having allowed himself to be smoothed down so far as to give an explanation, he added, " Well, now you know what you have to do."

He then whistled the dog, spat contemptuously, and marched off by a side-path into the wood, at the same time looking occasionally over his shoulder to see whether we were also returning.

We did so, with that crestfallen feeling which, whether reasonably or not, one has after such an encounter.

" That was a fine old Pan who came and drove us away, instead of the little one you had dreamt of."

" What a bear ! " she said sulkily, and imitated mockingly his hoarse bass.

The children laughed boisterously.

" Well, I suppose he was right after all, though a notice-board ought to have been put up," she said. " If I were a forester, I should also be annoyed with all these people who come running about in the woods. But you really ought to feel it more than I, being the son of a ranger. Was your father like that, Harald ? "

" My father was a Royal Forester, this one was only an impolite steward."

" Aristocrat ! "

" Well, you yourself do not speak exactly like a democrat about people who roam about the woods."

" That is quite a different matter."

" No, not at all."

In this way we argued gently and joked for the rest of the way. Indeed, in the end we even played tig with the children, and came home hot and out of breath and in the best humour in the world.

CHAPTER X

THE following day, when Mrs. Hertz had spread the table-cloth in the summer-house and her husband was just sitting down with his newspaper, we appeared on the scene arm-in-arm, and in this manner betrayed our secret from afar.

This could not have been received with more hearty joy, even had Minna been their own daughter, and I a millionaire. A bottle of Rhenish wine was sent for from the hotel, and our healths were drunk in the little arbour, where the evening sun stole in between the foliage, and sparkled like gold in the brownish green glasses. Hertz spoke much about the interesting Faust manuscript, the authenticity of which he did not doubt ; the discrepancies, however, were fewer and of less importance than he had expected. This led quite naturally to a discussion as to whether it was right to publish such an early and, according to the author's own judgment, unfinished sketch of a famous piece of poetry ; and the old man brought forward many good and striking arguments against those who, for the sake of a great feeling of veneration towards perfected works, insist upon suppressing the founts from which they sprang, which are, after all, of deep human interest and of great value for all artistic psychology.

But he spoke more slowly and with more effort than usual, and was often interrupted by a troublesome cough, that evidently distressed his wife. The fog, which

10

near the Elbe had been so unusually thick that it resembled the famous Rhine mist, had also not spared the Moldau Valley ; and in the narrow-built town of Prague it had lasted till far on in the day, penetrating everything with its wet cold.　In addition to this Hertz had for hours been in a loft, where this dampness had been accompanied by a dreadful draught.

Nobody had shown sufficient forethought to have the contents of this extraordinary chest removed to more habitable rooms, and besides there were also many book-cases and boxes which had not allowed Hertz any peace, and in which he had also succeeded in discovering one thing and another.　Notes from Carl August and Archduchess Amalia, original copies of a couple of books by Wieland and Herder with dedications, theatre programmes, etc.　A few of these things he had managed to buy, and he showed them to us with great joy when, a little before sunset, we went into the house.　But we could not hear this cough, which constantly interrupted his gay remarks, without the fear that he might have bought his treasures too dearly.

When we were going homewards, a little earlier than usual, Minna gave way to her distress—

" Hertz is weak, and he cannot stand much."

" It may be so, but that is no reason to fear the worst."

" Well, I am like that, Harald !　Your cheerful dis-position will be thoroughly tried by me.　I always meet troubles half-way, and it seems to me it does not make the way shorter.　Just look at me, I am now in reality as depressed as if the dear old man had gone already."

" Indeed it would be a hard trial, not only for his good wife, but also for my friend Immanuel.　I have never seen so charming an intimacy between father and son.　It reminds me of the patriarchs."

" Ah well ! It might well touch me, as it was so different from what I experienced in my own home."

"Aren't you fond of Immanuel ? He really is such a nice fellow."

" Yes, indeed—very nice——"

It struck me that she had never much to say about Hertz's son, and it also surprised me that *he* had never spoken to me about Minna, and that I had never seen her when I had visited him. Very likely in those days she had come less frequently, or at fixed hours of the day. As a matter of fact it was only in the last part of the year, before he left for Leipzig, that our acquaintance had grown so intimate.

I would willingly have continued this subject, but Minna had already put it on one side.

" By the way, when you come to town you will call to see mother—I have written to her. And listen—do not judge her too harshly."

" But, dearest girl, how can you fear—— "

" Well, well, I have not myself raised your expectations too highly. But there is any amount of good in her; truly she does not of her own free will harm anybody, and she is so fond of me—she really is."

" The last is enough for me."

" Do you know, Harald, there is one thing which pleases me."

" Well ? "

" But you must not be so delighted, it is not at all nice of me, but very selfish. Do you know, I am so pleased that you have no parents alive."

" Oh, why ? They would have been so fond of you."

" No, no," she exclaimed, in an almost frightened tone.

" How could they have been ?   They would have expected
quite a different daughter-in-law, and they would have
been right.   But as it is, there is no one but you who has
any claim on me, if only you will be satisfied with me as
I am."

" My own beloved wife ! But you are crying ? " I
exclaimed, as my lips met tears on her cheek.

" Never mind ! But it sounded so sweet, do say it
again ! "

" My wife ! "

Already we had more than once walked backwards and
forwards through the little village.   The night was pitch
dark.

The lights of the solitary windows, which were scattered
on both sides of the dark valley, added more to the cosiness
than to the brightness of the place.   Above the obscurity
of the heights and rocks sparkled the stars, keen and
restless, and now and again a falling star darted over our
heads.   Besides our own footsteps we only heard the little
brook babbling between the stones, and from time to time
a passing movement in the willows on its bank, as if an
enormous animal was suddenly shaking itself.

As we, for the third time, came near to the lights that
beckoned us from the Zedlitz Villa, our steps grew gradually
slower.

" You sigh ? " said Minna when, against our will, we
had at last stopped walking.

" I have something like a presentiment, I cannot help
it.   It seems to me so sad to part from Rathen, I feel
depressed—I fear something, I think."

" We have been so happy here.   But it is my own dear
town we are going to, I am looking forward also to our
walks there."

" It is only this. Our love is just like a plant that has grown up here, and now has to be transplanted."

Minna laughed, a subdued and wise laugh.

" No, it is only going to be removed. For it is a plant which has its root in the heart and not in any especial locality."

After a long, long embrace she glided away from me and disappeared in the darkness, while the tiny twigs still crackled under her steps, which tripped on the gravel path. Suddenly they stopped.

" Good-night, love ! " sounded her high, clear voice, surprisingly near.

" Good-night, little soul ! "

And again it sounded, but this time far away, as a voice from beyond—

" Good-night ! "

BOOK III

CHAPTER I

By five o'clock on the following day I was in Dresden. As soon as I had unpacked my things, and dined in my usual restaurant, I thought of going to see my prospective mother-in-law—not so much on account of politeness or inquisitiveness, as for the reason that I was thus indirectly communicating with Minna.

It was not many minutes' walk to " Seilergasse," where Mrs. Jagemann lived. The house was exactly like the neighbouring and opposite ones. Through the open front door one entered an arched, whitewashed passage that at the other end led into the garden, and in the centre had the usual winding stone staircase whitened with hearthstone, leading up to the upper floors. On the first landing I stopped at an open window and looked out. Just as the interior had already pleased me by its familiarity, so also did the view, which reminded me of the few places where I had lived, and of the homes of my friends. It was, in short, a commonplace Dresden home of the regulation citizen type.

The garden was joined on all three sides to other gardens, and these again to neighbouring ones, so that they formed a big garden square, surrounded by rather low two-storeyed houses. By this plan the Dresdeners gained air and light, even in the old, narrow parts of the town. The sinking afternoon sun beamed over the various trees, while the pathways and small lawns lay in monotonous shadow. In a neighbouring garden some young boys were running to and fro, in another several little girls were playing; in one place some drying clothes waved gently. The little garden beneath was empty. In a bed, in front of the vine-covered summer-house, roses were flowering; an acacia and a pretty cherry-tree stretched their branches over almost the whole space, and the elder-tree was not missing, " der Hollunder," in the absence of which, since the days of Kleist, one cannot imagine German love-scenes, and in the presence of which one cannot avoid thinking of them. It is true that the tree was not in flower, but at the end of August it could scarcely be blamed for that.

On the first floor a faded visiting-card in a small frame announced that College-teacher Jagemann lived there. I rang the bell time after time, but in vain. As I could not decide to leave this place, the only one in the beautiful town where I could find anything that was associated with Minna, I went into the garden and sat down in the summer-house.

It was almost as quiet as if one had been in the country, for only now and then did the heavy rumble of a cart remind me that I was in a town. From the garden in which the small girls were playing, voices could be heard constantly singing—

> " Here we go round the mulberry bush,
> Here we go round the mulberry bush,
> Here we go round the mulberry bush,
> So early in the morning."

This childish play made me think of what had happened in these gardens ten years before.

One of these voices was Minna's, and it was her pink dress which, through the bushes, I saw turning round like

a top. She was visiting a friend of hers, for here, on
account of her father, she did not dare to play with the other
children. But once he nearly caught her in this crime, and
I began to wonder into which of the two adjoining gardens
she might have escaped. Behind me was some wooden
boarding—that way was fairly barred ; to the left was a
hedge of hawthorn behind a paling, but it didn't look
sufficiently old ; opposite me the paling was a little higher,
but in the corner the ground sloped upwards, so that it was
easier to climb over ; and also this was the place most
hidden from any one who came through the entrance door.
All this I examined just as carefully as an historian would
inspect the localities at Pharsalia in order to get a clear idea
of the plan of Cæsar's battle ; and it cost me just as much
head-work to decide upon the neighbouring house and the
window from which her friend's beloved and his friend, her
first adorer, had made their salutations.

In the end the elder tree occupied all my attention. It
stood in a corner against the neighbouring garden, and
overshadowed a little bench which was made of two or three
boards and looked extremely old. I moved from my seat
in the summer-house to this one. It was not exactly a
comfortable seat for an old man who wished to take a nap
in the mid-day heat, but it was very suitable for a young
couple who didn't demand much comfort. And then this
romantic " Hollunder " ! It was not in flower now, but
it had flowered—for him ! Like the shadow from this bush
jealousy filled my soul, the jealousy which my feeling of
happiness and Minna's presence had so far kept away. I
wanted to own her altogether, would like to have seen her
as a child ; in imagination I could picture her leaving her
play-fellows in order to put her little plump arms round my
neck. If there were a pre-existence, it seemed to me that

this also should have been mine. But not even her first youth had belonged to me! Another had possessed this beautiful fragment of her life, and had kept it as a jewel with which to deck his vanity. In the end, however, it was I who had won the treasure, while he had been blind enough to be satisfied with a few baubles. This thought consoled me the more because it flattered my sense of self-esteem.

I got up and went out into the street. The twilight had deepened. On the one side some dark tree-tops over a garden wall had caught the roseate glow of evening, on the other it was quite dark between the houses, the upper windows of which sparkled like gold, while the lanterns were lighted at their feet. As I had no particular aim in view I went towards the bright side.

At the corner was, of course, the inevitable beer-shop.

A little old woman, who, in spite of the heat, was wrapped up in a thick woollen shawl, toddled in. This reminded me that Minna had said that her mother, towards evening, usually took her beer in " Zur Katze." The site of this restaurant I recollected well, for I had always noticed its very humorous sign.

So I directed my steps to the centre of the town and soon reached the brilliantly lit-up Schloss Strasse, which was crowded with people. Several oldish men were sitting in the restaurant. I saw directly that it was not a place that would tempt many casual visitors, but depended chiefly upon regular customers. One of the men, who had a bundle of newspapers and a portfolio in front of him, scowled at me furiously as I approached, just like a dog which growls when one goes too near its dish of bones. A well-preserved, clean-shaven gentleman sat in a corner and rather loudly entertained a couple of decayed

Philistines with the last scandal from the Court Theatre.

An open door led into a smaller room. I peeped in, and saw an old woman seated close to the door ; just opposite to her, in the big room, an old-fashioned mirror was hanging. As I wished to be undisturbed while I looked at her reflection in the mirror, I quickly retired, and once more seriously terrified the newspaper reader by sitting down next to him. By way of pretence I took up the paper he had laid aside ; but even against this he protested with a discontented murmur. The waiter placed a glass of beer in front of me.

I could not, however, imagine that the old woman in the inner room could be my future mother-in-law. Minna had said that there was some resemblance between them, and it was impossible for me to find any trace of such a thing. The forehead was not at all high, but strongly arched, the eyes were not deeply set, and the lips were thick and shapeless, as was the rest of her greyish face. It looked like a thing which had been so long in water that it had become soaked and puffy, and such a condition might—to be sure—have effaced any resemblance which had ever existed.

I called the waiter, so that I could pay him, and asked if he knew a widow of the name of Jagemann who was often supposed to come there. " She sits in the small room," he answered, and I got up immediately and went to her. She moved uneasily on her sofa-corner, and, as I stepped up to her with a greeting, she looked so terrified that one would at least have thought that she was alone with me in a railway compartment.

I told her who I was, and supposed that she through a letter——

" Yes, indeed, to be sure, Minna has written—that dear child, oh dear me! . . . Well, I *am* glad. . . . So you have come up to town, Mr. Tenger——"

" Fenger."

" Ah! certainly, Fenger, of course, you really must be kind enough to excuse me. It was in a letter, and the capitals are so much alike, my eyes also are not very good, and Minna writes rather indistinctly . . . don't you think so ? My good husband wrote such a clear hand, he also gave writing lessons, you know, and Latin as well. Oh dear me, yes, he really was very learned. . . . Minna, too, was well educated, it was quite different in my time, but the young people nowadays. . . . Won't you take a seat ? You really must sit down."

I placed a chair close to the table, and when I saw that she thought of offering me some refreshment, I hastened to anticipate her.

" You really are too kind. Indeed I don't know, perhaps for company's sake, but only a small glass, please. I suppose you drink many glasses. Young people ! Dear Jagemann was also a heavy beer drinker . . . from the student days, you know. Do you drink much beer in Denmark ? "

I tried in vain to start a sensible conversation while we drank our beer. Sometimes she became limp and stared stupidly at me, not answering anything but " Oh dear me, yes." Then, directly afterwards, she would start, as the Germans say, " to talk the blue off the sky " ; evidently not for the pleasure of talking, but from nervousness, and especially from a fear of being obliged to speak of the relationship between Minna and myself. It seemed to me that she had not much belief in it, and I thought that very likely she was judging her daughter by the standard of her own flighty youth. Sometimes, when she thought that I was not noticing, she looked at me critically, as if she was thinking, " What kind of fellow is this that Minna has now got hold of ? " Then if I looked at her she put her glass to her lips so quickly that she spilt drops of beer down her black shawl, which showed signs of having been dyed.

When we left, I wanted to take her home, but on no account would she allow me to go out of my way ; and, when I insisted, she told me that she had some shopping to do. She disappeared down the first dark turning, not, however, before I had given the promise, or the threat—I do not know which she considered it—to visit her the next day.

I went straight from the Polytechnic to her flat.

When I rang for the second time I noticed that in a window, which opened on to the stairs, a dirty little curtain moved slightly in one corner, and from the darkness behind, an eye peeped out at me, after which the curtain fell back in its place. Having waited for some time I heard shuffling footsteps, and at last the door was opened by Mrs. Jagemann, who, had I been the tax-collector, could not have looked more alarmed. I was on the point of asking her why in the world she was so frightened, when it struck me that very likely I myself was the cause of the trouble. She seemed to have forgotten that I was going to call, or she had regarded what I had said as merely an empty form of politeness. The dyed black shawl, which I had seen on the previous evening, enveloped her and seemed to be thrown over her chemise, while her skirt bore a marked resemblance to a petticoat. She took me to the sitting-room with many apologies, and then disappeared for half an hour, " so that she could offer me a cup of coffee."

The rather small room, facing the garden square which I

have mentioned, was bright and cheerful, and got plenty of sun. The furniture, however, was not only plain, and even partly broken, but everything showed symptoms of an entire want of order. The lid of the upright piano was quite grey with dust, and on the top of it, on a bundle of music, stood a plate containing half a smoked herring. It has always been a mystery to me how it ever arrived there, for I soon discovered that Mrs. Jagemann never inhabited this room, but muddled about the whole day long in the almost dark kitchen, where she prepared and ate her meals, slept, and read *Dresdener-Nachrichten*. In a corner stood a bookcase almost entirely filled with green-bound volumes which I at once recognised as Minna's classical treasures, the gift from that severe aunt who would haunt her as a spirit, if she ever parted with them. A door in the middle of one of the walls was covered with a green rug, and a sofa had been placed in front of it. With this rug as a background, an oil-painting was hanging, on which I saw part of a fishing village under low dunes, near a bay. In the foreground sat a couple of young girls netting, while they at the same time carried on a flirtation with a town dandy who was conspicuous by the addition of a paint-box and had an unmistakable likeness to Stephensen. His pointing finger and the laughing expression of the girls evidently suggested that a deeper meaning was signified in this netting. While the figures were as conventionally painted as they were tastelessly thought out, there was a good deal of freshness and nature-study in the beach and the sunlight on the sand-dunes, and the picture with its powerful bright colours beamed in the little room, to the more than plain furniture of which it stood out in striking contrast. Every one was bound to wonder how it had come there. And to me, for whom this question was answered beforehand, it spoke in a forcible manner of all that I would fain forget. Surely he appreciated her and their friendship, since, years after, he had sent her such a finished picture. But, at the same time, what indelicate coquetry, to suggest himself flirting with two young fisher-maidens in a gift to *her*! What feelings would it not awaken in a German girl, whose heart was full of love for the Danish painter, and whose fancy was full of poems by Heine! *"Du schönes Fischermädchen"* and *"Das Meer erglänzte weit hinaus"* would constantly sing out to her from this canvas, both awakening in her an intense longing after the unknown romantic charm of his fatherland, and creating a perpetual jealous unrestfulness. A refined self-love and a stupid heartlessness seemed to me to have drawn this bragging monogram on the stone on which the dandy put his boot, a boot, by-the-bye, that was so shiny that it could not possibly have trodden even a few steps on the dusty road.

Besides this picture there were two others in the room done by the same hand. They hung under one another between the window and the bureau : A pastel portrait of Minna and a pencil drawing of a middle-aged man with a high forehead, a straight nose and small, compressed lips— which combined with overhanging brows and deep-set eyes gave him a discontented and bitter look—thin hair and big whiskers, that did not conceal a small but firmly shaped and clean-shaven chin. Especially in the chin and forehead there was a striking likeness to Minna, and when I examined it closely, the shape of the lips also was the same ; but her nose was broader and shorter. This drawing was cleverly done and showed a good solid training.

But I could on no account reconcile myself to the pastel portrait. It was a head and shoulder picture in three-

quarter size. She was in a black dress without the slightest
relief, which rendered her much exaggerated paleness still
more striking, and the whole thing floated away in a blue
mist so that one would think it was a young tobacco-
smoking woman who had just enveloped herself in smoke;
only that this did not seem to stream out of her compressed
bloodless lips but rather from her indistinct, expressionless
eyes—an art which, as everybody knows, is not yet discovered. This kind of misty picture had in those days
just come into vogue. And this was a man who had
painted his beloved! Where was the love that goes into
all details, the jealous care that preserves even the smallest
of them, because it sees that which is greatest behind, the
self-forgetting losing of oneself in the object, the love's
realism in which there is only room for a loving idealism,
which far from hiding the individuality only wants to put
it in the clearest and truest light? Nothing of all this;
everything here was sketchy, and the whole thing done in
a careless sort of way in order to blur it in the indistinct
fashion of the moment, affecting an artistic " vue " rather
than giving a human aspect. The more I looked at this
portrait the stronger became my disgust and fury against
this man, who had painted Minna in such a way, this artist,
who so boldly had prepared a picture after the last recipe,
who had taken his beloved as a " subject " and had dodged
all the difficulties, and indeed everything that should have
been made clear. It seemed to me that, if he came into
the room, I should take him by the collar, drag him in
front of this sinful work, shake him soundly and shout
into his ear, " What a beastly modern and artistically
decayed ass you really are! Look there, you knight of the
palette, what a disgusting scarecrow of a lie in colours you
have made, with the most beautiful of God's creation

imaged in your eyes, nay, in your heart, too, if one could only believe you!" And I heard him answer: "And what kind of fellow are *you*, and what can *you* do? *I* have at least been able to paint a portrait of her, that anyhow can be recognised, and which every one will see represents a pretty girl, and in which an artist would see talent. . . . *Maintenant à vous, monsieur*. Take colour and canvas and place yourself, with your 'self-forgetting,' losing of yourself in the object, 'your love realism,' and then see what kind of a fright you will get out of it! But never mind, try all the same: they are very agreeable hours, I assure you; you have the sweet girl sitting in front of you, and can look at her to your heart's content; she will blush, therefore you must moderate the colour a little. I recommend you to tone the shades a little cooler than one usually does. . . ." In this manner I worked myself up to such a degree of jealous fury, that I very likely should have seized the picture and thrown it on the floor, had not Mrs. Jagemann at last appeared with the coffee.

It gave her a great fright to find me on my feet, and she hurried to get me seated on the little sofa behind the rather shabby mahogany table, on which she served the Saxon drink. An important change had taken place in her, and she had now quite a dignified matronly appearance in a dark blue, white spotted delaine dress, and a big cap with lilac ribbons. She herself sat on the edge of a chair just opposite me and sipped her coffee slowly, putting her head right down to the cup. I had already for some time noticed a sweet sickly smell which now constantly grew stronger, and I realised that on the other side of this covered door a very common tobacco was being smoked. Mrs. Jagemann seemed to guess my thoughts; and presently she began to cough—

11

" Oh dear me, yes . . . it's this tobacco smoke, it *will* make its way in here. Our lodger lives in there, a very pleasant young man, but he smokes all day long. Do you also smoke ? Please don't hesitate to do so on my account ; it tastes so well with the coffee, they say. We have lodgers, otherwise we could not keep the flat going, you know, and when one is accustomed to good living. . . . But it has its disadvantages, as now, this tobacco smoke. Of course one can get lodgers who smoke less, or who are not so much at home . . . there are even those who do not smoke at all, but there might be other objections. Dear me, Mr. Fenger, there are so many bad men in the world ! As, for instance, this lodger, there is not much to say against him. He always pays me, even if he is sometimes a month late, but, good gracious, there are also those who do not pay at all. I have had plenty of them ; they clear out suddenly, with promises, of course, that they will come and pay. . . . Oh, dear me, bad people, Mr. Fenger ! "

I again began to stare at the irritating portrait, and suddenly burst out with — " What a beastly modern artistically decayed ass ! " And Mrs. Jagemann, who saw what I was looking at, began at once to praise the portrait.

" Yes, that's a portrait of my Minna, as you can see. It is really very good, almost as good as a photograph. Oh dear me, yes ! What wonderful skill ! What they can do nowadays, Mr. Fenger ! In America they can now take photographs in colours, so the papers say. My goodness, what will happen to the poor painters ? What are they to do ? Art moves on, the one flies higher than the other, one's death is the other's bread, as the saying is. By the way, it was painted by a countryman of yours ; he was also one of our lodgers. . . . Mr. Stephensen was his name ; he lived here for six months."

She spoke slowly, with constant pauses between her jerky sentences, and she looked at me as craftily as she could with those dull eyes of hers.

"Yes, I know all about Stephensen. Minna has told me. She does not keep any secrets from me," I replied.

"No, of course not! Yes, he is a countryman of yours, and even an artist, of course you have heard of that," she said quickly, evidently satisfied to know that I understood what she was talking about, but at the same time anxious not to pursue the subject.

"Oh yes, such talent," she prattled, "you are quite right in that!" (I had not referred in any way to his talent). "And a nice man, so pleasant to have dealings with! He always paid me punctually, sometimes even before the time; not because I asked him to do so, but times were hard, and he was very considerate. He only smoked cigarettes . . . very different to our present lodger. By the way, he is also a painter, that is to say, he comes from Holstein. It's houses he decorates, ceilings and walls. . . . But Mr. Stephensen only smoked cigarettes. Oh, when in those days one came into the room, it was just like smelling the incense in the Catholic Church. Yes, you have been there? Dear me, so lofty, isn't it, and all the candles on the altar? Yes, and how they sing! It's just as if one heard the angels. I've been there with Minna. She said it was Latin they sang; my good husband was an excellent Latin scholar. Otherwise, I go to the Anna Church near here. It's a wonderful parson we have; he shook hands with me the other day and asked for Minna. He confirmed her, but for some reason she doesn't like him. She easily takes fancies . . . and of course she's right in a way, there are so many bad people. Good gracious, it is a trouble to know what to do among them all, therefore we have religion. What should we be without religion, Mr. Fenger ? "

" Well, I am sorry to say I am not very churchy, but I think that Minna and I also in that respect——."

" Oh, dear me, yes, young people, you see ! When I was young . . . it was just the same . . . then one only thought of amusing oneself. And, upon my word, why not, as long as one doesn't do anything bad ! "

" Anyhow, I think also about earning something, and hope soon to be in a position to marry. I have an uncle who is a factory-owner in England, and he wants me to go over there."

" To England, oh, I say ! I had a sister who was several years in England. Oh dear, what tales she could tell! It must be an awful town, London ! All the fog and smoke ! There also they live on several storeys, and the whole family take their dinner in the kitchen."

When at last it was clear to me that it was hopeless to try to lead the conversation into a sensible track, I let her babble on to her heart's content, and made no attempt to stop her. She had at first spoken fairly correctly, but as she got excited her provincial accent became apparent ; she said "m'r" for "wir" and "sein" for "sind," and interlarded her talk with many slang expressions and terms ; and it then amused me to remark that Minna, when she sometimes jokingly chattered her Dresden dialect, resembled her mother very strikingly, even in countenance and features. Consequently, I was as patient and attentive a listener as the old woman could have desired.

When I at last took my leave, she did not make any attempt to detain me, but accompanied me to the door with many curtsies and salutations.

Well, I had made acquaintance with my future mother-in-law, and was in a way not at all discontented with the result, however far it was from being brilliant. The reason was, that when I had pictured the future and imagined the happiness of bringing a beloved woman home as bride, I had always shuddered at the thought of a mother-in-law, and had been terrified by the prospect of marrying into a family which might provide me with a tail of brothers-in-law and sisters-in-law, and a new outfit of aunts and uncles, and so forth. Now in this case there was evidently no idea whatever of a family ; if Minna did not bring me any dowry in money, she did not bring me any superfluous relations. As far as the mother was concerned, of whom, I knew, that Minna had in her own mind formed an unusual but sound judgment, she seemed to be a rather modest being, who would certainly prefer to toddle about in peace in her kitchen, and take a nap in "Zur Katze," and who was so wrapped up in her Dresden customs that there could hardly be any idea of bringing her to England. Supposing that I had got a stately lady as " mamma " who embraced me in a motherly way, criticised my habits, was discontented with my prospects, mixed herself up in the household affairs, put the daughter against me as much as possible, insisted upon visiting on regular evenings ! My goodness, how easily I had got out of it with this homely motherly soul !

If I had written a diary, I should, that day, have put down : " At ease on one point, mother-in-law harmless."

CHAPTER II

Two days later, at five o'clock, Minna arrived by the steamer. I was, of course, on the landing-stage to receive her. As we walked together through the streets, it seemed to me there was something that weighed heavily on her mind, but I determined to ask no questions before we reached her home. Besides, I thought it was Hertz's condition that had grown worse.

When Minna had finished her dinner, and her mother had left us alone, my dear one became more and more silent. Sometimes she gave me a long sad look which almost brought tears to my eyes; soon after she began gazing, as if her thoughts were far off, and I felt very distressed.

"Do you fear that it is serious with Hertz?" I asked at last.

"Yes, I think so; you will see that he is going to die. And why not? It was searching for Goethe's manuscript in Prague that made him so ill. It is his hobby that kills him—there is something beautiful in that."

"But his poor wife!"

Minna rose with a sigh, and went to the window.

There she stood for a long time, looking down into the little garden. The setting sun cast its beams on her face, that with its air of seriousness and depression seemed to belong to a much older woman. The front folds of her light blouse rose and fell forcibly and irregularly. The right hand, hanging by her side, grasped tightly a small handkerchief; once or twice she lifted the other hand, shading her eyes as if she was looking for something definite, but just as quickly she forgot it, and either stroked the hair away from her forehead, or drummed upon the window frame.

I went quietly up to her and laid my arm round her shoulder.

" Has anything else troubled you, darling ? "

" I have received a letter—from him, an answer to the one I sent off the other evening."

" Well ? "

" It has given me pain, it was not at all what I had expected. He does not think of me as a good friend. It is as if he wanted to hurt me. I don't understand it."

" What has he written, Minna ? "

" Well, you shall see for yourself."

She went back into the room and knelt down by the little handbag that stood open in the middle of the floor. Taking a letter from a blotter she gave it to me. It was written on very elegant notepaper and had only some unimportant lines as introduction to a poem by Heine, which I did not know. It read as follows :—

> " Once more from that fond heart I'm driven
>   That I so dearly love, so madly ;
> Once more from that fond heart I'm driven—
>   Beside it would I linger gladly.
>
> The chariot rolls, the bridge is quaking,
>   The stream beneath it flows so sadly ;
> Once more the joys am I forsaking
>   Of that fond heart I love so madly.
>
> In heaven rush on the starry legions,
>   As though before my sorrow flying—
> Sweet one, farewell ! in distant regions
>   My heart for thee will still be sighing."

" Silly nonsense ! " I exclaimed, and involuntarily crumpled the paper between my hands. But Minna, who had again been looking out of the window, turned quickly, and snatching it from my hands began at once to smooth it out.

"I fancy it is a treasure!" I said, with a bitterness which I could not possibly conceal.

She looked at me reproachfully.

"If you ever leave me, even with far bitterer words, I would do as much for your letter, Harald." And she put back the letter in the blotter.

The touching faithfulness to all her heart's remembrances, that breathed from her words and manner, disarmed me, but a sting of ill-feeling was left behind.

"I was wrong, forgive me—but it is a letter which might make an angel swear, there is neither meaning nor sound sense in it."

"No; I do not understand him. It was he, after all, who wished that our intercourse should be friendship only, and who advised me to marry an honest man, and now he reproaches me for doing so."

"And in such a foolish way! Why does he not express his own feelings? A poem by Heine! It would be foolish even if it was appropriate, which it is not, by any means."

"Just so; it was that which also struck me so strangely as a false note. Otherwise, it would have hurt me much more, or perhaps it might have reconciled me. But at this I could not help feeling annoyed."

"His vanity has been hurt by your forgetting him for another, that is all. Therefore, he has nothing to say himself. Most men would have sought refuge in 'The Complete Letter-writer,' being an artist he betook himself to Heine."

"And yet, if he still loved me and suffered!" she exclaimed and clenched her hands.

"Loved? There are so many different ways of loving. Why did he leave you?"

" For the sake of his art. And is not that worth more than I ? "

" No, a thousand times no ! For the sake of his art ? A silly phrase. Such a miserable fellow ! How does he think he can produce art worth anything, when he is such a chicken-hearted fool, who does not dare to face life, and how can he expect to put real feeling into his pictures, when he plays with himself and with you ? "

" But suppose he had only *said* so. If for a time he had been obliged to work alone, and therefore wouldn't bind me, but trusted that my love was firm and constant enough to last, and he himself had waited faithfully, and worked, and now had been disappointed ? "

I walked irritably up and down the little room. The thought of Mr. Axel Stephensen as a faithful lover, sitting in Denmark, and working in order to be able to unite his life with hers, seemed to me, after all I had heard of him, to be so very far apart from the truth, that I was on the point of laughing ironically ; but a look at the beloved girl, whose misplaced belief did so much honour to her soul, disarmed my bitterness, and only a deep painful sigh escaped me.

Minna still stood close to the window with her back turned towards it, leaning on an old-fashioned chest of drawers that was covered with cheap knick-knacks and faded and soiled photographs. She supported herself on the edge with both hands and looked down on the floor.

" I am to be unhappy and to make others unhappy, too," she murmured, as if she was speaking to herself.

" Minna, Minna ! " I exclaimed in despair, stopping in front of her and stretching out my arms towards her, " You must not say that, with me and to me you cannot possibly say that."

Without looking up she shook her head very gently.

"But he thinks it is flightiness on my part, and I cannot allow him to think that. He must be able to understand that——"

"But you are not going to write to him after this?" I interrupted.

"Indeed, Harald, I shall do so."

"But why, dearest friend? Nothing but pain for all of us can come out of it. Put an end to this correspondence, it has already lasted too long."

"Then one more letter would not hurt, it will be the last one."

"I beg this much of you, Minna! Leave it off for my sake. I cannot explain to you, I myself don't know why, but it alarms me."

"I must," she answered, in a tone of fatalistic assurance. . . . "He and I cannot part like that."

"I wish you had never met," I exclaimed.

She looked at me for some moments with a strangely puzzled expression, as if she was unable to realise the vastness of this idea. Then she came close to me and put her arms round my neck.

"Yes, I wish to God he and I had never met. Why did you not come in those days? Why did we not come to know each other first? Then everything would have been right."

"It is going to be right all the same, my love," I said, and kissed her forehead.

We sat down at the open window and talked about that dear Rathen. Minna teased me by saying that, in a letter which I had sent to her two or three days before, I had confused one view of the country with another. This I denied, and demanded that we should examine the letter itself.

"Oh, it is not worth the trouble, anybody might make a mistake in writing," she said, and it seemed to me she was rather confused.

"But I am sure that I have not done it. Do let me see the letter."

"Then we will say that I made a mistake in reading it, I do not mind," she said, and turned crimson. It was evident she had a reason for not showing the letter.

The irritation which, during the whole of this conversation, had been lurking within me because she had kept his letter so carefully, now burst out with a jealous suspicion that she had handled *mine* more carelessly and did not know where to find it. I was not sufficiently generous to spare her, though I knew well enough that even the most precious letter can easily be lost, especially when one travels.

"You cannot possibly be so lazy as that. Your blotter lies there on the table."

"No, it is not there," she answered, getting up. "Obstinate! I must take the trouble to go out in the passage to fetch my travelling-bag."

"No, I brought it in; it hangs there, near the door."
She looked in the bag.

"Then I suppose it is in the trunk," she remarked, with a shrug of her shoulder. "'*Tant de bruit pour une omelette !*'"

"Thanks!" I said, with an ironical intonation of which she took no notice, for she laughed gaily while she went down upon her knees and started to turn over the things in her trunk. To me this laughter sounded a little unnatural, as the situation was obviously painful.

"You must not look, Harald, do you understand? My trunk is so untidy."

"Very well," I said, and stared irritably out of the window. At last I heard her get up and come towards me. She handed me the letter. The rather stiff paper was crumpled and twisted and bent in a strange way.

"I suppose you have used it for packing," I remarked bitterly, and held it up to her.

She did not answer, but smiled in a very peculiar way, which suited her admirably and both irritated me and made me madly in love.

"It does not seem that you handle my letters with the same care, or keep them as well, as those of Mr. Stephensen!"

Minna bit her lip, and peeped up at me with a teasing but still caressing look. I did not understand how she could take this matter in such a way, and should surely have been as angry as a Turk, had I not had a feeling of uncertainty and a suspicion that I was making a fool of myself.

"But you are quite forgetting to examine it, Harald," she said, as I continued to hold the letter towards her.

"Oh, you are quite right," I decided, without deigning to look at the letter, which I threw upon the floor.

Minna bent down very quietly and picked it up.

She gave me a reproachful glance, which made me ashamed, and I looked away, though I still thought myself right. Then, without withdrawing her eyes from me, but with a more and more tender smile, she unbuttoned the upper part of her blouse, loosened her bodice at the top, and let the letter slide down into her bosom, where it disappeared with the rosy shimmer of the last sunbeams which were glowing through the little room. I took her eagerly into my arms and covered her face and neck with kisses, while I stammered forth excuses for my uncalled-for behaviour, my jealousy, and my foolish suspicion, of which she, in such a touching manner, had made me ashamed. This repentance, and still more the happy feeling of being so sincerely and sweetly loved, caused my tears to flow so freely that Minna jokingly said she feared they would obliterate the writing on the precious letter. Her eyes were also moist as we laughed and cried at the same time, and kissed away the tears from each other's cheeks.

But before we could look round her mother had entered the room. Then we awkwardly released each other, and Minna tried, by a quick turn, to hide her rather disordered toilet. The old woman coughed apologetically, and even her careful steps in her almost worn-out slippers seemed quietly to whisper, as she crept out with the coffee cups: "It doesn't matter, my children, I'm no nun myself. I have also been young. Go on billing and cooing! Dear me, as long as one doesn't do anything wrong!"

It annoyed me that we should be subject to a moral indulgence which we did not need, and especially that an ignoble—and undeserved—construction had been put upon this scene. Minna must have shared my feelings, for, while she buttoned the top of her blouse, she shrugged her shoulders and murmured with a comical resentment—

"The old woman always comes creeping in at the wrong moment."

"Do play a little, Minna," I said. "I have not heard you play at all, and I have looked forward so much to it."

Minna implored me not to insist, but I pulled her to the piano. It was still light enough for her to see the music. She opened a Schubert album and played one of the

"Moments Musicaux," not without feeling, but nervously, as if she feared to touch the notes.

"It is awful," she exclaimed, just as she played the final chord. "May I not stop? You cannot pretend that it is a pleasure to listen."

"Yes, I can, and also you ought to be ashamed of being nervous before me."

"Nervous? I am trembling all over!"

"You cannot see properly any longer. I will fetch the lamp."

"No, for God's sake, let me, at any rate, have that excuse."

The exceedingly lively, and at the same time fantastic and deeply-moving, impromptu, which she now started, was treated with much more ease and courage, and though she failed once or twice, I had a sincere pleasure in her really musical rendering. After this I expected that she would want to stop, and I was prepared with persuasions to make her continue. But she had scarcely taken her hands off the notes, before she took down the "Sonatas" of Beethoven from the top of the piano.

"If it has to be, let it be," she exclaimed gaily. "One might just as well be bold. I should like you to fetch the lamp, Harald, so that I can see all my dropped notes lying upon the floor."

I had expected that she would play "The Marche Funèbre," the first movement of "The Moonlight Sonata," or something equally manageable, one of those pieces about which one can say that they are naturalised in the drawing-room; but to my surprise I heard, while I lit the lamp in the passage, that it was the grand Waldstein Sonata she was attacking, and playing with no lack of passion. She had evidently sent me out for the lamp so that she might begin before I returned, with the idea that when one has taken the first plunge and cannot feel one's feet, one is obliged to swim. And she really swam; even the depth and movement of the waves helped to bear her up.

As I came in just at the moment when from wild runs and violent octave passages she reached the calm of the rich chords that sustain the hymn-like melody, I was struck by a strange expression of energy and enthusiasm on her face. This Beethoven glorification of all her features appealed to me so deeply, that a joking encouragement, which I had on my lips, was suppressed. I quietly placed the lamp on the chest of drawers behind her, and as a big piece of the globe was missing, I turned it so that the light shone through the hole on to the music; a necessary action on my part, for surely this lamp had never given an effective light, and it looked as if it had not been cleaned during the whole of the summer. I seated myself far back in the room, where I could not disturb her, but could see the soft, shaded bend of her cheek, and her neck where the knot of hair glittered in the lamplight, while I lost myself in an enjoyment, that perhaps is the noblest of all—to have Beethoven played by one's beloved.

In this mood even the unfinished execution was rather advantageous than otherwise; the very modest surroundings were not in accordance with concert demands, and one enjoyed so much more the conquering of difficulties, even if these victories were not won without loss of men in the note-army. In spite of all, her playing was artistic, because she was quite lost in it; she played as a musician who has got a difficult manuscript on the music-stand; now and then she grumbled with disgust at having stumbled, sometimes when she had struck a wrong chord she sent an exclamation after the false note, which was not far from a little oath, and when her hands dragged behind the inspired will, then she loudly sang the melody as if to make the fingers ashamed and force them to follow. In this way she had stormed through the grand Allegro's sunlit mountain-land and descended peacefully to the Adagio's lonely valley, with the deep shadow round the still, shiny water mirror, where the mind searches its inner life, but still with the gaze wistfully uplifted towards a hoped-for glory; then again to soar into the ethereal regions, where the Rondo lives in a heavenly light and undisturbed splendour, joyously warbling and trilling as a blessed spirit of a skylark that dwells not among clouds but between stars.

Minna threw herself back in the chair; I went up to her and pressed a long kiss on her forehead. " Thank you," I whispered.

" What a thing to thank me for ! " she said, and looked at me in astonishment, as if she feared I was making fun of her.

" How can you say so ! I am absolutely astonished. I knew well that you were musical, but I had not imagined you could play like that."

A sudden heartfelt joy beamed up to me in her eyes; but she lowered them at once, and her lips curled in a good-natured, ironical smile.

" Yes, is it not true ! I am quite a Rubinstein in striking wrong notes."

" Why do you mock ? I know quite well that it was not perfect, but all the same you played beautifully."

" Oh ! That is what almost makes me desperate each time I play, to hear it so beautifully and not be able to produce it. And especially when, as I sometimes think,

I might have been able to play fairly well, if I had ever had the chance to work at it constantly."

" Well, it is not too late yet; it seems to me you have your life before you."

" Perhaps, but there is always the same hindrance in the way. I cannot endure the strain—you have no idea how it affects me; I have now at least played away my night's rest. Why am I so feeble ? Ah, if you could imagine the melancholy which in these years I have played myself into, each time I touched the piano ! It was just like something closing over me, and the more beautiful the music the darker it was around me. Sometimes I could not leave off, but often it was so dreadful that I dared not go on any longer."

" But all this will disappear, dear one ! I shall manage to get you sound and strong, and when your playing makes me happy you will also be pleased. I am a grateful listener, even if you never play any better than you do now, and in the future you will be able to devote yourself to music."

My words did not seem to make much impression on her. She placed the lamp on the table, seated herself in the chair I had left, and leant her head on her hand.

" I can feel it in my head ; it strains and thumps in there." She laughed as if by a sudden inspiration. " Do you know, if ever I should wish to get rid of the little sense I have, I think I could play it away."

" What an idea ! "

" Indeed, that was also a way to commit suicide. It was the mode of Frants Moor, ' to destroy the body through the mind,' applied to suicide."

" Minna, you must not speak like that—it's a bad joke."

" Anyhow, it is a truly "practical joke " when it is put into execution. But one doesn't know what tricks one might need in life. 'It is a trick which deserves you as inventor,'" she recited, with a comical imitation of a fashionable actor. "Have you seen him here in the Court Theatre? How affected he is! Ugh!..." She posed as Frants Moor in the beginning of the second act, and mimicked the face of a scoundrel so funnily that I could not help laughing. Urged on by this applause, she began to imitate the false means of effect which the aforesaid actor had invented for this monologue of meditation: to give questions and answers with two different voices, a high falsetto and a deep ventriloquial voice, while she turned first to the one side then to the other. "What species of sensation should I seek to produce? Anger?—That ravenous wolf is too quickly satiated. Care?—That worm gnaws far too slowly. Grief?—That viper creeps too lazily for me. Fear?—Hope destroys its power. What! and are these the only executioners of man? Is the armoury of death so soon exhausted? How? no! Ha! *music*! Of what is not music capable? It can breathe life into stones; would it not be able to kill a Minna?"

She laughed gaily and embraced me.

"I have been very naughty, Harald, and you were so kind and thanked me so prettily for my music, you dear sweet friend! But I did appreciate it, though I do talk such nonsense. I cannot help it, it often pains me so much; it seems to me it must be so beautiful to be an artist, to be able to make others love and admire what touches one so deeply. But I promise to make you a good wife! And do not mind what I said before; as long as you are with me and care for me I shall not destroy myself with the sweet poison. But, Harald, if you should ever care more for another——"

I closed her lips with a kiss—truly not a very logical argument, but in this case, perhaps, more convincing than any other.

Her mother came in with tea and white bread, for which, as a treat, she had bought honey in the comb and fresh butter. When we had finished eating she placed herself in a corner in a queer triangular arm-chair with straight sides. It had originally been the end of a sofa, and the *disjecta membra* of this piece of furniture were scattered about in the flat. In a very few minutes the old lady was fast asleep.

Minna was also tired after the journey, and when the hideous alabaster-columned clock on the chest of drawers, after a long threatening rumble, had made up its mind to strike four strokes, which echoed in the piano with a long note, thereby calling our attention to the fact that the time was really ten o'clock, I insisted that she should go to bed.

Without waking up her mother, Minna lighted me out. To her great terror I went " with my chin on my back "— as she expressed it—down the steep spiral stairs, without being able to take my eyes off her, while she stood bending over the balusters, with a smiling face strongly lit up by the outstretched lamp.

Down below I stood for a long time sending kisses up to her, until she began to scold me, and as that had no effect she suddenly began to make faces and produce such dreadful caricatures à la Wilhelm Busch that at last I broke out into loud laughter and fled.

CHAPTER III

THE following day Minna showed me a copy of the letter that she intended to send to Stephensen.

We read it together in the little summer-house, because one of the aunts, who "was not all she ought to be," had turned up, and from her company Minna was anxious to save both herself and me.

The letter calmed my feelings, as it seemed well-fitted to make an end of all this misunderstanding. It was without any bitterness and free from any trace of sentimentality, and was also written with more dignity and calmness than I had expected her to show under circumstances that so deeply moved her feelings and remembrances.

While we were together at Rathen I had sometimes looked forward to walking with Minna in her own beautiful town, and I begged her now not to waste any time.

We went through several rather plain-looking streets and lanes, all alike, which, with their entirely flagged pavement, and without gutters and cellar-stairs, made a neater and cleaner impression than a Dane expects in such quarters. The two-storeyed houses only vary a little in grey or yellowish colour ; but now and again a low building extends, the big sunken roof of which peeps down on the street through many of those real Saxonian lattice windows, which are shaped like half-closed eyes and, when placed close together, give to the tiled roof the impression of a long wavy movement. The low buildings are old farm-houses, proving that not so very long ago these were the outskirts of the town.

Everywhere a rather comfortable and familiar informality prevailed. At the open window on a ground floor a young woman gave her child the breast; opposite, in a sunlit window above, a man in shirt sleeves smoked his pipe and stared across at his neighbour's roof, on the ridge of which a white cat was walking cautiously. A well-dressed man, who looked like a student, passed us with a glass mug filled with foaming beer, which he had fetched from the beer-house at the corner.

The children playing in front of the houses greeted Minna, and a little urchin of a girl, three to four years of age, with curly hair and a face full of dimples came flying along, with her poor naked legs as bent as swords, and was not content until Minna had chased her into a passage, where she allowed herself to be caught.

Less pleasing was the attention from the bigger children. A tall, bare-headed girl, with dirty stockings and trodden-down slippers, continued to shout after Minna, " Who's 'e ? " And a shoemaker's boy walking in the middle of the street, who, to my astonishment, was whistling the Actors' march from the *Midsummer Night's Dream* so that it sounded through the whole neighbourhood, must have found something Jewish in my appearance, for he suddenly interrupted his occupation and continued to shout after me " Itzig." Sometimes all voices were drowned in the rumble of an immense waggon, the barrel-shaped canvas roof of which swayed up to the height of the windows on the first floor; a couple of heavy horses, with thick necks and muscular haunches, pulled it with a slow lumbering walk while they shook their shiny brass ornaments of rings and crests ; the chains rattled, it creaked in all the fastenings, the wheels grated, and under the enormous moving mass the cobbles groaned so that one was tempted to cover one's ears. Nothing of all this was new to me, but with Minna as my companion it assumed a different and familiar aspect, for I regarded the smallest details with love, because they belonged to the associations which from childhood had both surrounded her and influenced her imagination.

This cosy bit of the old city was suddenly cut in two by the distinguished Prager Strassë, the modern artery of the residential quarter with its pulsing life of moving carriages, gaily dressed crowds, and handsome shops. We came into new broad streets, which, apart from a few lonely pedestrians and crawling cabs, were quite empty. The rows of flowers on the balconies showed up brightly against the grey mass. There were hardly any shops ; on every second door was written " Pension," and over its neighbours " Hôtel garni." This did not suit our taste ; in order to reach the villa quarter in our mock " house-hunting," we should have chosen the shortest way, if in this rectangular quarter the distances had not been the same length.

We soon had fine gravel under our feet, and were walking under the shade of a small avenue of maples. Dark acacias, glittering silver poplars, transparent birch tops, massive domes of plane, lime foliage, and copper beach, mixed with numerous varieties of rare bushes and trees, towered on both sides over railings, hedges, and low walls. Here and there the white limbs of a statue shone between flowers and leaves, or the fine spray of a fountain mounted and descended with gentle splashing in the middle of a fertile mass of foliage. Villa followed villa, glorious mixtures of country seats and palaces with fine façades of yellow-grey sandstone which still possessed some of its granulated sparkle. Where the big plate-glass windows stood open the outer pair of cream-coloured net curtains waved gently, and in the sombreness of the room the prism of a chandelier sparkled or the edge of a golden frame shone with a subdued light.

In a loggia formed of Doric columns with Pompeian painted walls and Caset ceiling some people were drinking coffee. Down a double zigzag staircase, which was surrounded by flowering plants, a slim lady with the tail of her riding habit over her arm was being escorted by a cavalier in bronze-coloured velvet. In a covered drive, which on the side of the villa formed a beautiful portico copied from the Villa d'Este, a landau was waiting, and a pair of chestnut horses were prancing impatiently and pawing the red gravel.

This kind of covered drive especially delighted us, and under no circumstances were we going to content ourselves with one made of iron and glass. It was settled beyond doubt that we were to have a carriage at the time when these luxurious plans were fulfilled. The aforesaid pair of chestnuts pleased us very much; at the same time we also had a strong liking for a black pair. Much consideration was naturally given to the style of the villa, and our tastes coincided, as we both preferred a not too rich renaissance. An ideal one of this kind we found at a corner near the park. It was a massive building of considerable size, stamped by a real aristocratic simplicity without the slightest sign of parvenu pretentiousness, but with imposing, grand, and noble proportions; it seemed to have been built by Semper himself, or by one of his best pupils.

" That is the one, that is our villa ! " Minna exclaimed

at once. She laughed hilariously at this castle in the air, but I already took it more seriously. After all, why was it impossible ? It was not an unprofitable art in which I indulged; besides, I had good connections and might perhaps inherit something. Eventually, why should not one, after a life of work, be able to retire here as a rich man ? My youthful courage seemed to possess unlimited power. And as I knew myself in safe possession of that which is the aim of youth, all my thoughts and dreams began to centre themselves towards that of the man : a glorious fruition of active work. The scepticism of Minna almost hurt me, as if it was a disbelief in my capacity and energy.

"No, to tell you the truth, Harald, I do not believe that it would suit me at all. Just think what such a house involves—all the servants one would have to manage. It also strikes me that with so much money I should be everlastingly wondering whether I was using it wisely, and one would be almost obliged to entertain largely. I am sure that all this would not suit me, and that I should feel much happier in managing a small homely household. For that reason I do not envy the rich at all; on the contrary, it pleases me that others, who are better fitted for them, should have such luxuries. But when I am in a selfish mood I imagine that all this is there for my sake, in order that I should have so many nice things to look at when walking with you, and so that we may have an excuse for such a foolish conversation."

We continued along the Zoological Gardens, entering " Grosser Garten," where we chose the least frequented wood-like road that curved between tall pines and broad oak trees. At last we sat down on a little hillock with a fine view to the north of the Hercules Avenue, the magnificent lime trees of which cast their shadow far away over the stubble fields in front of us. To the left, strongly lit by the sun, lay the heights on the opposite side of the Elbe, with its wood-covered banks and hollows surmounting the villages, which, with the help of the villas, form an almost continuous border of gardens and houses. The steep slopes are intersected by the terraces and walls of the vineyards, and here and there high-roofed country houses, encircled by Italian poplars, are interspersed, while on the heights above are dotted the little cottages of the vineyard workmen, looking like small watch towers. All these details continually repeated themselves, dwindling and becoming less clear and closer to one another, until they melted into an almost indefinite tone of colour at the point where the brow of the hills sloped down towards the plain. This latter stretched far away in a blue mist, and in the dim distance appeared more hazy mountain shapes floating like a sediment of the blue in the atmosphere, rather than a rising of the earth. But as the shadows on the fields grew longer the contours came out more solidly, and among them we recognised distinctly the familiar profile of Lilienstein. While on the right Loschwitzer bank the window-panes flickered like the beginning of an illumination, and we could distinguish the stone-quarries of Lilienstein as a lighter line below. It was queer to think that in this mountain-picture, which was so diminutive that it could be painted on the nail of the little finger, we could with a needle point out the place which had held so much of our happiness. Silently we pressed one another's hands, and our eyes filled with tears as we gazed towards it. It seemed to both of us that the idyll had grown to the place as a delicate flower which will not bear transplanting, and that we had left it there, and only there would be able to find it again ; an irresistible home sickness overpowered and united us.

Though only a few days parted us from that time, and we sat together just as happy as we had been then, and though we looked forward to a happy union,—in spite of all this it seemed to both of us that we saw a lost paradise revealing itself out there in the glow of the setting sun, with tiny rosy clouds like Cupid-feathers floating above in the light colourless sky, little by little to glide away under the shadow of the soft wings of the night, which found us still sitting on the same spot with our arms around each other.

This constant, tender sadness in looking back on things, is it but the reaction from an idealising power which the memory itself possesses, or does it perhaps rather proceed from man's never-ceasing fear—the feeling of everlasting uncertainty with regard to the unknown fate, that by a mere mood is able to rob one of everything, except what one has experienced—an uncertainty that not only threatens from without, but also seems to warn from within, and against which perhaps only our Ego's hidden kernel in rare moments of expansion can place an equal force ?

CHAPTER IV

As we came out of the house on the next afternoon, Minna took my arm and turned me round quickly.

"Do you know where we are going to-day? To-day we are going to Zwinger. I want to take advantage of all you have told me about architecture, and especially about the Rococo style. Now we must repeat it in Reality's great picture-book."

And we went to Zwinger both then and on many other lovely afternoons—to Zwinger, this Palace Court of pavilions and galleries, which is an epopee in stone from a time when fondness of life and its pleasures excluded all poems except of the material order, in which one could move and enjoy, drink, dance, fence, love, ride roundabouts, and bathe in the basins of fountains under the open sky. This master-piece of a luxurious and fantastic style, which an insipid after-taste of the Empire has taught an unproductive generation to look down upon with pseudo-classic contempt, but which now everywhere is again recognised with honour and glory. Zwinger, which seemed to be built by Saxonian gnomes, led by a faun who was in love with a muse. . . .

On other days we visited our godly hostess from Rathen, "the mother Elbe," in her town residence, where she is lodged between both parts of the town in a grand dwelling, which is parted into two banqueting halls by the rows of columns of three bridges. On the famous Brühl-Terrace we intoxicated ourselves at the sunset hour with the glorious metallic colours that shone and glittered between one another in the whirling of the river, until far away it bent into a golden arch in front of the blue vine-hills. Or we walked on the quay, which is ornamented by a long row of small curly poplars that seemed to be taken from a child's box of toys.

I remember a gloomy day when the sun in the last minute broke through the bank of clouds, and the sudden illumination of the windows gleamed down over the stream ; it was as if Mother Elbe had unveiled her banqueting hall— a colonnade of twisted columns embossed in the purest gold.

Twice we went on board one of the little steamboats and sailed out to the idyllic vine-trailed Loschwitz, the native town of " Don Carlos," or to the Schiller garden of its neighbour Blasewitz, where Gustel of " the Camp of Wallenstein " lived.

On the way back through the town Minna usually had to make some purchases for our supper. I waited outside the sausage-maker's dainty shop while she did her catering at the marble counter.

One evening, when we returned after a long walk, her mother had gone out, and Minna had no key. We were both very hungry, and, as we had warm sausages with us, we did not hesitate long ; Minna went off to the baker at the one corner and I to the beer-house at the other, and bringing respectively a " Zeilen-Semmel " and a tankard of " Kulmbacher " we met in triumph. In the dark summer-house we enjoyed with jokes and laughter the best supper I had ever eaten.

We did not visit the picture-gallery. Minna never mentioned it, and I dared not propose it for fear of bringing back painful recollections. But we often went to see the excellent collection of plaster casts, in which antique art is so well represented in all its stages.

I was surprised at the instinctive sense of art in Minna and the originality of her criticisms. She was amused over the "Æginets'" set smile, whether they killed or were killed, but at the same time remarked how advanced art already was in the treatment of the body and its movements. It struck her for the first time that an art can be at such a standard that its technique is almost perfect in certain directions, while there is something higher towards which it is moving with the uncertain footsteps of a child. And she questioned whether this was not also the case in a lower degree, with what we recognise as perfect art.

In the Parthenon Hall it was especially the Torsos from the gable groups which impressed her. But what struck her most of all were the master-pieces of the after-classic art " The Gaul," " The Grinder," " Venus of Milo "—most of the other statues of Aphrodites she passed by with indifference. She pointed out to me many details that I had not remarked myself, the life-like touch of reality in a hand or foot, remarking that in statues of modern artists which she had seen these were often made too " beautiful."

Sometimes a personal interest in these plastic studies was awakened : " How nice to have such a beautiful straight Grecian nose ! " she sighed more than once, " then you would love me still more. Oh yes, you would be bound to do so."

And after having inspected a whole collection of goddesses: " But they have not got such very thin arms ! "

" Why should they have ? "

" I thought it was ugly to have strong arms," she answered, the blood rushing into her face as she turned away.

But our enjoyments in art, in this town where one *can* enjoy art, culminated ecstatically when we heard Wagner's "Valkyrie." The noble and melancholy love of these two Völsungs etherealised in a beauty of tones, the fervour of which has eternity's clear depth. How profoundly did it not penetrate our souls, uniting them in an endless sympathy! Our love reflected itself in this heavenly flow of melody as a narcissus—and loved itself.

In the beginning we whispered an occasional outburst of admiration to one another ; later we were silent.

Minna pressed my hand at the words—

> "When in winter's frosty wildness
> First my friend I found."

And when Sieglinde distinctly, so that every syllable was heard in the dead silence of the theatre, and with such pathos as only Wagner has ever inspired an opera singer, sang—

> "How fair and broad
> Thy open brow,
> The varying veins
> In thy temples I trace !
> I tremble with emotion
> Resting entranced "—

she gave me a look which I know I shall feel on my death-bed. And at the end, when the curtain did not *fall*, but was drawn together . . . oh ! I still see her standing up in the box, clapping with all her might and main, with sparkling eyes and moist traces of tears on her blushing cheek, more beautiful than I had ever seen her, more spiritually beautiful than anything I have seen or shall see !

We went down into the glorious *foyer*, the marble walls and columns of which gleamed in the late daylight. It

was overcrowded with well-dressed people. Minna's dress
was plain, though not so plain that it was striking, but many
eyes were turned upon her. She was too moved to be
worried by the attention paid to her, or even to notice it.

We stepped out upon a balcony where a mild summer
air met us refreshingly. The beautiful open square,
surrounded by monumental buildings, lay calm and
deserted under us, while crowds swarmed over the Elbe
bridge ; the wood-covered heights were bathed in sunshine
and seemed to be quite close. A feeling of endless happiness and richness overcame me.

" You are sighing ! " said Minna, who was leaning upon
me.

" It is only because I am much too happy, much more
so than I deserve," I answered. " Do you know, it was
rather presumptuous of me to propose to you."

She looked at me with a questioning smile.

" As I did not know all that was in you, I ought to
have waited until I knew you as I do now. I discover
new treasures every day. I am getting richer and richer."

Minna said nothing, but pressed my arm firmly to her
bosom.

CHAPTER V

Mr. and Mrs. Hertz had now returned from the country. We had each of us visited them in turn ; then they wanted to see us both one afternoon to coffee, according to our Rathener custom. The old man was obliged to keep quiet in the evening. Coughing and pains in the chest continued to worry him ; he was only able to get up in the middle of the day, and even this was rather the result of an obstinate determination not to give in than because he felt the better for being out of bed, where the doctor wished to keep him.

Mrs. Hertz was rather distressed about him, and thought that it would really be better if we waited for a week or so, but the old man would not hear it of : " But why ? Not for my sake, as if I am not able to see anybody ! Of course they must come to-morrow, but I will send them away when I get tired. For now I usually get tired a little earlier in the evening," he explained to me.

So, towards four o'clock on the day after we had heard the " Valkyrie," we started into the heart of the Alstadt, where one still sees with pleasure the old Rococo houses, with their irregular roofs and twisted shell ornaments, and the miniature palaces in Baroc style with pilaster-striped façades ornamented with medallions in which were to be seen images of Mars and Athene adorned with helmets and perukes. Between these plainer houses are to be found, in a rather indefinite style but of a thoroughly German character ; their cosy bay-windows making a row of cupboards along the street and forming at the corners hexagonal projections tapering down to fine points—inverted cones, scaled like pineapples and ending in a big knob beneath. Several of these houses have stucco ornaments of flower garlands, or draperies made of stone, hanging down from their windows ; now and then, too, one comes upon a frieze with enormously stout angels, so thick with paint that at a casual glance one might take the whole thing for a piece of *natura morte* of cabbages, apples, and big branches.

In such a corner house, where four streets met, the old couple lived on the first floor. There was an everlasting rumble of large covered country carts, goods wagons from the railway station, and all sorts of business vehicles, and it was evidently this noise of a busy traffic which pleased the old Königsberg merchant, and made him prefer this situation to a more airy but duller quarter.

The coffee-table was laid in Hertz's study, where he preferred to be. He rarely came into the drawing-room, but liked his wife to take her needlework in to him. It was a middle-sized room with old mahogany furniture, among which no comfortable chairs were to be found, but an arm-chair had now been moved in from the drawing-room.

Against one wall stood an ordinary writing-table with eight fragile legs, a tobacco table, and a bookcase ; just opposite was a desk of the same kind as the one beside which Kant was painted (the old colour print again presided in its usual place over the writing-table). On each side of the desk hung a couple of valuable oil paintings, life-size portraits of Beethoven and Frederick the Great in their youth. Over it were placed some daguerreotype pictures, on which, however, one could never discover anything but some shining metal spots.

13

Behind the glass doors of the bookcase there was no show of any special binding, but the outwardly homely-looking company, which displayed sulky, leather-covered backs and torn or dirty bits of cardboard, consisted only of original editions, among which—on the middle shelf—were many of Goethe's and all Schiller's works, from *Zwoote verbesserte Auflage*, of *The Robbers* with the lion rampant as vignette, and the inscription, "In tirannos," to a *William Tell* with a dedication written by Schiller himself. Several of these books we got out, not so much for curiosity's sake, for it was not the first time that the bookcase had been opened for us, but because we knew it always pleased the old man.

Minna was also privileged to unlock a drawer in the writing-table and reveal the most precious of all the treasures; it was a snuff-box which Schiller had sent to Kant, a rather big, circular-shaped box, on the cover of which was painted a beautifully designed miniature copy of the Schiller portrait by Graff. Hertz found in it a resemblance to my most unworthy self—especially in the long neck and nose, a discovery which made Minna so delighted that she kissed him.

It began to rain, and suddenly became as dusk in the room as if it was the hour of twilight. The bluish spirit flame which licked round the copper kettle shone on the old man's white beard and on his moist under-lip while he talked—slowly lisping and interrupted by coughing—about life in Riga, where he had been instructed in mercantile business for two or three years. In the Exchange an old-fashioned custom ordained that the bankrupt had to sit on a sort of stool of repentance, while a doom bell was sounded, a sort of moral execution.

"One laughs at such old symbolic customs and finds

them barbaric," he said, " but perhaps they have also had something good in them. How distinctly I remember the day when Moses Meyer had to stop his payments. He was chief in one of the two richest Jewish commercial firms, and had ruined himself by rivalry with Wolff—they had always been enemies. There was a dreadful uproar on the Exchange, some were malicious, but the Jews were all very down-hearted. 'Will Wolff come?' was asked everywhere, but most of the people thought that after all he would not witness the humiliation of his rival. It struck twelve, the hour at which the ceremony was to take place; the chairman was just going to ring the bell, when Wolff's landau drew up at a gallop, and Wolff rushed into the hall and shouted breathlessly : ' The bell is not to ring; Meyer is not to take the bankrupt chair.' He had at the last minute, surely after a hard fight, decided to supply his rival with the necessary amount in order to prevent the Jewish congregation from being humiliated; and the two old men cried in each other's arms."

We stared in astonishment at this old man, who seemed at this moment still more venerable, on account of his remembrances of a time that had such a far-off and patriarchal character.

With what pious meditation did we regard some dust and pebbles in a bottle, earth from the Holy Land, which an old Jew from Riga, who had made the pilgrimage to Jerusalem on foot, had brought home in a pocket-handkerchief.

From such Jewish tales the conversation gradually diverged to the Jews' share in liberal-minded literature and centred principally on Heine.

As soon as the coffee-table was cleared Hertz had his Heine portfolio taken out. It contained many letters both to and from the poet, some proof-sheets, and a few small manuscripts. I took up one of the proofs and, as it was still very dark at the table, I went to the window in order to make out a very much erased portion.

I accidentally looked down on the street corner and started. It seemed to me that the slim, very fashionably dressed man with pointed and well-twisted fair beard, who was passing by, looked like Axel Stephensen. But no, this man was taller and older than the Danish painter, and as he took off his hat to an acquaintance I even saw that he was bald.

My feeling of alarm vanished.

At the same instant Hertz started with his feeble, husky voice to read aloud from a manuscript sheet—

> "Once more from that fond heart I'm driven
> Which I so dearly love, so madly;"

Minna and I exchanged a meaning look; she grew pale, and her pallor showed out still more clearly in the stormy light, which seemed to penetrate through an ashen rain, so dirty and yellow was it.

"It is a beautiful poem," said Hertz; "do you know it?"

"Yes, we know it."

"Oh, they are reading Heine together, the young hearts," Mrs. Hertz exclaimed. "A beautiful time!"

Soon after we took our leave.

We went towards "Grosser Garten."

The rain had stopped. After we had walked a little, Minna exclaimed—

"How strange that he should have the manuscript of just that poem!"

"Yes, a strange coincidence!"

"There is not such a thing as chance."[1]

[1] "Es giebt Keinen Zufall!"—*Wallenstein*, Schiller.

But as we were half-way up the lovely plane avenue which runs across the fields between the city and " Grosser Garten," it flashed into my mind that the rings which we had ordered were promised us without fail for this afternoon.

We at once agreed to go back, though it took us right into the quarter of the town from which we had come. It was not one of the larger goldsmiths, but a workshop on the second or third floor, of which Minna knew. The rings were ready, and the old woman who gave them to us bestowed them with many congratulations and blessings, to which she also added many regards to Minna's " mamma."

The distress, or rather despondency, which had taken possession of us since that unfortunate poem had been mentioned, gave way to the golden magic of the engagement rings. The weather had changed to the most beautiful sunshine, and we decided to enjoy it on the terrace near by.

The terrace was swarming with people, as is always the case at this hour in fine summer weather. We heard sounds of the concert in Wienergarten on the other side of the river ; it was the finale of the *Valkyrie*, and we stood still and listened. Distance blotted out the defects in the execution. " The renunciation," during which Wotan kisses away the godlike power of Brynhilde, so that the long swooning sleep falls upon her, came clearly over to us in its melancholy rise and fall.

" I heard this very thing on the evening I decided to spend my holiday at Rathen," I said.

" A blessed evening it has been for me," answered Minna," though I at that time had no notion of it. It is strange to think how quite an unknown human being's decision can so completely alter one's whole life. Therefore I do not believe in chance in such things."

"It has been a blessing for both of us," I exclaimed, "and blessed be the place. I will now show you where I sat, over there, outside the little Café Torniamenti, between the columns. Do you see, just there where the gentleman, no, not the old one, but the one who is now getting up and is paying the waiter——"

I felt myself kept back by a sudden grip on my arm.

Minna had stopped and stared—But, good God, with what an expression upon her face! She was not pale, but her eyes were unnaturally open—Macbeth might have looked on Banquo's ghost in that way when the courtier showed him to his seat.

I followed this look to the spot to which I had myself directed it.

The gentleman, who had paid the waiter, looked towards us and quickly raised his high silk hat.

BOOK IV

CHAPTER I

THIS smart gentleman was Axel Stephensen.

At once he began to take off his right glove and to walk towards us; Minna also began to unbutton hers, but it fitted tightly, and she was still pulling at it when he stopped in front of us.

"Oh, please, Minna, don't trouble, between old friends——"

But Minna continued determinedly to stare—with a queer smile—at her glove, for the obstinacy of which she was perhaps grateful. At last she got the hand free—the hand that now wore my ring. It appeared to me that she caressed this magic love-token with her eyes, and that Stephensen stared at it morosely. She glanced at him in shaking hands, and with a gesture which made the ring sparkle she introduced us to one another.

"My fiancé, Harald Fenger."

We bowed almost too politely and assured one another that it was a pleasure and an honour, but I noticed that his aplomb in this ordeal was greater than mine, and this added to the irritation that his sudden appearance had already aroused in me.

"You have come here"—Minna was on the point of making the same unnecessary remark which her mother had bestowed upon me, but she had enough presence of mind to insert a " suddenly." " You have come suddenly to Dresden." And in recovering her self-control she looked at him steadily for the first time. " In the letter you sent me a fortnight ago you said nothing about it."

In Germany it is not so unusual as it is in Denmark for young girls and young men—brothers' friends, distant relations, or even acquaintances—to call one another by their Christian names ; and therefore Minna could not feel that Stephensen, by still taking advantage of this privilege after she was engaged to a countryman of his, meant to emphasise to me the nature of their intimacy and to equalise our positions.

She turned and began to walk slowly back towards the steps. We accompanied her, one on each side. It was evident that Stephensen was annoyed that this letter was mentioned in my presence, and his annoyance was the greater because I assumed a defiant air, as much as to say, " Indeed, sir, I know quite well your beautiful Heine effusions."

" Quite right," he said. " I got the order after I had written. I have come to copy Correggio's Magdalene. I suppose you remember the copy of it I made a couple of years ago, Minna ; you were kind enough to take an interest in it, and to come and watch me at work "—here he smirked under his moustache with a vain and insinuating smile which made my blood boil. " I, at any rate, have not been able to forget the pleasant hours we used to spend together in the gallery." He glanced up in the air with a vague far-away look, and paused so that Minna might have an opportunity to agree with what he had said. But, as she continued to look silently at the ground, he proceeded in a lighter tone—

" As I think I wrote to you, I sold that picture to a

merchant. A Mæcenas of ours has now been so uncritical as to fall in love with it."

" You speak a little too modestly about your art for one to be able to believe in your humility . . . especially as I suppose there is no reason for it." This latter I added because Minna looked at me reproachfully, as if she feared that the conversation might take a pointed and personal character.

Stephensen laughed and stroked his beard.

" Well, I have at least reason to wish that this new client will not be too critical, for such a hazardous under-taking does not succeed twice. But, anyhow, it is a good thing to be acquainted with what one is going to represent, and as to the good Correggio I have long ago found him out : the lady is by no means studying the Holy Bible, but reading a pastoral novel, and an improper one, too, I should venture to guess."

Though I, in reality, found this remark quite striking and could not help smiling, there was something so irritat-ing, yes, even insulting, towards Minna in the self-satisfied smirk with which he accompanied it, that an almost irre-sistible impulse seized me to take him by the collar and push him down the steps at the top of which we were standing. I reflected whether in such case there was any possibility of his breaking his neck, and pictured to myself Minna's terror, the crowd of people round, and how the police would arrest me.

And all the while the unsuspecting man stood expatiating upon the beauty of the town that was stretched out in front of us. He was especially pleased with the Catholic church which, in the foreground, presented its two storeys of massive weather-beaten sandstone, in the elegant forms of a noble Baroc style. Between the clustered columns of the open tower the yellow gleams of evening were shining, and over the copper roof, that just peeped through the balustrade as a green field through a fence, the row of statues were silhouetted sharply in characteristic decorative positions. Stephensen reminded Minna that she had drawn his attention to a group half-way in front of the tower, where a nude arm darkly outstretched on the sky's golden ground made an extraordinary effect.

"Whenever I have thought of Dresden I imagined myself here and at this hour, and it always seemed as if that arm beckoned to me, perhaps also on account of the precious remembrances which were associated with it. But what a lovely place it is! This treasure of a church, and just behind it the palace tower that is so all-powerful, though at the same time so far from being massive. Soon the tower-watchman's light will be lighted above. Do you remember how often we have pondered over that strange life up there above the busy traffic of human beings? . . . And how I love to see the people swarm in and out of the George porch and enter the town through a house. . . . And then on the other side the river quarter, the old bridge under us, and the Maria Bridge which stretches its whole length over the shiny water, and the Lösnitzer Hills, purple-coloured and so graceful in shape, they always remind me of the Janiculum by the Tiber. At the same time such comparisons are odious. One calls Dresden the Elbe-Florence, but Florence itself has no square near the Arno which can compete with this, not by a long way."

I, an untravelled man, could never have been able to pay Minna such a compliment, and each word of praise of her beloved town was bound to please her. For the first time she glanced at him with a kindly look, which he caught without turning his eyes towards her, apparently quite lost in contemplation of the town ; he even for a minute spread out his arms as if he would embrace it, and this enthusiasm, which was perhaps not wholly feigned, was not unbecoming to him.

"What a pity one does not live here and enjoy this view every day! An artist must live and breathe in artistic surroundings. I feel it every time I get out of Copenhagen : one degenerates there. Don't you agree with me that Copenhagen is a dreadful town ?"

"Detestable," I answered, though I had never thought much about it ; but I wanted if possible to overtrump him.

"All the same it drew you back when you were there," Minna remarked without lifting her eyes from the broad stone steps down which we slowly walked.

"What can one do ? A fellow must live, Minna ! "

"But you have just said that an artist must live in a place like this in order to be creative."

"That is right, but one must also sell. And works of art are easier sold where artists mix freely in society ; it is not flattering to us, but it is true. It was with a heavy heart I bade good-bye in those days, and I feel it doubly on seeing the town again. No, if I had been happy enough to be born here——"

"Surely then you would have found your way to Berlin," I said sullenly.

The tears came into Minna's eyes at his words, and possibly it was to turn the conversation that she exclaimed—

"Oh yes, it will be hard when some day one has to leave this sweet town."

"Anyhow, you will not have to go away alone, wherever you may go when you leave for your new home," Stephensen answered very emphatically.

"And we shall not stay away for ever," I added quickly

" but even if it is impossible for me to remove my business to Dresden—certainly I shall not have to go out to dinners on account of my wares, to be sure . . . but . . . at any rate, when we are getting old, and I can retire with a good conscience and a little capital, then we will surely live here, I have promised Minna ! We have even looked about for a house, and in case I should be a Crœsus we have fixed upon a magnificent villa by the Park. Perhaps Minna might then persuade you, for old friendship's sake, to come and decorate it for us."

Though this was supposed to pass as a joke I was not enough a man of the world to conceal the undertone of satire and insolence, which was much more apparent than it ought to have been. I immediately regretted what I had said, the more so because Minna looked with terrified eyes at me.

" I am not a decorator," Stephensen answered dryly. But directly afterwards he turned towards me with his most suave and courtly smile and continued : " I do not, however, mean to disparage that art, which would give you a false idea of my perception of things. Surely with us there is a certain prejudice against decorative painting with which I do not agree ; altogether I do not share many of our Danish prejudices. On the contrary, I highly appreciate decorative art, and when men pretend to be too grand to undertake it, the real fact simply is they haven't got the imagination for it. That is also the case with myself, only that I do not pretend to be too grand. And isn't it the same with all art ? We have not sufficient imagination to decorate life, therefore we only copy it and then pretend that we do it out of reverence and love of life. Nonsense ! To begin with we are pessimists, so we have neither reverence nor love of life ; and besides, even if we still have these—for we are also inconsequent—*la vie c'est une femme*, and they always like to be flattered. By the way, all art is originally decorative, and Apollo is in reality a *maître de plaisir* in Olympus. But to decorate! Great heavens! who can do that? Rubens could. Now we are far too earnest—that is to say, we are morose—and with reason, because we are anæmic and nervous, and get a headache if we have made a night of it. We pretend that we do not want to dance any more and we put on airs, but the truth is that our legs have become stiff and tired. Well, perhaps you do not share these views, Mr. Fenger. I know quite well they are not in vogue."

" I quite agree with you," I assured him, though I did so only in part ; but it pleased me to disappoint his hope of a dispute in which he, with reason, expected to get the best of the argument. Nevertheless, I quite understood that he did not mean anything serious by all this palaver, but that from the beginning he merely wanted to make it clear that he was worldly wise enough to understand my sarcasm ; and above all things he wanted to show off before Minna. He glanced constantly towards her with his half-closed eyes, and the self-contented smile seemed to say : " Did you notice how quickly I understood that the conversation must be turned away from the shoals on which this fool was just going to strand us ? I hope you are thankful. And cannot I discourse about art brilliantly ? He ought to try that, but he wisely keeps silent. Well I, too, know when it is time to be silent. *Assez d'esthetique comme ça !* "

When we were outside the theatre some ladies and gentlemen came out on to the balconies of the foyer. I thought of yesterday ; at this hour I had stood up there with her and had magnified my immense and still growing wealth. " Er stand auf seines Daches zinnen—Polycrates, Polycrates ! " [1]

" By the way," Stephensen began after a pause, " I paid your mother a visit and it pleased me to find her so well and active."

" Have you already ? And you came yesterday ? "

" No, to-day by the morning train."

" And leave again ? " I blurted out.

" Not exactly to-morrow," he answered with a mocking smile.

" I almost thought so," I answered, " since you were in such a hurry with your visit."

" And the picture ! That will not be finished in one day," Minna remarked.

" No more than Rome ! Fortunately the picture is free. I have already arranged everything with the custodian, and I think of starting to-morrow."

I had quite forgotten this picture, and he evidently had also forgotten it.

We had walked slowly through Zwinger, and were now passing through the gardens towards the post-court. Behind a group of acacias, with leaning trunks, a street-lamp, that was struggling with the last ray of daylight, spread a dull yellowish misty glare, out of which the dainty Gothic sandstone portal of the Sophie-Church appeared, while its slim open-work spires stood phantom-like over the dark summits of the trees against a twilight sky, that was almost colourless but for a couple of sloping feathery clouds still beaming in a rosy glow. I had often seen the place in this fascinating light during my evening walks, and now, to my disgust, it was Stephensen who

---

[1] Schiller's famous ballad " Polycrates " (" He was standing on his palace roof ").

pointed it out and in a way adopted it with his artist's authority.

"Just look how delicately it stands there; it is a pure *Van der Neer.*"

"Oh, one sees beautiful light effects here," I remarked. "The other day we saw 'a real *Poussin*' out in Saxonian Switzerland."

Minna bit her lip. Stephensen, who could not have had any notion of the reference, felt that I mocked at artists' expressions.

"Yes, I quite believe it. One comes upon subjects at every turn. But, *nous voilà*! I live at Hotel Weber, and will take my leave. Perhaps I have already intruded."

We assured him, of course, to the contrary, and he disappeared with quick steps which made a crunching sound upon the gravel.

In silence we walked homewards. Near the post office there was a crowd of yellow carriages making their way home like bees to their hives, and every moment a horn-signal resounded.

I silently cursed all letter-writing and the whole postal system.

CHAPTER II

Mrs. Jagemann opened the door to us in rather an alarmed manner. She drew Minna aside in the dark passage and whispered something to her, and as I closed the door of the sitting-room I heard Minna say—

" Yes, yes, we have met him ourselves."

" Oh dear me ! " the mother sighed in her stupid way.

This did not improve my temper. I continued to walk up and down, and without knowing it myself I shook my fist at Stephensen's *alter ego* on the sea picture. I caught myself in this act as the door opened, and I quickly dropped the hand and put it in my pocket.

Minna threw herself wearily upon the little sofa.

" What does he want from me ? " she exclaimed in a worried tone.

" You ? But he has come in order to paint."

She shook her head.

" He wishes to take possession of me again, that's what he wants."

" What a funny fancy ! How can you believe that ? "

" You have thought the same yourself," she said, and looked at me inquiringly.

" Perhaps for a moment. Queer ideas come to one under such extraordinary circumstances. However, there is no reason to——"

" Did you notice the way he said to me, ' Wherever

you go when you leave for your new home ' ?—
those words were quite clear; I know his way only too
well."

" But, indeed, it would be too bold. Just as we are
engaged ! No, had we even been married a couple of
years, then I should think it more likely that a fellow with
his easy-going ideas might think there was hope."

" For shame, it is nasty to speak like that, you have
no right to talk of him in that way."

" You defend him ! "

" Is that so strange ? You know quite well yourself
that it is unjust of you, besides, you ought to remember
that it grieves me when you express such a low opinion
of him ; for, after all, I have cared for him, and, of course,
still do. . . . And you have not been at all nice this
afternoon ; all the time you went on aiming remarks
at him, and I was so nervous ; you did not make it easier
for me, and it was quite difficult enough without
that."

" You are right, Minna ! Forgive me. I felt it myself ;
but you must be able to understand—in such a frame of
mind and under such conditions."

" It proves that you were afraid of him. You have been
as afraid as I have, all the time ; not only for a moment, as
you said."

" No, I have not. And, after all, it only shows that I
feel irritated in the presence of this man, who owns part
of your past, and that I must hate him."

" That is just it, he owns my past, all that has any
value in it, and he thinks it gives him a hold over me,
which perhaps it does."

" Minna, Minna, what is it you are saying ? "

" Oh, I am completely confused."

14

" Do you not know that you are mine, and I yours ? "

She nodded slowly, while she gazed in front of her and pressed her lips together.

" And that you love me ; don't you know that ? "

Minna got up and embraced me tenderly.

" Yes, my beloved, that I know."

" Then there is nothing to doubt, not even as regards him. He knows you sufficiently to be sure that you would not submit to a marriage of convenience, and of me he knows that I am neither a duke nor a millionaire."

I spoke to her long and soothingly, while we were sitting on the little sofa with our arms round one another ; it was so dark I could hardly see her. She seldom answered, and I doubted whether she really listened or whether her thoughts were completely wandering. Suddenly she pressed my hand and said—

" Let us go away from here, Harald ! At once, to-morrow."

" Go away, but where to ? "

" Out in the mountains, to Erzgebirge, to Blocksberg—anywhere ! " And she laughed with the natural gaiety that was always ready to break out.

" Yes, but, Minna, would that be wise ? "

" I dare do it. I have thought it all over—I have no relations for whose sake 1 need bother. I am my own mistress, and I dare."

" That is all very well, and I appreciate that you would in case of necessity ignore—ignore such ideas and formalities, but I think in this instance you ought to understand that your reputation is to me the most precious thing in the world, and I cannot see that it is a necessity."

" Indeed, indeed ! " she exclaimed decidedly, almost violently. Whereupon she laid her lips to my ear and whispered in the most insinuating voice : " Let us, Harald ; do say ' yes ' ! "

" Well, yes, dearest——"

" Yes ? "

" That is to say, suppose that we really were to leave to-morrow——"

" Yes, yes, what then ? "

" I have hardly any money, and I do not know how I, with so short a notice — I only know very few people here, the only one would be Hertz——"

" No, for God's sake ! Hertz ! What would they say ? I haven't given them a thought; how bewildered I must be ! "

" Yes, there you are, and it really is an important step, which requires to be most thoroughly considered ; one might suffer long for a hasty step."

The turn things had taken was rather welcome to me. I continued to speak soothingly to her, and already thought that I had got her quite away from her idea, when she suddenly said—

" Still, if we had money by us I would do it after all. . . That money should have such power, it is really dreadful ! "

At that moment her mother entered with a lamp, and I was struck by the expression of terror on Minna's face, perhaps exaggerated because of the sudden dazzling light. She seemed compelled to look towards the unavoidable fate, and I myself got a feeling of fear and discomfort as of impending danger, though I could not imagine that such was at hand. For, however painful it might be for poor Minna to receive Stephensen and listen to his undeserved reproaches and fruitless representations, it is the kind of thing one overcomes, and nothing in the whole affair seemed obscure to me.

I did not reveal my own secret forebodings, but so much the more allowed these reasonings to come to the fore. Minna seemed to agree with me.

As we spoke Danish the old woman felt *de trop*, and was just going to creep out in her quiet way when Minna begged her to stay, and began to talk Saxonian dialect and Dresden slang with her ; and in this funny language she joked so gaily, and put on such peculiar faces, that I soon quite forgot the feelings which had so recently depressed us, and the mother laughed till the tears ran down her cheeks.

When the old woman fell asleep after tea, Minna sat down at the piano and played a berceuse by Chopin. She also began to play a waltz, but over this she broke down more than once.

" I am not in form," she said and came to me. " I prefer to read to you."

She took *Käthchen von Heilbronn*, which we had begun and hoped to see acted in a few days.

We soon came to the charming episode where Kätchen will not lift her skirt when wading over the brook, and the old man-servant shouts—

" Only to the ankles, child, to the extreme lowest edge of the sole, Kätchen," but she runs away in order to find a plank.

" Yes, Hertz was right when he called you a Kätchen," I interrupted her. " Do you remember at the quarry, when we were going up ? "

" Oh, indeed, I can remember it. When you were so obstinate and nasty ! And if only you could have imagined how comical you looked, as if you had got on a mask which did not fit at all——"

Then she read the most touching and, in all its naïveté,

the most profound love-scene which the whole of dramatic literature possesses : Kätchen reposing in a half-somnambulistic slumber under the elder bush, and answering the questions of the Count. " Verliebt ja, wie ein Käfer bist du mir " (" In love, yes, like a beetle are you ").

" That is to you ! " Minna exclaimed. " I could also have said that to you in those days."

We laughed and kissed one another.

After having read fluently for about half an hour, she suddenly stopped and blushed crimson ; but I had hardly discovered this before I had the book hurled into my face ; she had only meant to throw it from her, but, as I was seated just opposite, it had struck me ; perhaps she also had involuntarily been annoyed because I had waited for her to continue.

" What have I done ! " she exclaimed, starting up and throwing herself on her knees beside me. " What a wretch I am ! Have I hurt you ? "

I laughingly assured her that I was more surprised than anything else.

" I could not read it to you—why does he write such things ? And I had not sufficient presence of mind to skip it."

I tried to take the book, but she snatched it up, and having smoothed out the crumpled leaves, she put it back in the bookcase.

" Poor man ! You had to suffer for it ! "

" Yes, just as I look up—Bang ! "

And we burst into uncontrollable laughter. The old lady had shown some signs of waking up when the book had come into contact with my head, and our laughter thoroughly aroused her.

" You make such a rumpus, children, that we shall soon

have the watchman up," she said. "It is already late. Oh dear me, yes! I wish I was in bed!"

She lit a little bit of a candle, which stood on the chest of drawers, and slouched out.

It was the hour at which I usually left, and I seldom stayed later because I knew that Minna had to get up early.

But she asked me to stay, for she said that she would not be able to sleep for several hours.

"I have read to you, now you might tell me tales," she said, and seated herself beside me on the little sofa. "I have told you so much about my own childhood, and have not heard nearly enough of yours. Do tell me."

I told her of the calm lonely life in a Ranger's home in the south of Zeeland. My mother I could hardly remember, but my recently lost father I described with all the grief which overwhelmed me by the thought that he would have come to love my Minna, and that she in him would have found a second father. He was in some ways rather peculiar, an old disciple of Schopenhauer, and a philosopher of nature; in consequence he was always quarrelling with the parsons of the neighbourhood, who had a craze to convert him. I shared his hermit life and, to the disgust of the neighbourhood, he brought me up in his free views.

Minna sang the part from the *Valkyrie* where Siegmund relates his youth:

> "Friendless fled
> My father with me;
> Lapsed my youth
> While living for years
> With Wolfing in woodlands wild."

"By the way, have you wolves in Denmark?"

"Of course we have, and polar bears go about on skates there."

Minna slapped me over my fingers.

" After all, it was not impossible ! They have wolves in Poland. I have stayed with a cousin who is married there, and have heard them howl. Yes, just you look at me, such an one am I !—By the way, why did you not take to forestry ? I should have liked to be a forester's wife ! "

" Well, you ought to have let me know in those days. But you forget, then we should not have met."

" Why not ? You might have come to the college in Tharandt. Those who are to meet will meet."

" Fatalist ! "

" Oh, you ought to know I am that ! But, to be serious, I should think it would have suited you well."

" I also had a taste for it ; it was only later I wanted to be an architect, and it had already been decided that I should be one when my mother's brother, who is a director of a large china-factory in London, offered to help me, if I would be a Polytechnic student. Well, it was more advantageous, and my father did not think we ought to lose the chance. Besides, he thought that it would be a good thing for me to take to a practical life, and not become such a lonely misanthrope and dreamer as he accused himself of being. "

" I am sure you will be that all the same. You are my sweet enthusiast. And with all this you have not told me a word of those with whom you have been in love. Do you not know that it is the custom for all engaged couples at once to boast to one another of their former sweethearts ? To have confessed before the engagement is an exception that confirms the rule, but you seem to imagine that you can break it altogether."

" Not at all. Be it confessed to you under seven-sealed

promise of silence, that in my first youth I sighed in secret for the daughter of a forester."

" Well, it is quite an idyll ! "

" No, only half a one. For she was so far from being a beauty that it often caused me an effort to keep up the illusion. But it seemed to me I ought to have some one whose initials I could cut on the bark of the trees with a burning heart above."

" Yes, afterwards you men can always speak with irony of your loves, and then it is for poor us to suffer. And who was the next one ? "

" There wasn't another."

" What do you say ? Look here, Harald, Harald ! "

" Indeed, I assure you, none worth mentioning. Perhaps I have fancied some pretty face I have seen in the street. I may have had a dream or two and built castles in the air. . . ."

" Well, for those you are a splendid architect. But I feel certain that you are deceiving me."

" What makes you say so ? Remember that I have had so little society, have met so few ladies."

" Yes, that may be the reason. Very likely that is why you care for me. When you discover that I am just like the others——"

" But you are not."

" Well, you don't know ! "

" I am sure of it, it's impossible. . . . And, after all, what do I care for the others ? "

Minna laughed heartily and pressed me to her.

" That was well said, and it came from the heart, therefore you shall have a kiss . . . if only you would always think so ! No, do not promise anything ; what is the good of that ? Kiss me ! "

The tower clock on Kreuz Church struck twelve, it was quite time to part.

The outer door had, of course, been closed long before. Minna had to go down with me and open it. In the cool cellar-like corridor we gave one another a long embrace. I was not to detain her when she opened the door, but quickly slip out so that no passer-by or late neighbour should see her. But the draught blew the folds of her skirt out as she was about to bang the door, and while I helped to free her, I couldn't resist the temptation to steal one more kiss, in spite of the fact that I had seen a man on the opposite pavement.

The light from the little lamp, which she had put down in the corridor, shone round her dark figure with a flickering glare which suddenly went out.

" Good-bye, good-bye ! " she whispered quickly, and the door closed.

CHAPTER III

I WALKED rapidly along : " A dream in the heart, on the lips the last kiss," as one of the German lyric poets sings. With delight I inhaled the fresh evening air ; my stick sounded on the pavement, and my firm steps echoed in the empty street. A man whose boots creaked audibly kept pace with me on the opposite pavement. Only a couple of lamps lighted the whole street, and both of them were on my side ; I glanced in vain at the stranger, who very likely had witnessed the tender little scene. Suddenly he crossed the road, cleared his throat, and lifted his hat. I was startled to recognise Stephensen.

" Excuse me, Mr. Fenger," he began ; " perhaps it surprises you at this hour, it might have the appearance . . . well, why not be straightforward ? I *have* been waiting for you."

" Indeed. Then you must have been wearing away the pavement for a considerable time."

" Just as long as you were later than usual in leaving your fiancée. . . . It shows that it was most important for me to meet you."

" You honour me too much. You wish——? "

" I should like to have an interview with you, upon a subject which is of the greatest importance to both of us."

" All right."

" Suppose we drink a glass of beer in a place where I am known and where we can be alone ? "

"A glass of beer by all means," I answered, with as cheerful an indifference as was possible, though I felt as if somebody had proposed to drink poison with me.

"I suppose you also appreciate a good glass of Pilsener, or Münchener beer ? As far as I am concerned I cannot stand our Danish beer any longer."

"No, it tastes more or less like water with gin in it."

"Quite my opinion ! And that we are proud of ! Well, *à la bonheur*, as the German says, anyhow it has brought us some statues.[1] Suppose we go to the ' Three Ravens '— very likely you also are known there ? "

"No, I have only been there a few times."

"Really ! I went there nearly every evening from the very same front door out of which you have just come. Perhaps you know that I lodged there ? I had, of course, my own key, and therefore had not the opportunity of being seen out in the pleasant way you were. Speaking of that, do you know the expression, ' A genius, who never has had his own door key ' ? I find it very applicable to our Danish talents, I came across it the other day in one of our new authors. I suppose you are up to date in our new literature, are you not ? Oh, one cannot deny there is a lot of ' go ' in it, otherwise I read mostly French novels. Well, here we are at the ' Three Ravens,' they have been illuminated, that's something new. After you."

He stood aside for me to go first into the lighted corridor, and then he took me to the left through a billiard-room, where five or six men were playing in shirt sleeves, to a smaller room which was empty. Before we had taken off our overcoats, a very fat and pale waiter, with leg-of-

[1] A wealthy brewer in Copenhagen made the collecting of modern sculpture his hobby.

mutton-shaped whiskers, appeared, and hastened to the assistance of Stephensen.

"Welcome, Professor!" he said, and so that he might leave no doubt as to his personal knowledge of the customers, he hastily added: "Arrived from Denmark in order to paint again, I suppose?"

"That's just it. How are things going on at the 'Three Ravens,' Heinrich?"

"As usual, Professor, as well as usual, I am glad to say; only that last year we stopped drawing Bohemian beer, which the Professor sometimes drank. Well, there was also a waiter on the staff—but perhaps the Professor remembers Frants, the tall fellow with the red beard?"

"Perfectly well; is he not here?"

"Last Easter he opened a bar in Friedrichstadt. He is supposed to be doing well, but I say, 'a bird in the hand——'"

"You are right. It would never do for you to leave the 'Three Ravens,' we couldn't do without you. Look here, could we be by ourselves, Heinrich?"

"Oh, dear me, yes, Professor. Shall it be Pilsener?"

"Yes, two—and——"

"With a lid, of course, Professor," the waiter said, anticipating him, and bowing and flicking the napkin under his arm, after which he quickly disappeared.

I sat down on a little velvet sofa with the depressing feeling of inferiority that one gets in a public place in the society of a regular customer, who is treated half as a prince and half as a comrade by the waiter, while whatever attention is shown to outsiders is given as a favour. And what a customer! Arriving here after a couple of years' absence, and being received as if he had left last night. Stephensen, "the Professor," evidently enjoyed his triumph, while he stretched out his legs, glanced in the mirror over the sofa, and fidgeted with his fingers between his neck and stiff little collar.

"What astonishing memories these waiters have," he exclaimed. "Upon my word, he remembers that I always ordered Pilsener beer drawn in a glass with a lid—it is almost absurd! By the way, I also had a curious experience with a porter in Berlin. . . ."

He started to tell some anecdotes in order to pass the time until the waiter returned. I felt as if he was playing with me, like a cat with a mouse, and was almost inclined to get up and go away. From the adjoining room one heard the monotonous counting. A hoarse voice shouted—

> "I am naughty,
> You are naughty,
> We are both naughty."

The waiter entered with the beer and disappeared immediately.

Stephensen lifted his tankard towards me, and took a long drink.

"Well," he started, "it was—— By the way, do you smoke?"

"Not so late in the evening," I answered, though I had a great desire to calm my nerves with tobacco; but my pouch was empty, and the thought of receiving anything from him filled me with disgust.

"Ah, you have principles," he observed, while he lighted his pipe. "Really, with principles, as with trunks when travelling, one ought not to drag about too many of them. . . . There are, for instance, art principles. . . . However, it was our concerns we were to talk about."

"Just so, I think it is time we began," I remarked irritably. . . . "Is there any way I can be of service to you?"

Stephensen smiled in a peculiar way.

"I dare say you can, but it is not about that I want to speak. . . . H'm! I said on the terrace that I had come in order to paint."

"That could not surprise me, as you are a painter."

"Quite right. . . . I am also going to paint, but it was not for this I came. . . . Two letters which I received from Minna, and in which she informed me of her engagement to you, brought me here."

"I don't understand why they should bring you to Dresden."

"Perhaps you will when you come to know what sort of association there has been between Minna and me."

"I know everything concerning this intimacy, but it only makes your presence still more mysterious."

"Indeed! It seems to me you ought to understand that the information that she was suddenly engaged to another man was bound to be a great surprise to me, and that I——"

"Pardon me. A surprise? And why? I think on the contrary you should have been prepared for it, and that it ought to have been welcome news to you. You have in days gone by flirted with her, unfortunately not without success ; you have assured yourself of her love in return, though you did not succeed in making her your mistress——"

"Mr. Fenger, what an accusation! I must distinctly refute this insinuation——"

"I am sorry, but you can hardly wonder that I believe more in Minna's assurances than in yours. As you, on the other hand, failed to have sufficient moral courage to take the responsibility which an engagement involved——"

"An engagement? That would be the last straw. My good Mr. Fenger, you are young enough and very likely still sufficiently Danish to be pleased with our four, five, or six years' engagements. For my part I am not. I would do much for Minna's sake, but to bring such an absurdity on myself, to go about as a proper patent Danish fiancé— No ! "

" Very well, so after all you also have your principles. Only it is a pity that as engagements are on the same lines in Germany, her German heart and understanding have perhaps not been able fully to value these motives. What, however, is still more to be regretted, is that you did not manage to impart to her your own view of the situation, but that she, on the contrary, believed that there were to be no ties between you and herself."

" In that she was quite right. . . . Of course I wished her to have her full liberty——"

" And you yours, especially the latter."

" What do you mean by that ? "

" No doubt you have taken advantage of your liberty, indeed I can mention a certain lady who was sufficiently ' well-to-do ' to inspire in you a desire for marriage."

Stephensen laughed mockingly.

" I must say that Copenhagen's old reputation for being a gossip-hole does not belie itself, since the gossip has its echo right down in Saxonia. I can imagine that you have not deprived Minna of this ' tit-bit.' "

" Think what you like, it's no business of mine ! But permit me to call your attention to the fact that you are not very consistent, when it surprises and annoys you that she, on her part, has at last made use of her liberty."

Stephensen was evidently very irritated at the turn the conversation had taken ; but he checked the sharp outburst that was on his lips. For several minutes he remained staring silently at the ceiling with furrowed brow, breathing

deeply and sighing.   " What does this mean ? " I thought.
The voices in the billiard-room had grown more noisy ;
the musical member sang with sentimental tremor on the
long notes : " *Gute Nacht, du mein 'he-rz-iges Kind,*" and
several voices joined in, howling the syllable " herz " in
a prolonged discord.   Stephensen smiled, passed his hand
over his eyes, and then looked at me vacantly.

" You do not understand me," he began, and his lisping
voice had again attained its gentle, rather sugary tone.
" What was it you remarked ?   I see, that she had only
used her liberty, and that it ought not to annoy me.   But
this is not the point !   I do not feel at all wronged.   And
it is not the fact that she has used her liberty, as you so
strikingly observed,—not at all.   If I had heard that she
had become engaged to a young man whom she had known
for a long time, with whose family she had associated, and
who was in such a position that he could soon marry her,
for instance the son of this Jew where she visits so often,
I don't remember——"

" Hertz, I suppose you mean ? "

As a mocking chorus they howled in the billiard-room—
" *he-rz-iges Kind.*"

" That is it, Hertz ; of course she could have married
him, and why not ?   Not a brilliant match, but a solid one.
Well, I should have been resigned, and should have silently
acquiesced.   Indeed, it would have been a case in which
my consent would neither have been asked nor required,"
he added, with a rather self-sufficient irony.

" Your last remark appears to me very sound ; would
it not also be applicable in the present instance ? "

" Not quite. Just place yourself in my position.
Minna and I parted as friends, who knew that they were
more than friends, not really bound in any way, but with

a mutual consent not to lose sight of one another. In consequence of this we have corresponded for a year and a half continually and rather regularly, a fact of which you are probably aware. Well, I am not exactly 'given to sentiment,' and even if our friend perhaps has got a vein of it, it followed naturally that neither of us overwhelmed the other with emotional outpourings or fond assurances. Fortunately, however, the art exists which is called, 'reading between the lines,' and by means of this art I can, without boasting, assure you that the letters, which I received two or three months ago, were written by a lady who was in love with me."

The little Danish Dictionary, which had been Minna's favourite book, came into my mind, and I did not dare to contradict him.

"Then suddenly I receive her confidential announcement that she is engaged to a young man, whom she had only known for about three weeks, and who—forgive my saying so—is not in a position to marry soon and offer her the comforts and security of a home. Excuse me, I must repeat it—it is very painful for me to touch upon your financial position—I know that the thought of not being able to support a family in the near future, or anyhow not to maintain it with ample means, is humiliating in itself, and doubly so when it is alluded to by another; but I place the greatest importance on this point, because it shows that she was not thinking of a marriage of convenience.

"Just the very remark I made to Minna, namely, that you would see this point, and consequently understand that it was serious . . ." I said, and began to stutter, for I was annoyed by my admission that Minna and I had been talking about the possibility of his interference; and he,

15

after a long drink, glanced lurkingly at me over the lid of his tankard, and then sucked the beer from his moustache in a very contented way, as if he was saying to himself : " Oho, my friend, you put your foot into it that time ! So you have already been talking about the possibilities ! "

" Serious ! Oh, no doubt of that."

" It is as much as to say that—that we both—in short, that there was nothing for you to do," I brutally broke through the difficulty, and looked at him fiercely.

" It quite depends, it quite depends, sir ! Your reasoning does not hold good. . . . At all events, I quite see what leads you astray. Of course you look upon the expression ' marriage of convenience ' as something depreciatory, and forget that I do not share this particular Danish prejudice, nor even all cosmopolitan ones. On the contrary I consider, taken as a whole, that the so-called ' marriages of convenience ' are those matches which have most chance of happiness, not forgetting that matrimony altogether is—I won't say a curse—but an anomaly. . . . In this case, however, a matrimony of interest is, as we have already agreed, out of the question ; here is supposed to be, forgive me, passion, enthusiasm, love—whatever you like to call it. Please do not misunderstand me ! I do not doubt that, as far as you are concerned, it exists, and I will go further : I will grant you that Minna also feels real affection for you, even—I don't mind saying—is in love with you ; only, the question is, of what description is this love ? "

" Is it not the most natural thing to leave it to her to decide this question ? "

" What are you dreaming of ! She is quite incapable of doing that. I am convinced that a certain impatience to break an intercourse, which to her was doubtful and unsatisfactory, has contributed more than a little to this new and sudden love. Besides, I have also a suspicion that the quite accidental circumstance of your being a countryman of my unworthy self has made the transference of certain feelings and impressions easier——"

An intimation in her first letter to Stephensen came into my mind, and certainly confirmed this supposition. I lowered my eyes, bewildered by his inquisitive glance.

"The favourable conditions, the loneliness have done something, and then, what I do not at all doubt, many excellent and lovable qualities in yourself——"

"Shall we not now leave off this rubbish!" I burst out, and got up suddenly. "I understand quite well your ideas, but what the dickens do I care about them? I do not recognise that you have any right to act as Minna's guardian."

"And what the dickens have I to do with your recognition? That is beside the question. I simply *have* the right to do the best I can to prevent Minna from committing one of those follies, which are not easily put right again, and as it is my own behaviour towards her which to some extent is the reason for this rash haste, it is even my duty —I don't know what you mean by your scornful laughter."

"I thought the feeling of duty belonged to those cosmopolitan prejudices which you did not share."

"On the contrary, it belongs to those which I *do* share. But there is one motive that very likely influences me still stronger. It is the circumstance that I love her—love her!"

He also had risen. We stood facing one another with the little table between us, staring firmly into one another's eyes. It struck me that the most natural and, after all, the most proper thing to do, would be to jump at each other and fight like a couple of tigers, instead of which we should no doubt continue to argue and perhaps even drink our beer together and politely say good-night when we parted. This consideration made me so irritated with the situation that I recovered my control. "Since we have begun, let us play the comedy to the end," I thought. Pushing the table away I freed myself from my closed-in position, in which I felt as if I was besieged, and began to walk up and down the room. Our neighbours sang with Teutonic enthusiasm "Die Wacht am Rhein."

"What the deuce, then, do you want?" I exclaimed at last. "Perhaps you think you can make me give her up?"

"Oh no, I don't ask impossibilities."

"Really not! So, after all, you grasp that it is impossible?"

"Of course, for the same reason that the Nürnberger could not hang somebody—they had first to get him."

"I know I have got Minna, just as I know she has got me."

"Those are mere sayings and even antiquated sayings. No human being can get and own another. Do you really think your engagement is going to frighten me? As if I could not long ago have been engaged to her."

"More fool you not to have been so!"

"Perhaps you are right. But I still have a chance, and she will have to choose between us."

"She has chosen."

"No, that's just what she has not done. Under the supposition that I would not marry her, she has given you a promise. Dare you say that you would have been accepted if she, the day before you proposed to her, had known for certain that I loved her and was longing to marry her ? . . . Very well, the supposition was false, and if you are a man of honour, you will not bind her to a promise that was given under such circumstances."

" I would never, under any circumstances, look upon her promise as binding if she herself did not feel that she was bound by it."

" Oh, but that is exactly where the shoe pinches, sir. I do not doubt that Minna has most of these esteemed prejudices, which are the chief ornaments of the weaker sex. Indeed, I mean it seriously : I, for my part, would not be without these prejudices in women, though no doubt it would make life easier and more agreeable. It is an extravagant luxury, but what are we to do ? Modern nature contains such contradictions. . . . Therefore, it is very likely that Minna is inclined to consider this engagement as a bond for time and eternity. She is not exactly what one would call a character, but she certainly is a nature—and a faithful nature ; and it would consequently be easy for you, without precisely forcing your claim or appealing to her constancy, still to keep her amiable, though somewhat narrow-minded, feeling of duty alive in your favour, not stretching the tie, but still holding it firmly, so long as she herself does not untie it. What I demand of you is, that you yourself shall let it go ; understand me rightly, 'not give her up,' as you say, but only not make use of the advantage which this half-legitimate position gives you. I demand it of you as a gentleman, and, understand, not for my own sake—you would, of course, willingly see me hanged ! But for Minna's sake you cannot wish—I will not believe that of a man to whom Minna has given such a promise—that she should be yours by compulsion, were it even *inward* compulsion, while she secretly grieved over not being able to be mine. If you notice, or even suspect, that she is on the point of committing such a folly, you will know that it is your duty not to accept such a sacrifice, but, if necessary, to open her eyes and give her back her liberty which she herself has not the courage to take. It is possible that you have driven me out of her heart, in that case the matter is already settled. But it is also possible that she loves us both, each in his own way. In that case she will surely have a great struggle to go through in order to come to a conclusion ; but she must fight it out alone, and we most certainly ought not to make the battle harder by forcing ourselves upon her and by dragging her in opposite directions. . . . Minna must choose between us ; for she *has* not chosen, and no power on earth can relieve her from making a choice. But she must be free to choose—that is all that I demand."

" I shall not put any hindrance in the way of her liberty, either direct or indirect, and I will submit to her decision without trying to shake it. I rely upon you to do the same. . . . And as I suppose your object in this meeting was to obtain such a declaration from me, I presume that we can now part—as enemies."

" But, at any rate, as honest enemies, who are fighting in the open and with equal weapons."

I took my hat down from the peg, gave a stiff bow, and left the room. In the billiard-room the game had ceased ; a couple of the shirt-sleeved men, who were standing with their hands on one another's shoulders, were assuring each other of their " absolute affection and unbounded esteem." The musical member, who sat on the corner of the billiard-table, sang : " Ein' feste Burg ist unser Gott." I guessed, with reason, from these manifestations, that the sublimest height of drunkenness had been reached, and that it was very late.

By a stroke of good fortune I succeeded in finding the fat waiter, and in paying for my own beer.

CHAPTER IV

No sleep came to my eyes during that night.

I heard the clock on the Kreuz church strike one quarter after the other while I tossed to and fro on my bed. Sometimes my thoughts began to ramble in the uncertain way that is so often the harbinger of slumber, but then a wave of fever-heat rolled over me, and I was wide awake again. Dull despair took possession of me, and made everything seem lost, and by-and-bye my tears began to flow.

The more impossible a misfortune seems, the nearer is its realisation as soon as it comes within the range of possibility, for because it has already taken the leap over the widest precipice, one cannot doubt that it will also have the strength to overcome the smaller chasm. Having developed to something from nothing, why should it not be able to become everything ? Certainties exist, which to us seem so incontestable that they are almost argued away, when we are brought to dispute about them at all ; for together with their indisputability their inmost being seems to disappear.

What can be a more certain possession, more remote from any danger, than a faithful woman's love ? I felt that Minna loved me, I knew that hers was, as Stephensen also had said, a faithful nature.

But the dreadful, Nemesis-like thing was, that this fidelity recoiled upon itself : it was her faithfulness towards older feelings that had been aroused to battle against later ones, by which she was tied to me.

How safely I had rested in my happiness! And now a stranger had told me, in so many words, that he hoped to tear it from me. And as far as I was concerned? Had I laughed in his face or turned my back on him as if he were a poor fool? No, I had entered into a quarrel with him, as if my happiness needed defending; still worse, I had absolutely arranged with him how best to act in the future, and in this way I had agreed to the possibility of his gaining the victory, and admitted that I did not already possess this happiness, but had first to win it.

The danger was not only possible but actual; it was upon me, and I groaned under its weight as if possessed by a nightmare.

How safely I had rested in my happiness! And yet it occurred to me now that I had in reality always suspected danger, and that there had always been a shadow hovering over the clear sunshine of this time. I remember how this suspicious letter had awakened me from the intoxicating bliss of the first kiss. I suddenly felt again the unaccountable terror which came upon me in Schandau when I heard her letter fall into the box. On my first lonely visit to the home of her childhood, a feeling of jealousy had overcome me in a manner that now appeared quite ghost-like. Then again, hardly had I enjoyed the bliss of reunion, before it was embittered by Minna's sadness, and by his reproachful letter which had created a foolish jealousy in me, and a less foolish fear; how persistently I had begged her to leave it unanswered, and she had replied, "*I must,*" with her peculiar fatalism that now also seemed to have infected me. And the following day, when she had written and shown me this letter, and we had sat together in the evening on the small hill in " Grosser Garten," and viewed the distant Lilienstein, did not a melancholy shadow creep upon our hearts, as if we looked back towards a lost Paradise ?

In this way the hostile fate seemed to be born at the same time as our compact, and threateningly to have approached, till it now—as Beethoven says—" knocked at the door of our existence." And it was sure to get admittance ; the strong one does not threaten in vain.

I forgot that the moment when fate knocks at our door, is the time to show that one is capable of receiving it and, if necessary, of throwing it downstairs ; otherwise circumstances, confident of our weakness, might easily take to masking under the cloak of fate.

A prey to such miscellaneous reflections, I was gripped at the same time and with equal force by a state of lethargy, and by a purely physical horror which caused me to rise in agony. I had a vision, I should rather say a feeling, of something enormous and unshapely, of greyish hue, that came out of the darkness and slowly and continuously approached. But even these vague expressions give perhaps a wrong idea of my condition, for this nervous impression was really indescribable, yes, even unfathomable ; it seemed to emerge from some part of my own nature which lay under the consciousness, and was as incapable of being bounded by our narrowed conceptions and imaginations, as are the enormous creations of prehistoric times to find a place amongst the now living species.

After awhile I shook off this uncomfortable feeling, dressed, and went out.

It was a cold dawn with mist and fine rain. All the cafés were still closed. Giddy and heavy in my head, and with the sinking feeling that follows a too early rising, I had to go without food for over an hour.

At last I found a café that was being aired and cleaned. I sat down in a corner, and the waiter, who had formed his own opinion of my requirements, proposed " a soda water."

" Coffee," I ordered peremptorily.

But the fire was not yet lighted, so I had to wait. I had a real, though not pleasant, sensation of travelling, with remembrances of hotels and the rush to catch early trains. To travel, away from here ! . . . It was just what Minna had wanted yesterday evening. Then I had persuaded her against it,—but now what would not I have given for us to have already started, for her to be sitting with me, and for the cab to be ordered for the early train ? Where should we go ? Anywhere, only away !

But it was impossible now, even if I had money. Stephensen had, with his frankness, really succeeded in paralysing me ; and very likely that had been his intention, though he had not suspected that we had been thinking of going away secretly. It was not so much that my pride prevented me from flying, though the idea that Stephensen, with some reason, might complain of my action, was revolting to me ; worse than this was the fear that I should for ever have the feeling of having gained my best treasure in a deceitful manner ; and still worse, the possibility that I might even be guilty of injustice towards her. For my part this flight could only have meaning under the supposition that Minna, after grave consideration, would have preferred Stephensen. But what right had I to prevent such a decision, even if I did so with her consent ?

And suppose it proved to be a hasty step ; suppose that later on she discovered that she had mistaken her feelings, how bitter would not that repentance be which came too

late ! No, we ought to remain, happen what would. And
still there was an inner voice, which continually whispered :
" Go away ! Surely she will still go."

Then came the programme for the day. The great
question was, should I go to her at the first possible
moment ?

My longing and fear urged me on, but my better judgment
said : " Why disturb her at such an early hour ? I shall
alarm and trouble her, and she requires all her calmness
and clearness. Besides, it shows that I myself am out of
gear ; it makes me appear nervous, perhaps even distrustful ! Very likely if I stay away there is a probability of his speaking with her alone ; that I cannot,
anyhow, prevent, so just as well now as later. . . .
Yes, they must speak together, curse it, I cannot possibly
propose for him. Well, either I have to run away with
her, or leave off playing Argus."

I decided to go as usual to the Polytechnic, and to put
off seeing Minna until after dinner.

CHAPTER V

WHEN I entered the little room, Minna was sitting by the open window. I could at once see by the look she gave me, that she had shed many tears.

" Has he been to see you ? " I asked at once, while I held her trembling hands in mine.

" Yes."

She allowed me to hold her right hand, while the other, with which she was crushing a small handkerchief, was firmly pressed under her breast, as if she was suffering acute pain.

" What he has said to you, dear Minna, I know beforehand after the interview I had with him last night. . . . He—after all—you were right yesterday, at all events with regard to the motive of his coming . . . unfortunately . . . though perhaps it is selfish of me to say so. . . ."

I hardly knew what I said, and even commonplace words were not any longer at my command, but stuck in my stifled throat. I watched the expression of her averted face, and waited for a word. But she, after one firm grip, suddenly snatched her hand from mine, sank down on the chair, and burst into a dreadfully violent fit of sobbing, with her face hidden in her hands. This heart-rending sound, and the touching sight of this delicate girlish form shaken by the elementary force of weeping, affected me to such a degree that I forgot everything else. I threw myself on my knees beside her, embraced and pressed her firmly to me, called her again and again by name, and implored her with foolish entreaties to stop, not to cry in that way, to take heart and spare herself. Soon my tears fell as freely as hers. Little by little the crisis passed over, she smiled languidly, dried my eyes with the little handkerchief, which was wet with her own tears ; and while she tenderly pressed my hand, she whispered several times—

" My dearest friend."

" That I am, Minna, that I am whatever happens. . . . But you must not take it in this way, do you hear ? You must not feel unhappy, for you are not going to be un-happy. . . . I would rather suffer anything than that, rather lose you, and so would he, I am quite sure of that. . . . We must be wise and you must make yourself strong . . . you must not consider *me* at all . . . only think of yourself, what is best for you, that must also be best for us. Only do what is right and follow what your own nature dictates, that is the main thing. . . . We shall both be satisfied, if only you will be happy."

" I—no, really I am the last one who ought to be con-sidered. . . . Oh, if I could make both of you happy by giving both of you up, I really think—yes, I am sure— I could make that sacrifice, rather than disappoint one of you. . . . And now I cannot give my hand to the one without taking it away from the other ; how then is it possible for me to be happy ? That is out of the question."

" Indeed, my dearest, that alone must be the question. I know that at the beginning you will feel very unhappy because you will be bound to hurt one of us so much, but there is time enough for happiness, as it concerns your whole life. . . . When you choose what is best, you will gradually feel content ; and the one who does not get the right to call you his—he will also in time resign himself to what is inevitable. Only if you choose wrongly, if you mistake your feelings, well, then you will make all three of us unhappy."

"It is dreadful! To be obliged to make such a choice! If only some one could choose for me, if only a duty existed in this case, which said: 'You must do this, otherwise you will be doing wrong!' . . . But I do wrong whichever way I decide, for I have already done wrong, and it will continue."

"No, no! You must not yield to such thoughts! Do not add scruples of this kind to all the rest——"

"Harald!" she exclaimed, getting up and looking steadily into my eyes, " dare you make the choice for me? Have you the courage? Understand me rightly, I mean is your conviction so strong, that you with a clear conscience can say: 'Your duty is to come with me. You have given me your word, and I cannot give it you back because I am convinced that if you act otherwise it will be your ruin'? . . ."

A shiver of joy passed through me, as I suddenly saw our fate placed in my own hands, and the comforting knowledge that I only had to grasp it made me momentarily forget the seriousness of the responsibility. But before I could answer, Minna stretched out her hand, as if she would place it on my lips, and with an anxious pleading look continued—

"But do remember, Harald, that although you get a wife who loves you, and whom you love much more than she deserves,—indeed I know that—she may not ever be able to make you happy, for she has an inner wound which will never quite heal, and which might kill her. I should never be able to forgive myself for being unfaithful to my first love. . . . No domestic happiness would quite be able to drive away the image of him, to whom I owed my first consciousness, my first thoughts, my independence, the awakening of my best and purest feelings —a life and feelings which rightly belonged to him. Oh, how fondly precious has not his image been to me—and now it must come as a ghost accusing me of giving all this to another, while he confidently waited for me, worked for us both, for our future! No, no, never can I be really happy or give you such happiness as you deserve!"

I stood terrified and almost stunned by the despair of this outburst; my eyes turned away from hers while I tried to collect my thoughts, and to unravel the tangle into which my mind had been thrown. It was quite plain to me, that a girl with her pure and faithful nature could not help putting the most flattering interpretation possible upon Stephensen's conduct. Already in consequence of his letter with the Elegy by Heine she had held forth his faithfulness as a supposition, and after my interview with him yesterday I had not doubted that he, making use of his knowledge of her heart, would let this very flattering, almost melodramatic, light fall upon the obscure interval of time which separated them. For my part I looked upon this through such very critical glasses that every bit of romantic glamour was taken away; and it seemed to me that in time its true character was sure to become clear to her also, for which reason the danger of the ghost did not seem to me quite so great as she had imagined. But, unfortunately, even *I* was not quite sure of my case, and I was obliged to admit to myself, that as I was possessed with a very natural antipathy towards Stephensen, it was not impossible that this led me to judge him unfairly. And in that case . . .

I still faltered, and already the favourable minute had slipped by.

"See, you hesitate, you dare not!" she exclaimed. "And still you have only us two to consider. The third, to whom you would do the greatest harm, is to you only a stranger, yes, even a man you hate. . . . Then consider how dreadful this choice must be for me, as I know that to whichever side I turn, I must cause unhappiness to one I love."

"It is just that which makes it so difficult for me to put myself in your place. I do not understand this. . . . You say you love me, I feel it, I will not doubt it, but at the same time you mean that you love Stephensen. It is a problem to me. I do not think that what you feel now for Stephensen is love at all, but only remembrance of past love, and that certainly is too frail ground on which to build a matrimonial life, and especially so, when a new passion has sprung up in opposition to the old one."

Minna shook her head.

"You love, really love, two men? Impossible."

"I do not know what is called possible and impossible, my friend! But consider all that you know yourself and then acknowledge, even if you cannot believe it, that I *must* love him. I have shown you, as well as I could, what he has been to me, you know that my love was constant during the long separation, yes, in spite of my belief that his feelings had changed, you saw—it was indeed the first you saw of me—how even a poor dictionary could give nourishment to my enthusiastic remembrances by teaching me words of his language, and by creating the illusion that I was learning it in order to speak with him. . . . And how could I, only some weeks after this, have grown indifferent to him! If I had heard something disparaging

16

about him, or even, that he loved another—but what have I heard! That he, in the midst of an active and social life, which offered him so many different and stronger induce- ments, has retained his affection more faithfully than I, who had nothing to distract me. Oh, how meanly and miserably have I behaved! If he had held me in contempt! Oh, I have not the heart to wish it, and still perhaps it would have been better for all of us! But instead he comes here, as if his life and happiness depended on my decision—*mine!* Poor me! That so much love should be able to be a curse for one—love which, otherwise, is the greatest blessing."

She turned away, struggling to repress her tears.

"Dearest Minna," I began, laying my hand on her trembling shoulder, "you are right, I could have foreseen all this, and I ought to have. I now think that your feeling towards me is rather an enthusiastic friendship than a real love."

"Why?" she exclaimed, and turned towards me with swimming eyes—"why cannot I love you both? Perhaps I do in a different way, you are not alike and the conditions are also now quite different. Perhaps in reality I love you best——"

"Oh, Minna!"

"And am most in love with him," she added faintly, lowering her eyes.

My outstretched arms fell, and I started as if I had received a blow. Now I felt how that elementary power, which my jealousy had ever secretly feared, was rising against me, scattering my hopes, overthrowing all my nearly victorious efforts, carrying the day with the irre- sistible birthright of love. But in a moment Minna was embracing me with genuine tenderness.

"No, do not take it in that way, Harald. My God, I have hurt you! I did not mean it like that. It just came to me, but all words express so badly what we mean. . . . Perhaps it is not at all like that, I do not know, I understand nothing any longer. I only feel that both of you belong to my life. I am torn in two directions. Oh, my God, what will become of me!"

"You will become a sound and true woman, my own dear girl, by your own strength, when you have overcome these fights and struggles. . . . God knows how willingly I would assist you, but you see I cannot. Nobody can do it, not even Mrs. Hertz, with all her love for you. It is a temptation to me to advise you to confide in her—there is at least a great probability that her counsel would be in my favour, but that does not matter. I do not think that you ought to ask anybody but yourself. Your own nature will perhaps suddenly, instinctively, choose what is best for it. . . . More important than all, neither Stephensen nor I must from now add to your agitation, and especially not, as to-day, by our alternate presence make the task of deciding more difficult for you. You cannot stand that, and very likely it would end by your taking a rash decision, as was the case just a moment ago. Both of us have now seen you alone and have pleaded our cause. From this time . . ."

"Pleaded your cause!" Minna exclaimed, and looked at me with a candid smile; "but, dearest Harald, you have not done that at all."

"Have I not?" I asked timidly. "Do you think I have taken it too calmly?"

"No, no, my dearest, I understand you so well, you are so tender and loving, so careful for me, you want to save me from the reproaches that you might charge me with ; oh, but be sure, so much the more bitterly do I reproach myself ! "

" Not for my sake, Minna ! you have no right to do that. . . . What should I have to reproach you with ? As if I could wish this time had never been, even if it is to bring no future with it ! I am so grateful to you for the love I have felt——"

" No, Harald ! Oh, don't say that——"

" Does it pain you ? Then I will not speak about it any more. Still less ought I to frighten you by picturing the tragic consequences of such a loss to me. . . . What has to be borne must be, and, on the contrary, I promise you that I shall do all in my power to get over it sensibly— and—though I cannot attempt to forget you—nor will——" My lips quivered and my eyes filled with tears. " No, no." I continued, " it was not this I wanted to speak of. Besides, your heart will tell it all to you. . . . I made the suggestion that from now Stephensen and I must agree not to see you again until you have made up your mind. It would be better, if you could leave the town for the present, if you had relations in the country whom you could visit——"

" I have a cousin in the neighbourhood of Meissen, her husband has a farm there. I could easily visit them, they asked me only this summer, and I need not even write beforehand."

" So much the better. Can you leave to-morrow ? "

" To-morrow ? Oh well, I suppose I could."

" Then do it, Minna, It is better not to put it off. And when you have made up your mind, I suppose you will write your decision."

Minna nodded. She had again seated herself on the chair by the window, and was staring at the gardens.

I took my hat, which was lying on the table, and turned it over and over in my hands, waiting for her to look round. At last I approached her and touched her shoulder. She turned her head, and her tearful eyes gazed in astonishment at my outstretched hand, and at the other that nervously fidgeted with my hat.

"What is this? You are not going?"

"Yes, Minna, I must—it is already—I mean, as you leave to-morrow, I suppose you have a good deal to arrange and pack up."

"Well, it is not to Siberia I am going."

"No more it is, but I must go—in order to——"

"It is not true, Harald! But perhaps you are right in going and leaving me to myself, though that is just what I fear, but I must grow accustomed to it. . . . When are you coming again?"

"I am not coming again."

She jumped up.

"Not coming again? What do you mean by that? . . . Will you not spend this evening with me?"

"I do not think it would be right, as we are no longer engaged."

"Not engaged? It seems to me we must be still, as long . . . at any rate nothing has happened so far."

"'Still,' until you perhaps 'break it off with me.' But you must not be obliged to do that, you must never have the feeling that *you* have severed a pledge. Whatever decision you come to, you tie a new bond. It is *I* who have broken our engagement, you must feel yourself free."

"Oh, Harald, how sad and bitter it is! Who would have thought of this yesterday, when we exchanged rings?"

She looked down upon her ring, which glittered while she clenched her hands.

"By the way, the ring," I exclaimed, and with the feeling of an heroic effort I began to wriggle the ring over my knuckle.

"No, not that," she cried, and laid her hand preventingly on mine, "oh do not give me back the ring, do not demand yours!—Why should we be so cruel to one another?"

I sighed, smiling, pressed her hand tenderly and kissed it, grateful that her unerring instinct spared us an unnecessary pain, perhaps the bitterest of all; because by touching the magic symbol the full meaning of the pledge is realised. How many a knight has felt the announcement of the dishonouring doom less terrible than the breaking of his shield by the hands of the executioner.

"Are you not coming, Harald? Engaged or not, we are after all the same."

"Dearest Minna, imagine for yourself how much determination it will take to remain away. I really hardly know how to bear it myself, when I realise that this is perhaps the last evening I can spend with you."

My emotion overwhelmed me; I pressed my lips together, and while I looked away in order to avoid her glance, my eyes fastened on a boot-shaped spot on the homely grey wall-paper. It would be untrue to say that there was anything pretty in it, but all the same there was real dread in the thought: "Perhaps you will never see it again." Minna looked helpless at my grief, and I was conscious of her expression, though I still kept on staring at that spot. A minute or two passed before I could continue.

"But it is after all best like this. . . . Quite true that we are the same, but we shall be different to each other, and that will be painful for us. Besides, it is also

more correct now that we have taken such a decision,—
I mean it looks more fair towards Stephensen."

" But suppose he came this evening ! "

" Has he spoken about it ? "

" No, I only thought that he possibly might do so,
perhaps only to prevent your being alone with me. He
very likely thinks you will come as usual."

" You are right, anyhow I will not leave the field open
for him. If he comes, then send for me ; there is, I suppose,
some one you could send such a short distance. . . . Look,
here is my pocket-book, I will leave it with you. If I
have that sent to me, then I shall know that I am to
come. Just let him know that you are sending it to me,
it is better for him to understand that I am not coming
uninvited. . . . Farewell, my beloved, no one can forbid
me calling you that."

I gave her my hand, which she pressed impetuously,
while she looked penetratingly into my eyes with a
frightened and questioning smile, and her face approached
a very little nearer, perhaps unconsciously to herself. I
then drew her to my breast, and our lips met in a long
kiss, as if each of us would forcibly imbibe the other's
life in order to have it safe and impregnable. At last
I felt that she relaxed from my embrace, and in stepping
back, still with my arm round her waist, I noticed that
she could hardly stand, her head fell on to her shoulder,
she gasped for breath and trembled. I led her carefully
across to the little sofa, on which I allowed her to slip
down, and then I pushed the cushion under her head.

Thereupon I opened the door and called her mother,
who at once appeared out of the obscurity of the kitchen,
and, when I had told her that Minna was unwell, she again
disappeared to fetch some water. Nimble and confused,

always bent like some gnome on the stage, she quickly rushed into the sitting-room ; the alarmed expression simultaneously made her coarse features still more grotesque and gave them a rather spiritual beauty, inasmuch as it made visible her great tenderness for Minna. When I saw her tending the half-conscious girl I hastened away, for I felt certain that Minna would have no peace of mind while I was present.

CHAPTER VI

ON the table in my little room were two letters, the one with an English the other with a German stamp. I knew both handwritings, and quickly opened the letter from my uncle.

He wrote, in his usual short and business-like manner, that on account of a change in the staff at the factory it would be better if I came to London within four weeks. I should thus be obliged to give up my studies at the Polytechnic, and forego the chance of passing my examination, but it would not harm my career, and it was very necessary not to lose this favourable opportunity of beginning practical work. In a few days he would send me sufficient money for my outfit and travelling expenses. He asked for an answer by return of post in order that he might know that his letter had been promptly delivered. This communication, or rather order, put me into a state of great excitement.

It was evident that if the worst happened, if the bond between Minna and me should be broken, then nothing could be more desirable—if wishes and hopes could then any longer be spoken of—than this arrangement. I should at once be removed from these surroundings that would be so full of heart-rending associations, and where, perhaps, for some time I should be likely to meet her, in order to be thrown into work under new conditions which would require me to strain my energies to the utmost. But naturally my thoughts did not willingly linger over a desire, that was founded upon so painful a supposition. On the other hand if I was chosen, it would be as inconvenient as possible to leave her while she was still shaken by the emotional crisis through which she had passed, and would, more than ever, be needing a faithful support—to leave her just at the instant when a constantly renewed and strengthened feeling that the love, to which she had given herself up, neither could nor would forsake her was of the greatest consequence to her welfare. To leave her alone, perhaps for years, with nothing left to her but correspondence and—the Danish Dictionary ! The possibility that quicker than I expected I might gain a position to justify my marriage seemed not to make up for the misery of a separation at this moment.

But the terms I was on with my uncle, whom I only knew, or did not know, through letters, were not of such a nature that I dared to think of trying to alter his decision ; and besides, just at this moment when I was to give an answer, I was prevented from confiding in him.

A bit of English sticking-plaster, in case I got a deadly wound, and if I conquered, a peremptory command, which would draw me away from the happiness I had won, this was the not exactly brilliant promise that the letter held out. I felt even more miserable than when I had entered the room.

Outside it rained heavily, and the narrow street darkened the room so much that I was obliged to go to the window so that I might read the other letter. It was from my friend Immanuel Hertz (he was named after Kant) in Leipzig.

After having congratulated me on my engagement (he begged to be excused for his congratulations being a little late—" much business "), he added that he had been very upset to hear through his mother that his dear old father had not yet got rid of the cold which he had caught in Prague; he feared that his mother might be keeping something back in order not to alarm him, and asked me to say openly what I thought of his father's illness.

I was, of course, too selfishly absorbed in my own grief to let old Hertz's cough appear fatal to me. Therefore this inquiry did not give me much thought, whereas I pondered, with an interpreter's profundity, over his congratulatory remarks, and tried to imagine that they were rather forced. The honest Immanuel Hertz began to have an especial interest for me. I remembered how Minna had always avoided speaking of him; and Stephensen's remark of last evening regarding Minna and him, seemed, though quoted as an example, to have something behind it. All this pointed in the same direction; and, besides, to know Minna and to love her were in my eyes two things so indissolubly united, that my supposition very soon grew into a certainty.

So he had burnt also himself!—How had he got over it? He was surely no easy-going character, but perhaps he had a more self-controlled than passionate disposition, and therefore the wound would hardly have been incurable. New surroundings and hard work had, anyhow, surely been the remedy for him also.

However detestable the thought was that for me also this panacea might be necessary, I, nevertheless, gradually lost myself in fantastic English dreams of the future, which, by the way, left out the most important item—the work— as something taken for granted; but as a reward I imagined my own dear self, two or three years older, galloping in a grand cavalcade through Hyde Park (which I supposed to be like "Grosser Garten"), dancing at balls, which were sparkling with all the diamonds and stars of "High life," or moving as guest in an old country-seat hidden in tremendous woods and deer parks; an honoured guest, the champion at tennis, riding to hounds, and presenting myself in evening dress on the signal of the dinner bell, "the tocsin of the soul," as Byron has it. Of course, in Hyde Park, in the ball-room, and at the country-seat I was surrounded by those young ladies, who have the name of being the most beautiful women of the world, all of whom were heiresses to millions of pounds, though not by any means scornful of the homage that a broken heart still owes to beauty and attractiveness. . . . But then, as the image of Minna appeared very vividly before my mind's eye on this background, which brought out its unpretentious and simple grace, as a dimly seen tapestry of fantastic, luxurious Gobelin that the effect-seeking hand of an artist has painted behind the portrait study of a dark and calm woman's form—these dreams at once dissolved into nothingness. Not because I looked upon them as impossibilities; but because even the realisation was bound to be empty and without value in comparison with the pure and gentle ideal before which all that was noble in me seemed to rise to the surface, and all the baser and lower elements of my nature to sink into the soul's unconscious depths.

Ashamed at having at this moment unfaithfully allowed myself to be led astray by such digressing fancies, I offered them as a sacrifice on her altar, and I hastened to resign all these glories (which naturally would come to a youngster in a subordinate position at a china factory), and to give myself up to the bliss of possessing her or to the grief of losing her.

I was overwhelmed by a feverish longing to see her, and

could not imagine how I should bear to remain the whole evening in solitude, knowing that she was also alone and within a few minutes' walk. Dusk had already fallen, and it did not seem as if I was going to be sent for. Now I realised quite clearly that I had all the time supported myself by the hope that *his* presence at the Jagemanns' would also make mine necessary.

At last I began to light the lamp, in order to write to my uncle. At the same moment the bell rang.

I placed the globe of the lamp on the table—or rather on the edge of the table, and heard it crash on the floor before I reached the door, which I only just opened. As far as I could make out, I had been interrupted by a coal-heaver. Furious and desperate, I was going to bang my door, when I heard a weak childish voice exchanging some words with the servant, of which one word had a faint resemblance to my name.

I listened breathlessly. Tiny pattering steps approached, and I heard a gentle tap at the door.

Again I opened it; in front of me stood a tiny girl about seven years of age, with a tear-stained face, which I recognised; the child lived in the same house as the Jagemanns, and old Mrs. Jagemann was very interested in her and her little sisters.

" Do you want me, my little friend ? "

The child looked down and snuffled.

" Have you any message, or have you brought me something ? "

She now howled and rubbed her eyes with the one hand ; the other she kept wrapped up in a handkerchief. I dragged her inside.

" But what is it, then ? Perhaps you were to bring me a little book ? "

But now she absolutely yelled.

"Good gracious, what does it all mean?" I thought, and fidgeted about in impatient despair.

"It's not my fault," she started at last. "I had—I was to—it was the little Jagemann—she gave me the little book, and the big Jagemann gave me a cake—to eat on my way, and then it happened——"

I rushed forward and seized my hat. The child took her left hand out of the handkerchief, and stretched out the soiled pocket-book to me.

"Couldn't help it, it was a nasty boy—he pushed me, and then the little book fell—into a pool—ugh! in Dibbels-walder Square—ugh!"

I hastened to find a silver coin, which I pushed into her small wet hand, and flew out at the door past the servant and the coal-heaver, whose laughter followed me down the stairs.

In a few minutes—how precious they all were now!—I reached Seilergasse.

CHAPTER VII

MINNA opened the door for me. She gave me a firm shake of the hand and whispered, " Thank you for coming."

I stepped at once into the sitting-room, hat in hand. The lamp was lit. Stephensen sat talking to Mrs. Jagemann, who was wearing her linsey dress and best cap. It was evident that the piratical suitor sailed under the neutral flag of a visit to the family. She entertained him about the lodgers: " Bad people, Mr. Stephensen! Indeed, we have often wished you back. But, oh my, there is nothing to say against the present one; he is also a painter, that is to say in another way, . . . he is in the decorative line, you know."

Stephensen had risen. We greeted one another very politely, and I even compelled myself to give him my hand; for, after all, Minna was fond of him, and her feelings should protect him against my dislike. His thin and delicate hand was very cold—the heart perhaps, according to the old saying, was in consequence so much the warmer.

I pressed Mrs. Jagemann's soft and flabby hand, and after a wandering glance round the room I spoke to Minna—

" I thought I had forgotten my pocket-book; it was for that reason——"

" But we have just sent it," the mother shouted. " We thought you were sure to miss it."

" Indeed! Then my landlady will keep it for me."

Stephensen smiled a little ironically, as much as to say :
" Is it for my sake you take all this trouble ? "

" But you will now remain here for the evening ? "
Minna said, and bent her head over some music through
which she was looking.

" Yes, of course Mr. Fenger will stay. We shall have
a jolly time," the mother said.

I expressed my thanks, and sat down near the window.

The long box with the ferns had been put out on the
window-sill. In the midst of all her troubles Minna had
still been tenderly careful that they should have the
benefit of the rain. The single-leaved ferns, which we
had found together, stood in the middle and noddingly
moved their slim stalks. Some acacia leaves and a bit
of bent cherry branch glittered in the light from within.
The thick, fine rain sounded like a low whispering, and with
it a water-pipe mingled its babble. From the sombre background irregular dotted panes stood out, between which a
few staircases mounted up like interrupted columns of
light. I stared out, and was suddenly overcome by the
strange depressing feeling of the sadness and monotony
of human life. It was to me a very extraordinary idea
that all these lights were signs of just as many existences,
in which possibly there was not to be found any similarity
except modest conditions, disappointments, and emptiness,
a miserable and joyless fate, like the monotonous darkness,
which at the same time isolated and collected the lights.
" But," thought I, " could there in any of those rooms be
so queer a party as was collected in this ? "

" Jolly " was not exactly the correct expression for
our mood. Minna, absent-mindedly, struck some chords,
as if she had not much wish to play, but still would do
her best to break the silence. The mother, who had

nothing more to say, gave a deep sigh—that was *her* contribution. I felt the pressing necessity of making some remark, but Stephensen anticipated me.

"Is it pretty in the neighbourhood of Meissen?" he asked, evidently to let me know that he was aware of the plan.

"Oh no, I cannot say that it is. It is the contrary to that of the south, where Saxonia increases in beauty the farther one descends. Don't you know our beautiful rhyme—

> "'Denn gleich hinter Meissen—
> Pfui Spinne!—kommt Breissen.'"[1]

She said this, in spite of a certain nervousness, so funnily, that we all burst out laughing, her mother as heartily as any of us.

"Oh yes," she whimpered, while she dried the tears from her large cheek, "Why should you now get this sudden idea to visit Wilhelmina . . . when you have been away all the summer? Surely you must have had enough country air! Honestly I believe there is too much fuss made about this fresh air."

The naïve explanation of Minna's trip came as a relief, though I had an idea that it was not quite genuine. If all of us had understood the situation, it would have been too trying, and we should have felt that we might as well speak openly of what we all knew. The good woman's presence placed us on those more conventional terms which are so well fitted to hide the real emotions.

"And such cosy evenings we might have had," Mrs. Jagemann continued. . . . "We might, for instance, have

---

[1] "Then just after Meissen—
Damn it—lies Breissen" (Saxonian for Prussia).

arranged for whist. Can you remember, Mr. Stephensen, how often we amused ourselves in that way when you lodged here, and my good husband still lived ? . . . Oh dear me, yes, those were happy times, such a family party, h'm, so to speak, . . . true, I was always being sat upon by my partner."

"Not by me, I hope," Stephensen said with his most amiable smile.

"Oh dear no, Mr. Stephensen ! You, who always are so considerate and tactful ! But my good husband was often nasty; he also got angry when he had no luck. Indeed, upon my word, he did . . . oh dear ! Poor Jagemann could not endure misfortune."

" He was a good player, I remember."

"Good indeed, I should think so; he really was good at everything he undertook, was poor Jagemann. . . . But it's just the same in cards as in other things, what can one do with bad cards ? "

Or with a bad partner, I thought.

"Oh dear me, yes, my good husband surely might have been something more than a poor teacher in a public school, but what are we to do? Bad people, Mr. Stephensen ! Oh yes, and then fate, as you know—misfortune."

Stephensen tried to look sympathetic. I had not taken my eyes away from Minna. She still sat at the piano, but was half-turned towards us. It was evident that this talk irritated her; the smile round her lips grew more and more mocking, and every now and then she shrugged her shoulders.

" I think it is a good likeness you have caught in your picture there of Jagemann," I remarked to Stephensen.

" Oh yes, something of the old ' Tartar ' has got into it, though he could look more amiable."

" It reminds me very speakingly of father," Minna said.

" Oh dear me, yes, indeed ! "

" At times I have good luck with such light pencil drawings, but the pastel of Minna, which cost me so much trouble, is really a smudge. I ought not to allow it to hang on the wall."

" Please don't, Mr. Stephensen. How can you say so ? That beautiful painting ! At that time we had not one other one in colours ; at least there was another one with children in a boat, and I honestly thought it was very pretty, but Minna wouldn't allow it to be here, so I had to put it into the bedroom. . . . Well, later on you were so kind as to send that lovely picture over the sofa. . . · But Minna's picture, no, you mustn't say that, one can clearly see who it is meant for——"

" But only very dimly who it is," Minna said.

" Oh, you really are a naughty child ! "

Stephensen laughed.

" There you are, Madam ! It's no use for you to be so kind, the picture can't be saved. But one might make a new one, and, for instance, just such a pencil sketch."

" Have you painted at all to-day, Mr. Stephensen ? " I asked.

" No, the light was too bad. . . . I could only soil the canvas over, so that to-morrow, anyhow, I may not look at the white stuff."

" Do all painters use such disparaging expressions about their art ? " Minna asked. " It seems that one never hears anything from you all but ' soiling,' ' daubing,' or, at most, ' smearing.' "

" Quite right," Stephensen answered, smiling ; " it is a rather ordinary artistic *façon de parler* ; there is a bit of self-criticism in it, and still more affectation and perhaps perverted vanity. I will try to get rid of that habit. By the way, you ladies have a similar habit when speaking of your 'strumming,' what you were doing a minute ago."

"Oh, really you can't compare that!" Minna exclaimed, insulted on behalf of his art. "You are trying to make me appear foolish."

We now both asked her to play seriously. She at once turned towards the piano, opened some music, and started a Prelude by Chopin. Stephensen went into the hall and came back with a sketch-book in his hand. I thought he was going to draw Minna at the piano, though in reality his position was not suitable, but I soon felt that his attention was fixed upon me. I was annoyed that he should sketch me without my permission, but he smiled—one could not deny there was something attractive in his smile—and pointed with the pencil to Minna. "Is it really for her he is going to draw me?" I thought. "It is a queer idea, but in a way rather a nice one." And I sat as still as a mouse, listening to the music.

One Prelude followed the other. She played absent-mindedly and with not nearly her usual amount of expression. One could hardly expect anything else, but I regretted it; I was very proud on her behalf, and should have liked to see her showing off—even to Stephensen. He, for his part, was hardly a very attentive listener, as he was busy drawing, sometimes bending forward in order to see better, or measuring with the pencil in the air.

When Minna had played about half an hour, she turned towards us: "Have you had enough now?" Without waiting for an answer she jumped up and exclaimed, "What is it you are doing there?"

"Oh, it's not bad at all," she said, looking over Stephensen's shoulder. "It's a good likeness."

" Well, it might be worse."

" Oh, I say! Sweetly pretty!" the mother exclaimed.

" If only, I think——"

" What ? " Stephensen asked and looked up.

" No, perhaps I'm wrong, and it is impertinent of me to make suggestions."

" Not at all! A fresh eye easily discovers something, and you know the face better than I do."

" I think the chin ought to be larger."

" Really ? " Stephensen measured, rubbed out and corrected, bent forward in order to see, and altered again. " Yes, indeed, it improves it; I even think it might stand a little more. You have a good eye, Minna ! "

" Perhaps you ought also to let the Adam's apple be a little more prominent, it is so characteristic in him. Just see how it has helped ! "

I got up, curious to see my own likeness. The drawing was only lightly sketched, but firm and true in the lines. As one does not know oneself in profile, I could not have much opinion as to the likeness. But Minna was satisfied, and it secretly pleased me that she had taken a small part in the finishing touches. Stephensen's smile betrayed the childish pleasure that an artist always feels when he has succeeded in something. He signed and dated it, loosened the leaf with his penknife and gave it to Minna.

" Thanks ! " she said heartily, but without showing any surprise. " It pleases me immensely ! There is something much more satisfactory in such a drawing than in a photograph—more charm. I don't know quite how it is, but I believe it makes me think of olden days, when everybody did not have dozens of photographs of themselves to distribute among their friends and acquaintances, and when people must have been so happy to get such a portrait of a person dear to them."

"That hasn't occurred to me before," Stephensen said. "It's more natural to me to think of the art value, but there is much in what you have just said."

"Quite true," I remarked. "It is the way of getting a likeness which always has existed, and it has not only the aristocracy of many ancestors, but is also free from the tiresome democratic point, that Jack and Tom have the same picture which is precious to us."

"Oh dear me, yes!" Mrs. Jagemann exclaimed. "The world has been progressing since I was young! Photography is indeed a wonderful invention, and it produces better likenesses than anything else."

Minna smiled at her mother, who had no notion that her remark was so little in harmony with the reflection to which it was supposed to give support.

"Yes, you are quite right in that," Stephensen admitted with his flexible readiness to smooth over a difficulty, "only there is something in the art of photography which is called re-touching and which indeed can produce strange results."

"Have you never tried to draw yourself?" Minna asked him.

"Not yet. Strangely enough I have not so far received any summons from the Uffizi Gallery in Florence to contribute to its unique collection of self-portraits."

"Suppose I ask you to do so now?"

"Then I will try during these lonely evenings, if the hotel mirror does not make me too crooked. . . . But I must now make use of the time and draw you."

"Am I really to pose? I don't know anything worse."

"At all events it's a long time since I troubled you,"

Stephensen answered gently, and with a strange sorrowful tone in his voice that was quite new to me, and that clearly enough said : " And who knows whether I shall ever do it again ! "

Minna sat down without any further objection, and altered her position once or twice according to his directions. He began eagerly to sketch. But soon he stopped, discontented with the light ; I placed the lamp in a better position for him. In so doing I noticed that the old globe with the break had been changed for a new one, in honour of Stephensen, as it seemed ; but whether Minna or her mother had been so tender over his artistic susceptibilities I did not know. Most probably Minna would have had more important things to think of than the broken globe, and Mrs. Jagemann had evidently not only a deep reverence for " Mr. Stephensen, artist," but also a certain motherly feeling from the time he had been there as a lodger. She gave him now and then an affectionate side-glance, while she rocked her big head over her knitting, as if she said to herself : " Oh dear me, yes, there he sits again ! Yes, my word ! Why didn't you come before ? "

I did not doubt that, if the choice had been left to her, I might as well have retired at once. And though I was quite sure that Minna was far from wanting to take her advice, and that on the morrow she would be quite free from her influence, I had all the time a painful sensation that I was out of favour.

Minna, on the contrary, shared her kindness equally between us both in a natural and unhesitating manner, which astonished me, as if it did not give her the least difficulty to steer between her two suitors, each of whom seemed to have the same claim to her future. As she had hardly expressed her pleasure over possessing the drawing

of me, before she asked Stephensen to draw one of himself
for her, so she did not once allow either one of us to get
anything at the cost of the other ; even if she employed
a little art and calculation in this impartiality, she used
still more natural feeling and instinctive tact. She talked
to both of us—the subject of conversation was the German
Theatre and Dramatic Art—but as she was being drawn
half-profile, she could seldom look towards Stephensen,
and even when she answered him her eyes and attention
seemed to be fixed upon me. He was very much occupied
by his work, but liked her to talk so that her face might
retain its liveliness.

Only when he drew the important part round the mouth
she was to sit silent, and she then made her mother praise
the old days at the theatre. Truly enough it did not
appear that Mrs. Jagemann had often visited the theatre,
but she had been captivated by Devrient, whom she had,
however, seen more in her father's restaurant than on the
stage; and what she had heard from others, who had more
idea of art, was so mingled in her rather muddled brain
with the little she remembered herself that she grew just
as sentimental as if she had lived and breathed in the
temple of Thalia and Melpomene.

" Oh dear me, yes, in those days we had artists ! You
ought to have seen our theatres then, Mr. Stephensen !
Davison ! surely you have heard of him ? You know the
beautiful villa which he built, just opposite the Bohemian
railway station ; in those days it was something new, we
have so many others now. Yes, he made a lot out of it,
but it was also worth the money to see him. As Mephi-
stopheles, terrifying ! Now I would not dare to see it for
anything. But at last he also went off his head, you know.
And Emil Devrient, that was in quite a different way,

elevated, ideal, Max in Wallenstein, one was transported ; the present generation cannot realise this at all. Poor Jagemann said the same—he would not go to the theatre any more. Surely you remember, when you praised anything which you had seen here, he always said : ' No, you ought to have seen so-and-so.' *His* favourite, however, was Madame Schröder-Devrient; indeed, I myself remember her too, grandly tragic, plastic, ' classic plastic,' poor Jagemann said; he never missed an evening when she played. It was before we were married, she left the theatre before she was fifty. Oh dear me, yes, . . . such artists . . . indeed it was a glorious period."

" But it is everywhere the same, Mrs. Jagemann ; also in Denmark the old generation say they can't stand the theatre any longer, and that we poor things never have seen proper comedy.",

" Well, there you are, bad times, Mr. Stephensen ! . . . No, it was different in those days, it was nice to be in Dresden then. One did not see all that stiff Prussian Military, and we were not burdened with all these taxes. Oh, what couldn't one get for one's money ! Meat has now gone up one-third in price . . . oh dear, oh dear ! "

And, shaking her head, she got up and went towards the door.

Minna laughed and recited—

> " How love and truth and religion
>   From out of the world had fled,
> How very dear was the coffee,
>   How scarce was the gold, we said."

" Well, you have not forgotten your Heine," Stephensen remarked.

" Oh no," she exclaimed eagerly.

I thought of the way in which Stephensen had shown his

knowledge of Heine, and I suppose that I did not look very cheerful. Minna, who seemed to read my thoughts, sighed deeply. Stephensen placed the sketch-book on the table, and leaned back with his hands behind his back.

I think we were all surprised by being so suddenly brought back to ourselves and our conditions, and that we felt how impossible it was to get away from them.

Mrs. Jagemann came in with the table-cloth, and Minna got up and offered to help her to lay the table. But at supper our silence was much greater than our appetites.

Still the picture was unfinished, and Stephensen started again directly after we had risen from the table.

" Well, now it will have to be finished, it is also getting late, and I suppose Minna will have to rise early on account of the journey," he said, after having worked for about a quarter of an hour.

I went up to him and could not restrain an outburst of admiration. The drawing was not so firm and boldly worked as the one of me, but even this apparent anxiety gave it a certain pleasing grace, and the expression was none the less successful from being given very sketchily; one anticipated something more than was seen.

" It might be better, but even if I had the time I should be afraid to try and improve it."

He also loosened this leaf with his penknife.

" And who is to have that one ? " Minna asked.

Stephensen handed it to her : " You, Minna, in order to give it to the one of us whom you think will need it most."

There was a deep and sad earnestness in his voice, which trembled just a little with an exceedingly sympathetic sound. It was the only hint that had been given in the course of the evening of the decision on hand, and nobody had so far been more considerate in keeping the conversation in safe channels than Stephensen. The unexpected plainness almost frightened us — perhaps not the least himself, but I, for one, was pleased that we had not during the whole evening deceived ourselves as to the solemnity of the situation, but for a single moment had looked it straight in the face. It was like a solace for the conscience. I even felt a certain gratitude to Stephensen for the moral courage that he had shown. But, to tell the truth, a bitter feeling soon mingled with it : the recognition of his superiority. I was certain, that had I tried to say something like this I should have failed—it would have come out in a clumsy, upsetting manner, and would only have left a painful discord, instead of being followed by a sigh of relief. Just in the same way as on the previous day upon the terrace, and also during this evening, he had succeeded in keeping everything on neutral ground, so was he followed by the same success, when now, stepping outside this ground, with bold hand he touched what we had considered "tabooed." This success only depends upon assertiveness, and it was this very assertiveness that extorted the silent confession from me, the most painful of all towards a rival suitor—that he was more of a man than I. I tried, to be sure, to console myself with the reflection that this " manliness " was but the outward appearance of manliness, which, after all, only proves greater experience in social life ; but all the same it was both mortifying and alarming.

Minna accepted the leaf without a word and with downcast eyes. She placed it in her blotter next to my portrait, and this proximity I considered to be of good omen.

I also remember looking for that boot-shaped spot on

the wall-paper, which was not so easily found in the lamp-light, so that I might prevent the bad omen which might have been in that fancy, when I took leave of Minna : " Perhaps you never will see this spot again." If I had neglected to look at it, that omen might still be in power ! I was in these days as superstitious as an old witch, because only my sphere existed, and everything was bound to have a meaning for it.

Mrs. Jagemann sat in her chair, dozing with open eyes ; she understood nothing of the feelings which stirred us, but murmured mechanically—

" Sweetly pretty—oh dear me, yes, that's talent and no mistake."

We still kept on talking for a quarter of an hour about indifferent things—in order to postpone the moment of parting. At last we tore ourselves away.

Minna lighted us out to the stairs. The front door was still open.

I let him step out first. He turned, and lifting his hat, held his right hand towards me.

" You said yesterday evening, Mr. Fenger, that we parted as enemies. Just look, now we have spent quite a friendly evening together. In reality, we cannot hate one another ; for whichever of us is going to be the favoured one the other is bound to wish him happiness—for her sake."

" You are right, Mr. Stephensen. But our paths lie in different directions. Farewell ! "

We parted.

It had stopped raining. Between the ragged clouds a star sparkled here and there over the shiny roofs. The wet stones and the pavements shone for a long distance with a deserted and sad light.

CHAPTER VIII

THE following day I went, as usual, to the Polytechnic.
But before going I wrote to my uncle.

I visited the Hertzes after dinner, in order to be able
to give my friend some information about his father's
condition. The old man was in bed; he coughed and had
a little fever.

Hertz inquired at once for Minna, and asked why she
had not come.

"We thought you were inseparable," Mrs. Hertz
added.

It was a good thing that the yellow venetian blinds were
down; otherwise the distress caused by her words would
have been evident. I felt that I changed colour, and that
a sudden spasm of pain had taken away my breath. In
as indifferent a manner as I could assume I said where she
had gone, and gave them her love.

The old people seemed very astonished that she had
gone away so suddenly without saying good-bye. "And
the day before yesterday she had known nothing about
it!"

"She only had the letter yesterday," I said. "Her
cousin wished so much that she should come at once,
she was not well—depression, I think."

"Yes, then I can imagine she had to go," Mrs. Hertz
said; "Minna is always so kind when any one is ill."

"What a pity it should be just now," Hertz complained. "I had looked forward to her coming in these days, she might have played to me. The drawing-room door could have been left ajar, she plays so beautifully."

I hurried to get away from this dangerous subject, and told them about my uncle's letter, which called me to England much earlier than I had expected.

"Already, in the course of the month!" Hertz exclaimed. "Yes, Dresden is just like an hotel, where one comes in and the other goes out. Only such old folks as we are stick, till one fine day we are buried here. Last year the painter Hoym moved to Berlin, and Professor Grimm, who was a very learned Kantian, went to Hamburg a couple of years ago. . . . Well, you are young and had to start work one time or another."

"But there is one for whom that time in Dresden means a lot," Mrs. Hertz remarked.

"Yes, poor Minna——" Hertz was seized by a fit of that dry cough which every now and then interrupted the conversation.

"I have not yet said anything to her, the thought of having to leave her has already made me quite desperate. I have been very doubtful whether I ought not to try to make my uncle give up this plan."

"No, no, dear Fenger," the old man said eagerly, stretching out his hand—"don't do that. Work cannot be controlled, controlled by our inclinations. . . . First duty, work the sooner the better. Man's love works—woman's abides."

"You must not talk so much, it strains you," Mrs. Hertz told her husband. "But it is like that, we two old ones have known it too, once upon a time. . . . Don't worry too much over it. Minna is a sensible girl and a faithful soul, she will also have confidence in you. . . . Be sure she will get through the waiting time more easily than you now imagine."

" I hope so, dear Mrs. Hertz. At the same time I believe that you always had a calmer mind and more balanced temperament than Minna, and therefore in your youth suffered less from such a separation."

" Yes, that's true," said Hertz,—" for Minna, it will be more difficult. . . . But we must all struggle, each one with his burden, and it is well for everybody that it should be so."

" Anyhow it is not in those kind of struggles that one succumbs," said Mrs. Hertz cheerfully. " I do not think one need even fear a wound, and the hardships one is sure to get over. And of one thing you may be certain, we shall be all we can to the dear girl, and as far as an old couple like ourselves can help her she won't be in need of friends."

" I could never wish better friends for her, and it is the greatest consolation to me that she has here a second home, where she will always be understood, and where the dear remembrances we have together will be treasured."

I got up and gave Hertz my hand.

" Now you must rest and not be tempted to speak. I wish I could play to you. When I get home I shall write to your son, and then I can give him fresh news."

" Yes, give him my love, and tell him not to worry. I mean that he is such a loving son, but you see for yourself it is nothing serious."

Mrs. Hertz nodded, with her calm, habitual smile.

" It is good of you to think at once of writing to Immanuel. Now, you will not see each other for a long time, and he is so fond of you. You must look him up on your way."

" I had already decided to do so. . . . Good-bye ! "

During this conversation, I had momentarily forgotten the dreadful uncertainty in which my love was involved. But though this consciousness now returned with full force, the danger seemed less, and I was more inclined to take a brighter view of the future than I had been since my interview with Minna. This kind Philemon and Baucis couple were so intimately interwoven in the peaceful idyll of our love, that it needed only this meeting to refresh its colours and infuse them with a life-like light that drove away all fear of an impending tragic shadow. I had found them true friends, still possessed with the same confidence in our mutual happiness as before, and at a moment when this happiness was, I knew, in peril ; and I considered this confidence to be still more valuable, because it rested upon ignorance, a circumstance that would, surely enough, have diminished its value in other people's eyes. But I just needed a support that had not even felt the shock. " Their confidence is not destined to meet with disappointment," I said to myself, " all will turn out for the best,—old Hertz shall not die, and I shall not lose Minna."

This conclusion was not exactly logical. But even had it been so, at this visit to the sick-bed I might, had I been less occupied by my own fate, have remarked many signs to fill me with fear that a stronger Disputant— the strongest of all—would say, " *Nego majorem.*"

CHAPTER IX

WHEN I had finished the letter to Immanuel Hertz, I went out for a walk. With yesterday's rain a change in the weather had set in. Clouds drifted over the sky and a piercingly cold wind blew, as if it were November. I strolled about in the Villa-quarter, sauntering through the park—where the ridiculously dressed-up gigantic nurses promenaded with the perambulators—and roamed over the Grosser Garten, constantly looking up the roads and paths where we had walked together. At last I sat for a long time on the little hill at the Hercules Avenue. It was the hour of sunset, just like that evening a fortnight before; but all the fascination of the light was missing, and one saw nothing of the distant mountains of Saxon Switzerland. My head was heavy and incapable of thought; the sanguine feelings that had cheered me after the visit to the Hertzes had disappeared, without, however, allowing the previous melancholy tendencies, which considered everything as lost, to take their place. I was filled with a strange and dull restlessness.

When I went home I lay down on the uncomfortable sofa; so short was it that I had to place my legs over the one arm on to a dirty antimacassar. I did not light the lamp; a street-lamp threw enough light into the room to enable me to distinguish the objects, and to prevent me from being troubled by the darkness; I was neither tempted to sleep, nor in fact to do anything. As I lay in this con-

18

dition for hours, I mentally reviewed all that I had experienced in these last days, beginning with the previous evening at the Jagemanns', and proceeding backwards from my discussion with Minna, to the one with Stephensen; farther back I did not get. There was sufficient material; I recalled every word that had been exchanged, the tone of voice, the expression of face, gestures and movements, as precisely and carefully as if I had a special purpose in doing so, or as if, somewhere behind me, a secretary had been sitting to whom I was dictating. When, at last, I went to bed, this train of thought, having once been put in motion, could not be checked. But instead of appearing in order, as before, in its proper place and turn for a perspicuous inspection, the whole mass now thrust its way rebelliously forward, while each separate item wanted to assert itself, and the last would be the first. Had all the soldiers in King Mithridates' army appealed at the same time to his famous memory, and rushed forward pell-mell in order to catch hold of him and shout, " Do you remember *me* also ? What's my name ? What country-man am I ? Where have I distinguished myself ? Where did I get this scar ? "—then that royal master of mnemonics would have found himself in an overwhelmed condition, similar to the one which kept me awake until daylight began to steal into the room.

Late in the forenoon I woke up with a painful heaviness in the back of my head. I did not want to go to the Polytechnic ; these last weeks' study would not be of much importance, and, besides, I could hardly remember a single word of the previous day's lecture. I went out in the hope of curing my headache, and strolled about near the Zwinger and in the Theatre Square. But I was not accustomed to see the town by mid-day light with Minna, and it therefore appeared to me without charm and painfully strange ; all that I saw displeased me, just in the same way as it would have done to walk about in Berlin or Copenhagen in this state of mind.

On a theatre placard stood " Kätchen vom Heilbronn." We were to have seen it together this evening !

I soon went back to my house, the lodging-like discomfort of which abolished the idea of " surroundings," and isolated me, as it were, in an empty room. There I lay on my bed—the sofa was too much of a wreck—and kept reviewing these numerous, closely united remembrances, like a dying Alexander who is bidding good-bye to his soldiers ; they haunted me on my afternoon walk like a hearse, new crowds joining on at each new street, road, and pathway, and when I at last went to sleep, it was in the shadow of the banners borne by the death-watch.

While I was dressing on the following morning, I felt slack and disheartened at the prospect of the amount of worries that I had conjured up and could not drive away.

I now only wished to get free of the spell.

" Could one but kill time during these dreadful days of waiting," I thought, " or escape from oneself and all one's thoughts."

I recalled the one day of waiting in Rathen, and how then a fat novel had kept me company. At once I hurried to a library and asked for *The Three Musketeers*, which I thought would be suitable. While the librarian was looking for it, I opened a thick book lying on the desk. I got a sort of stab when my eye fell on the name " Minna." " Minna's matchless beauty and elevated mind conquered all his hesitations "—I still remember every word of the sentence. I turned the pages over, opening here and there—almost everywhere, " Minna " ! She was sailing on the mountain lake in moonlight—was dressing for the ball—was casting herself crying, and sweetly blushing, into her mother's arms.

" Is this book disengaged ? " I asked the librarian, who had brought *The Three Musketeers*. He said that it was, and I took both books home with me. I had not even looked for the author's name—both this and the title I have now forgotten. With regard to its contents and style, the Rathen novel was in comparison a true masterpiece, and I should surely have thrown it aside after reading the first twenty pages, if the heroine had been named Adelheid or Mathilde ; but I now read it faithfully through line by line, and the constantly recurring name put me into a rather excited, but still benevolent mood, while the sometimes trivial, sometimes fabulous, incidents that befell only most uninteresting people, just sufficiently occupied my mind to keep me from thinking.

During the afternoon I interrupted the influence of this narcotic in order to call on the Hertzes.

" Is Mr. Hertz still in bed ? " I asked the old servant who opened the door.

" Indeed the master is in bed, indeed he is," the old woman answered, and shook her head. " Please step into the drawing-room, Mr. Fenger. I will tell the missis ; she will be pleased to hear you are here, sir."

The drawing-room gave the double impression of too great order, and yet a certain disorder, which a room gets when it has not been used for some days. The chairs stood exactly in their places, but on one of them a forgotten duster was lying. On the corner of the table nearest the hall door several newspapers were heaped up, one on the top of the other, as smooth as when they had been delivered. The draught of air from the unclosed window had blown an open letter to the floor. However natural all of this was, it added to the uncomfortable feeling that had been aroused by the old servant's troubled manner; and a deafening noise from the street corner, where all the different kinds of vehicles passed, quite confused me.

I was still standing with my hat in my hand when, after a few minutes, Mrs. Hertz entered. She had weary, perhaps tear-stained, eyes, and the smile on her lips only seemed to linger there from habit.

"My husband is sleeping, dear friend," she said, giving me her hand. "He is not getting on at all well."

"Is he worse?"

"Yes, the fever has increased; he also has pain in his side when coughing; the one lung is attacked."

"My God! You don't anticipate danger?"

I turned quite cold with fear, not so much because of the dear old man's life being in peril, but because of the fixed idea which had constructed a connection between his health and my love.

"Good gracious," I thought, "supposing he dies after all, and I lose Minna!"

Mrs. Hertz, who could not, of course, have any idea of such a thought, regarded my evident emotion as a pure sign of sympathy and friendship for her husband; she thanked me with a grateful look, as she answered—

"Danger there might well be in such an illness for an old and feeble man. I must be prepared for the worst."

She sat down on the sofa, and asked me to sit beside her.

"I can see you wonder that I speak so calmly and openly about it. . . . Perhaps my nature has something to do with it, but I also think that the parting by death looks much more terrifying to a young person than to one who anyhow can only have a short time to survive and to miss. You are now thinking to yourself, 'If I had the danger of losing Minna, how different and heart-broken should I be—after all she must have a cold heart.'"

I looked down, and the whole room seemed to swim. How did she get this idea? Why did just these words come to her lips, that in quite a different way than she could suspect were exactly upon the track of my most secret thoughts? Wasn't it an inspiration, a voice of warning? Perhaps it meant that I ought to give her my confidence. I could not make up my mind, and all the while I mumbled thoughtlessly—

"Surely not. How can you believe it? I could never entertain such a thought!"

"See, now you already have tears in your eyes!" she exclaimed, and patted me in a motherly way. "You are very sensitive—unusually so, but don't be ashamed of that, at least not towards a woman; you will be a good husband. How can I believe it? Because it is natural for you to think that. But if you had lived a married life with Minna, and you both had grown old in love— for one can do that without love degenerating, believe me—then you would look on death quite differently. You would only see in it a short separation, yes, hardly even that . . . for I don't suppose you are a materialist, Fenger?"

"Materialist? No, I don't think I can be called that, but——"

"But perhaps you have your doubts as to the life to come. Or perhaps you have not thought much about death, and in that you have done right. Life still for

a long time offers you more than enough to think of. . . .
With regard to myself, I have always wished that I should
be the one to close my husband's eyes. Should I die
before him, the thought would trouble me dreadfully that
he would be left alone for his last years. It is so much worse
for an old man who all his days has been accustomed to
be cared for and looked after—we women know better how
to take care of ourselves. Then I also have Immanuel,
thank goodness ! "

" It is a loving and beautiful thought of yours, Mrs.
Hertz, but surely you will both still live many years, and
your wish may all the same be fulfilled."

" Perhaps. Will Minna soon return ? "

" I don't know."

" Have you not had a letter yet ? "

I became very confused, and thought that my embarrassment must reveal to her that there was something amiss.
But she laughed.

" It's true she has only been away two days, so I
suppose it was too much to expect. Perhaps she
knows from you how Hertz was when you were here
last ? "

" No . . . I . . . really have not yet written."

" How is that ? It is not like you, Fenger."

The old lady looked at me as if she suddenly suspected
that there was something odd about this journey ; and,
had not her own grief so completely occupied her mind,
my agitation must have betrayed me, and she would
have compelled me to tell her everything. But now
the womanly instinct was unfortunately blunted ; she
at once forgot her former thoughts, looked past me, and
sighed.

" I am going to write to-night ; I postponed it until I

had been here. And of course I will tell her what you have said. But won't you write yourself? It would be better if she heard directly from you how things are; surely she would come at once, immediately."

"I should like it very much if she came; but it is too painful for me to summon her here, as if to say good-bye —I *dare not*. Perhaps it is *superstitious*, but one ought not to anticipate misfortune."

"But I? May I not ask her to come?"

All my hope came to life. I saw an infallible way to salvation, if she was safe inside this house before she made her choice. Everything here would plead my cause, dumb but insisting, if she was silent; eloquent and persuasive if she gave her confidence. What was Stephensen here? A sick, perhaps dying, old man's blessing would seal her pact with me. My conscience had forbidden me to make her seek advice from the old folk in her trouble, but it surely permitted me to take advantage of a coincidence, which seemed to me a finger of fate.

"Yes, write, dear friend! But you must try not to exaggerate the danger, for her sake also, the dear child! She will take it to heart! She will judge best herself what to do, therefore do not urge her too much to come—perhaps her cousin needs her still more."

"Oh, I do not think there is anything much the matter with her."

"Then I do not understand how you can let her waste several days of the few weeks you still have left here in Dresden. So you have not yet told her that you have to leave so soon for England?"

"I have . . . just to-night I was going to write it— after all I could not call her back the next day, but the combined news will make her come at once, very likely the day after to-morrow. . . . Now tell me, can I help you in any possible way ? To fetch medicine ? No ! But perhaps if I came round to-night to help you with the sitting up ? "

" I sit up myself most of the time, and a night nurse is coming, a Sister. Besides you look yourself as if you needed rest ; you must be overworked, my dear ! I suppose it is to drive away the monotony while Minna is away that you overwork yourself, but that you mustn't do, do you hear ? Farewell ! "

I went straight home in order to write the letter.

How happy did I feel at again being able to write to her !

Willingly would I have filled one sheet after another, but I only permitted my pen, as shortly as possible, to inform her of Hertz's critical condition and of the curtailment of my stay in Dresden owing to my uncle's altered plans. Certainly I should have liked to have kept back this last information until she had made her decision, and then, if she had decided in my favour, to have told her myself. But it would not do for her to come to Hertz without knowing it.

Though I had considered it my duty not to give way to my feelings, a strange tone had involuntarily stolen into the letter, which disclosed all my despair and anxious longing for her. It struck me on reading it through, and I was pleased by it.

I at once took the letter to the post-office, though it was too late for the night mail, and I might as well have dropped it into a letter-box. It calmed me immensely to communicate with Minna, and in such a way that nobody could blame me for it.

The next day I went at once to Hertz.

The fever had been rather high in the night, but had now subsided, as is often the case in the morning. I only saw the servant ; Mrs. Hertz was resting. I promised to call again in the evening.

I spent the day alternately reading and giving myself up to the dreams of memory. I also rang the changes on the following thoughts : " Now she has at least received my letter. . . . Surely there is still a train from Meissen (I got the newspaper from my landlady in order to make sure)—and she has only half a mile's drive to the station. Perhaps—yes, very likely—she will come to-night—and it's possible—yes, it is almost certain that I shall meet her at the Hertzes', she will at once hurry to them. . . . She will be much upset, the motherly Mrs. Hertz will treat her as being engaged, perhaps the old man is conscious, and will enjoy seeing us together. When the evening or night has advanced a little she will have to go home. I will of course accompany her,—that will be almost necessary,—and the whole thing will come right by itself, as if there had never been any Stephensen in existence."

Twice, at the hours when the post arrived, I became excited ; never can a lover have been farther from wishing a letter from his sweetheart than I was on that day. But the critical times passed by without result, and after the last delivery I breathed freely.

It was quite dark in the room when I prepared to go to Hertz.

Suddenly the door opened a little : " Here's a letter for you," the girl said, and handed something white to me.

I became completely rigid with terror. At this hour ? I told myself that it was impossible !

The letter was large and stiff, and this soothed my feelings. Something from the stationer, I thought.

I quickly lighted a match, and at the same moment gave an involuntary scream. The handwriting was Minna's.

BOOK V

CHAPTER I

My hand shook so violently while I lighted the lamp that I very nearly broke the chimney.

There was no mistake. On the table-cloth was lying the big strange letter, containing life or death, or what seemed to me much more glorious, and much more terrible, than life or death. For a moment I had the greatest inclination to run away. Then I nervously tore open the envelope.

The first thing that met my eye was the pencil drawing of Minna.

Just as suddenly as the image of Portia in the lead casket revealed to Bassanio his happy choice, so in the same manner did these lovely features announce my unfortunate lot.

The room swam round before me. I sat down on the sofa and took up the letter. The words danced and spread out before my eyes; two or three minutes passed before I could read—

"My dear tenderly loved Friend,—It is all over! I must be his. I have lingered and would still like to linger, but I feel that it will not be otherwise. I feel powerless to break with my first youth, to take your dear hand and start anew, and I should have to write a whole

book if I would tell you all that moves me. But at the
same time it appears to me that after this everything I
can write to you is of no account, and besides you know it
all. There is only one thing which I must tell you in order
that you shall not misunderstand me.

"I have not taken this decision because I expect to
be more happy with Stephensen than with you; on the
contrary—no, it really is impossible to explain myself
properly, still, after all, perhaps you have understood me.
I mean to say that it is not regard for myself which has
decided me, and—yes, I mean especially—(it was therefore
I wrote 'on the contrary!') that if there were no past,
no reproaches to be felt, or, in short, had it been something
quite fresh that began, then I should have been much
more certain of being happy with you than with him. But,
do you see, *now*, as it is, I should not be able to make
you happy, as you deserve. I should feel a traitor
towards my first love. It is true that this feeling
perhaps might cease; but circumstances might also arise
that made it unnaturally intense, and with your tender
loving nature you would in that case suffer terribly
under it.

"Perhaps you think I start with over-strained ideas of
Stephensen, when I fear to have too much to reproach
myself with, if I leave him. Not at all! I know quite
well that he will not do himself any harm, and that one
would hardly be able to say that I even made him unhappy, though he really loves me passionately; but perhaps
I should still do him irreparable harm. A nature like his
is exposed to many dangers. It is difficult to make clear
to you what I mean; I might easily seem vain, conceited,
or overrate my influence—though no, you think much
better of me than I deserve, perhaps you, in return, think

too little of him. I can only say that he himself fully and firmly believes that a union with me, and *only* with me, will act ennoblingly (I really am ashamed to write it, but it is his own expression) on his character and art. In the past I myself sometimes thought the same, at least not exactly like that, only that marriage and family life may do an artist good, bind him more closely to humanity and infuse warmth into his art. I express myself badly, but hope you will understand,—but in those days (as we have openly discussed, when he lived here and I hoped that he would marry me)—in those days he always stuck to his idea that an artist must be free, without such ties ; he had so much to struggle with in relation to his ideal of art. Now he has come to my view, he has learnt, he says, that he cannot be without me ; he hardens, gets narrow, has nothing to live for, he stretches out his hand for me, the very hand which has pulled me up out of a moral dullness and the swamp of nothingness. And now is it possible for me to refuse him ?—No, no !—You see, it is my duty and my destiny—yes, my destiny !

" May God make it so that we may meet and be together, many years hence, when time has taken away the passion. The friendship it cannot touch ; I know that neither of us can forget the other. But I suppose you will have to live abroad ; it would be too much happiness to have you near by as friend.

" Farewell, my beloved friend, farewell !

" MINNA."

I read the letter through several times. Its loving tone calmed my pain—yes, there was even a moment when it called forth in me a certain renunciation. But the reaction soon followed.

"No, I will not, I do not recognise this settlement. What is it? It is *I* whom she loves—*I*! With him it is nothing but a reminiscence and duty—yes, and 'a destiny'! A nice destiny! To lay her fresh warm life as a plaster on his blasé existence. . . . But it is, of course, my own fault! Why did I not take the settlement into my own hands? What a fool I have been! All this scrupulousness and generosity and care, that wind and sun were equally shifted; it was nothing but pretence for want of will; and so I allowed myself to be overawed by him. He has indeed 'pleaded his cause,' as she said that day. 'He could not be without her '—no, I should think not, when he has had enough of the flighty girls and been thrown over by rich coquettes, then he has come to think whether 'the best one' might not still be got—for old acquaintance sake. Or perhaps does it only come to this: he could not bear that another one got her, that is the real truth, I suppose."

Yes, I have been a weakling, a young fool! Would a *man* have given up such a woman?

In this way I scourged myself—yes, I even reproached myself for not having that night in Schandau gone to her room, then she would have been mine and no choice left her; I forgot that in order to let this happen, we should both have required different natures. For the nearer an action lies to its opposite, the deeper is often the natural barrier that parts them.

But now, what was to be done? Go to her, take back my words, bind her by her promise and be myself responsible for all, past and future? Yes, but where was I to find her? It was likely that she was no longer in Meissen, or in any case that I should not find her there to-morrow.

My head was aching, my confused thoughts jumped nervously here and there. It was not possible for me to keep my mind fixed to anything. How I needed to seek counsel with somebody, some person with more mature experience! My motherly friend, Mrs. Hertz, seemed my only refuge.

Yes, I would confide everything to her at once.

CHAPTER II

At this moment the door opened, and Immanuel Hertz came in.

His good-natured but plain face had a very alarmed expression.

"Hertz, you here! I hope your father is not——"

"My father is very ill. . . . I got a wire from mother, just in time to catch the train. . . . Father did not recognise me, he was in a high fever. I am afraid . . . that he . . . will pass away."

At any other time these words would have caused me the most acute grief, but now my first thought was: How shall I be able to worry Mrs. Hertz with my own sorrow, when her husband is lying on his deathbed? That Hertz was going to die seemed to me quite natural and necessary, and at the same time I felt my own hope vanish. . . . However, I tried the usual cheering phrases.

"Father is dozing now. I therefore ran over to you. . . . Come home with me, Fenger! And remain with us for the night; I know it will please father to see your face——"

His eyes were filled with tears. I quickly picked up my hat and put out the lamp—at the same instant he caught sight of Minna's picture.

"Oh, how lovely! And I have quite forgotten to congratulate you, but you will understand at such a time. But now I do it with all my heart, for I *can* do so, it is not among the instances where one says it as an empty form. . . . Minna! One can indeed call that good fortune!"

He pressed my hand as in a vice.

"Thank you, dear friend!" I murmured and turned away my face from the faint light, which the street lamp threw into the room,—"it is so kind of you, in the midst of your grief. I know how much I sympathise with you . . ."

We went down the stairs and he kept on talking about Minna. "Well," I thought, "indeed you do wear your heart on your sleeve." And in reality my surmise was right; open-hearted and indiscreet, he expected the same qualities in others.

"Indeed you have reason to consider yourself lucky. Minna, such a girl! How I envy you,—at least, not exactly envy you, though really . . . I suppose Minna has told you that I was very fond of her, more than a mere friend?"

"No, she has never even hinted at anything of the kind; altogether she has spoken very little about you, though I know she likes you. But I must admit, now you touch upon it yourself, that I have had a suspicion . . ."

"You see, I never told her, I mean proposed to her, but she felt it; women always do. No, I kept my feelings to myself; I think her heart in those days did not respond to such a feeling. Her father had just died, and also there was something else, but perhaps you know more about it than I. . . . My mother, in whom I confided,— it's no good hiding anything from her, she looks straight through one, indeed, one can with truth call her a judge of human nature; mother was of the same opinion, however much she would have liked her as a daughter-in-law. Then also I had to go to Leipzig. But I shall never forget her! Well, now you can understand how pleased I am that it should be just you whom she gets."

I felt as if I should begin to yell if this continued, and thought myself lucky when, reaching the corner where the Hertzes lived, he began to express his anxiety about his father : " So changed he looked, quite hollow-cheeked ! "

The doctor had just called. I gleaned from Mrs. Hertz, or rather felt, that she had not much hope. He was lying unconscious ; the temperature was alarmingly high.

Immanuel Hertz and I soon went into the drawing-room. I recalled the case of a delicate old lady, who for a couple of days had been almost given up with inflammation of the lungs, and who, after all, pulled through ; it also occurred to me that I had heard from a doctor that Jews have strong vitality, even in an advanced age, and get through such illnesses. It evidently cheered up my sanguine friend.

He often went into the sick-room, and stayed either for a few minutes or longer ; Mrs. Hertz remained there all the time. Occasionally I went with him, but generally I remained sitting in the drawing-room curled up on a chair, a prey to dullness and irritation. I was in the house of sorrow without being able to take my share of the grief and trouble ; I was unhappy myself, but could not weep. It was so late that Minna could not any longer be expected. Everything was indifferent and tedious to me. Yes, I really was wearied and had a feeling that this state of tediousness would last for ever, and grow more and more unbearable until death at last took me. I would willingly have exchanged places with Hertz—if one could say that there was anything I would willingly do.

In the middle of the night I had at last succumbed to a dull drowsiness, when young Hertz came in and said :

"He has recognised me. Father is conscious ; do come in."

The patient faintly smiled when he saw me and said : " Dear Fenger ! " " Minna ! " he murmured a little while after.

" Surely she will come to-morrow," Mrs. Hertz said.

" Then she will play to you," I added, though I felt tongue-tied and could scarcely speak.

" Beethoven," the old man whispered, and closed his eyes.

Mrs. Hertz arranged the pillows more comfortably ; she then took the temperature ; the thermometer had gone down to a little under 106°. Shortly after he began to say that time and space were forms of perception, but the soul was a " Ding an sich " (a thing of itself), a substance, a " *Noumenon*," " *Intelligibile*,"—these words he continually repeated.

The son, who was grieved and alarmed by these thoughts that seemed to indicate death, took his hand and said—

" Now you must not think, father, you must rest."

" Perhaps Kühne will come to-morrow, then you can philosophise together," Mrs. Hertz said.

" To-morrow ! " he sighed, with quite a strange accent.

Mrs. Hertz turned away.

" Yes, indeed, wait till he comes ; he understands it better than we do."

" Progressus," the old man said.

" Amen ! " the Sister murmured, and crossed herself. She thought that he had called upon a saint, or perhaps a prophet.

Immanuel and I, who had heard it, could not help smiling a little. I wondered that I could still find anything to smile at. No one would have been more pleased with the humour that lay in this mistake than Hertz himself ; but he was already dead to his surroundings.

For a long while Hertz remained passive, then he began to wander. The fragments which we caught seemed to indicate that he was back in the days of Königsberg and Riga. I several times heard him say : " The bell is not to be sounded,"—and I thought this was a reminiscence of that occurrence on the Exchange of which he had told us so recently. I saw again the whole of that cosy coffee-scene in the dull rainy light, with the glare of the spirit-flame flickering over Minna's dear face ; it was so close to me and smiled so confidingly. Mrs. Hertz noticed a tear on my cheek and pressed my hand, touched at my sympathy.

Towards daybreak, when Immanuel and I had fallen asleep in the drawing-room, old Hertz died, without his wife, who had not moved away from his bed or taken her eyes off him, being able to say when death had come.

The nurse had been sleeping soundly for some hours.

CHAPTER III

HERTZ was buried three days later in "*Der weite Kirchhof.*"

I do not know whether the Jews in Dresden do not keep strictly to the Mosaic churchyard, or whether this unorthodox family had long before left the synagogue. At the time I did not think about it; I thought of nothing,—indeed I hardly realised anything. Therefore I have no idea whether an address was given, or whether it was a Jewish Rabbi or Christian priest who performed the ceremony; if an eye-witness insisted that it was a Dervish or a Druid, it would be all the same to me. The whole thing stands to me as a bewildered dream. I remember that the giant Italian poplars rustled heavily and soothingly, and that some little birds twittered in the sharp cool sunlight. And then I see, a little in front of me to the right, Minna's black-draped form. It was for me, for her also I should think, not so much the dear old friend we buried, as our own short and happy life together,—our love. At the gate of the churchyard we pressed each other's hands firmly and long, the last time for many years.

Minna had told Mrs. Hertz everything.

"You have acted rightly," said the old lady to me the following day. "And poor Minna! She anyhow thinks she has acted for the best. But it pains me dreadfully, and not least for her sake."

I heard from her that Stephensen was going to Denmark in a few days in order to prepare everything, and that

Minna was soon to follow. With regard to myself—I only thought of getting away. My uncle had no objection to my immediate arrival, and a week after old Hertz's death I was ready to start.

Mrs. Hertz presented me at parting with the little original manuscript of Heine's poems. How truly and bitterly it now suited my case! And still it was so precious to me. I have kept it as a treasure, the unattainableness of which had brought English collectors to despair.

.   .   .   .

Year after year passed in almost constant, strenuous work. It followed naturally that at first I hardly saw anybody except the workmen at the factory and the employees, and later on it became a custom that pleased me. I got on well enough with my uncle, though I never became very intimate with him. He was pleased with my capacity for work. After two or three years he feared that I should exaggerate it, be "a business bachelor," as he called it. He tried to persuade me to take some part in social life : a man in such a position ought to form ties.

Little by little I gave in, and gradually changed my habits.

There was neither talk of cavalcades in Hyde Park nor holidays spent in country-seats, but I made the acquaintance of some nice middle-class families, almost all well-to-do factory owners. The young ladies were not heiresses of millions, but no less beautiful for that (those who *were* beautiful), and none of them would go into matrimony empty-handed. I had, however, another ideal in my heart, and my coolness often irritated my comrades, who considered it humbug.

At last I became acquainted with a young girl, who made a certain impression on me, and who, so my uncle assured me, was not indifferent to me, an assertion that certainly greatly flattered me. She was the only child of the owner of a cloth-factory, who was more than well-to-do, at least after Danish ideas. She showed me much kindness, though only in a social sort of way. I was not quite sure that my uncle was right in supposing that should be able to win her heart and hand, but I thought that there was a possibility of it. At any rate I partly wished to do so, and began to pass on to less " social " terms.

It was just after Christmas, the fourth since I had left Dresden.

One evening it happened that, at a concert, I was introduced by a friend to a German musician who might have been a year or so older than I, perhaps even more.

He had played a violin Cavatina, it was a small, half-private concert ; his appearances at grand concerts were very rare, though I think he was talented enough to do so. He made an ample income by giving lessons in both the violin and the piano. In his appearance there was something distinguished and something rather indolent.

It happened that we walked home together. The German was very talkative, making great game of the good English people's musical ability, and told several anecdotes with a good deal of humour, amongst others one about a rich young lady who had come to him in order to learn to play " The Moonlight Sonata " (of course the first movement) in the course of eight days, although she had never touched the piano before !

We went into a restaurant to have supper, and asked for some ale.

" Your good health," I said, and drank to him. " What an excellent drink it is ! "

" Well enough in its way," the German murmured, and brushed a few drops off his moustache. " But still, I say, I wish I was sitting in ' Drei Raben ' with a good glass of Spaten-Bräu in front of me, as I have done so many excellent times at this hour of the day."

" So you know Dresden ? " It flew out of me. Drei Raben ! The whole scene with Stephensen stood quite vividly before me.

The German laughed a little.

" I should think so, but I didn't know that you had been there. For long ? "

" For two years. I went to the Polytechnic. It's now four years since I left."

" H'm. I was there two years before. Played with Lauterbach. . . . That was something different to London. What an opera ! Oh yes, yes ! "

He strummed with his fingers on the table, and glanced dreamily in front of him.

" Waiter, Johannisberger Schloss ! With the German remembrance German wine ! "

" The golden days of youth, artist life," I thought. " He also clings to his Dresden memories ; but oh, what could they be compared with mine ! "

The wine came ; he poured it out. " A glass for our Elbe Florentine days ! " We clinked glasses, emptied them, and stared long and silently in front of us.

" I suppose you also came often to Renner, in ' Drei Raben,' I mean ? " he asked in a distrait tone.

" No, I have only been there once. Perhaps you lived in the neighbourhood ? "

" Yes, quite close by."

" Where ? " I asked at once, for my heart was beating furiously.

" Perhaps you remember a little street—Seilergasse."

" Seilergasse ! " I repeated, and stared at him.

He smiled.

" Perhaps you also lived there ? What a funny coincidence ! "

" No, I did not exactly live there, but I went there very often. I knew a family there."

" I see ! Well, well. . . . In these little streets everybody knows one another. Perhaps you have by chance heard about the people with whom I lodged ; the landlord was a teacher at a public school."

" Jagemann ? " I exclaimed.

The musician just raised a full glass to his lips, and spilt it so that the golden drops ran down the lapel of his coat.

" Yes, it was with them I lived," he said, and wiped himself carefully.

I now knew who my companion was. It was her first, half-childish love, the musician to whom Stephensen had seen her give the farewell kiss.

" And it was those people I used to visit," I said ; " at least—Jagemann was dead—it was madam and the daughter I went to see."

" Minna—she was a lovely girl ! "

We both stared down our glasses, as if we, with Heine, saw everything there—

> " But most of all the face of my loved one,
>   That angel-head on the Rhenish wine's gold ground."

" Do you know if she—Minna Jagemann—whether she since—has got married ? " he asked at last.

I told him that she had married a Danish painter, made

some remarks about his position and circumstances, and related the little I had heard of them from acquaintances ; that she had had a daughter, who had died about a year ago.

The musician sat silently opposite to me, often emptying his glass and not always remembering to fill mine—he had ordered another bottle, and dedicated it with a glass to "Die schöne Jagemann." I also was silent. "*Wir schwiegen uns aus*" (We exhausted our silence), as Schumann once is supposed to have said.

When I was in bed on that night I realised that, in a moral lethargy, I had been on the brink of committing a dishonourable and foolish act, though no one would have called it the first, and all would have called it wise. From that day I ceased to visit the house of the owner of the cloth-factory.

My uncle reproached me for my fickleness. I complained of home-sickness, and told him that I wanted to visit my old friends. A week after I was in Copenhagen.

.　　.　　.　　.　　.　　.　　.　　.

My acquaintances in Denmark were not many, and none of them associated directly with the Stephensens. But, thanks to the gossips of our capital, I heard a good deal about them at second or third hand. There could hardly be anything remarkable in my asking about the fate of a Dresden acquaintance in Denmark; and if some people suspected a deeper interest, I did not care much what they thought. I wanted to know the real truth.

The usual opinion was that they lived happily together— it was a love-marriage, affection from youth, perhaps first love. Others said that his flirtations—a sharp tongue called them liaisons—could hardly escape her knowledge, and that she seemed to be rather passionate and impetuous. On

the contrary, some insisted, she was gentle but silly.
" Silly ! " several explained, " she can sparkle with original
thoughts, but this habit is not aways agreeable to every
one ; she has a very critical eye for the faults of others."
" Anyhow, she's interesting," said an elderly man. " But
she's without interests," remarked a young journalist. A
lady, however, who lived in the flat above the Stephensens
stated that she was at any rate a passionate lover of music,
as she usually played half the day. This astonished everybody, as in society she had never been known to touch the
piano, and she was rarely seen at concerts. Her appearance
was almost unanimously admired.

I had been nearly a fortnight in Copenhagen, and still
had not caught a glimpse of her. Should I simply go and
call upon her ? I considered this question for the hundredth
and which time God only knows, when rather late one
evening I entered Café à Porta. In the outer room there
were only a few visitors. Looking round in order to choose
a place, I heard from a side-room a voice that could not
be mistaken : it was Stephensen's, only a degree more
lispingly sweet than formerly. I placed myself as quietly
as possible where I could best overlook the adjoining
room.

The only one I knew of the lively party within was Minna,
whom I saw almost in *profile perdu*, hardly half a dozen
paces from me. Stephensen apparently was sitting on a
corner sofa, of which I could only see a little of the farthest
end. A smiling blonde leaned her arm upon it, and
evidently conversed with him ; her face had a certain
vulgar beauty ; every minute she laid her head on one
side, so that the reddish hair touched her half-bare shoulder,
which peeped through a broad insertion of black lace.
The laughing glances that she constantly flashed towards

the hidden corner, whence Stephensen's voice sounded, proved that she was—I will not say exactly jubilant—but rather in a condition of electric illumination. One of the gentleman addressed her by a name which I had already heard in gossip connected with Stephensen's. Minna sat leaning back and seemed to be looking down in front of her, but it was evident that she was constantly watching them.

The waiter came up to me to take my order. I was in a dilemma, as I feared that my voice would at once be recognised by Minna. But just then the whole party, with the exception of Minna, began to laugh in the boisterous manner that usually follows a story more vulgar than witty, and under cover of this noise I gave my order without disclosing myself. One of the gentlemen—very likely I should have known the famous name, which I do not doubt was in his possession, had I not been such a newcomer—expressed indignation on behalf of the party at Minna's reserve. " Why do you sit like a stick amongst us, Mrs. Stephensen ? Take things more lightly, and don't be a German Philistine. . . . Remember you are amongst artists. . . . Empty your glass."—" I am only tired," Minna said.—" Then you must just drink."—" But I don't care for champagne." —"Ah, ha! Too French, too light and spirituous, it is not for you. But Rhenish wine, that you surely like ? . . . Ah, I thought so ! Very well ! Waiter ! " The waiter flew in.—" No more of this foolery, please ! " she said, half angry and half amused.—" Really not ? I mustn't ? " —" No, but I thank you for your kindness. . . . Only let me sit and look after myself; I am so tired, and have a headache."—" You do not want to go home already, I suppose ? " Stephensen's voice sounded, this time very morose. Minna did not answer, but yawned in her handkerchief; she leaned back and looked down sideways. She really appeared as if she was tired, not with an acute but with a chronic fatigue. Her face, of which I had by this time obtained a better view, was almost unchanged, only the cheeks were a little less full. I had remarked that she spoke surprisingly pure Danish, the foreign accent was very slight.

The conversation round her now grew very lively. It centred on aestheticism, if one could call it so. Names such as Ibsen, Zola, Dostoevsky, Wagner, Berlioz, Millais, Bastien-Lepage, even such scientific ones as Darwin and Mill, almost buzzed round one's head. In spite of this medley I was not so very much surprised, as during my short stay I had become acquainted with the general tone. At first it had certainly made a great impression upon me. Good gracious! what must not those people have read and heard, such an education and insight, and so many interests! But soon I grew more critical; I perceived that those who talked most were least interested, and that many who "aestheticised" most loudly did not go even so deeply as I myself, who in these years had been too occupied with business to be "up-to-date," and who, through residence in England, had been reading the works of very different authors from those who were fashionable in Denmark. I even had a suspicion that the good Stephensen himself was no adept in literature, though he grew more and more talkative; very likely he wished to sparkle before the blonde, who really seemed to be on the point of fainting with admiration. The gentleman who had wanted to order the Rhenish wine for Minna, a big man with a glorious fair beard, excited him to a constantly growing exaggerated radicalism, and altogether seemed to fool the whole company.

Stephensen's eloquent sentences at last degenerated to an absolute harangue about the art of the future. He flung about apothegms like "the democratic formulae in art," "a scientific illustration of life, in contradiction to the decorative luxury," and finished up with something to the effect that the brush in the true artist's hand ought to be a probe in the wound of society.

"Then my advice is that they should first be thoroughly washed," the fair-bearded man suggested.

The wave of laughter for some time overpowered the discussion, but Stephensen's hollow talk kept afloat like a cork. Minna lifted her eyes and looked at him. Was it possible that she was imposed upon by this bosh ? I thought. The expression in her averted eyes I could not see. But then, with eyes half-lowered, she turned her head in more than profile, and I grew almost terrified by the smile of cold disgust that played round her lips, and the annoyance that darkened the brows and shone from her eyes. Thus she had looked at him, and had turned away because she felt that the expression of her feelings was too evident. Little she realised that she turned her face to one who could read its language line by line like his mother tongue, while the others, at most, could only make out a few words of those which are the same in all languages. "Weakling," whispered these firm lips; "Liar, fraud ! " this open forehead cried out ; "Faithless !" exclaimed those clear eyes, which could look so tenderly and now stared so hard ; but the whole hard-set face sighed : "And *he* was the love of my youth ! "

"But Raphael ! " a youthful individual of the party objected, "one cannot quite in that way——"

"Bah, Raphael !—'distance lends enchantment,' " the big good-natured man with the fair beard said loudly.

"The distance of hundreds of years, that's what makes it. Just let Stephensen be stored for two hundred years, then you will see what kind of fellow he will turn out."

"Yes, but," the blonde exclaimed, "then all this that we now . . . our art . . . would also be antiquated, just like the old one is in our days ? "

"Oh, logic ! " the fair beard shouted, "your name is *simplicitas profana* ! Indeed, madam ! everything is relative ! Even our great Stephensen is not quite absolute, therefore beware, don't take him too much *au serieux* ! "

"You with your irony," Stephensen said. "Yes, let everything be relative, but we——"

He was then brought to silence, even he, by a laughter that seemed to freeze the whole party, and which I can never forget. It was Minna who laughed. She got up, held her handkerchief to her mouth, and burst out again as she turned from the party.

"What is there to laugh about in such a way ? " Stephensen said, and his voice was extremely irritable.

"*Nein, es ist zu drollig !* " (No, it's too funny), Minna murmured. At the same minute her eyes passed over me, but if they stopped, it was only for such an atom of time that it was not possible for me to decide whether she had seen and recognised me. She slowly went towards the adjoining empty room, where the gas had already been turned off.

"Where are you going to ? " Stephensen asked.

" I feel suffocated in here," she answered, and disappeared in the dark space. I heard her open a window.

The indefatigable Stephensen started again. Directly afterwards, the robust bearded man got up and went into the dark room. I put on my fur coat, for I also felt suffocated. While I paid the waiter, a strong manly voice

20

called from the inner room: "Waiter! A glass of water."

Shortly afterwards the bearded man rejoined the party:

"Now, enough of your foolery, Stephensen. Your little wife is unwell, and upon my word she's worth more than the whole of your 'art of the future'!"

.   .   .   .

The following day I had a letter from my uncle in which he asked me when I could tear myself away from Denmark to go to Stockholm and St. Petersburg, where he had business friends with whom he wanted me to become acquainted.

Yes, I could tear myself away from Denmark, I had seen quite enough; help I could not. Run away from the place I could, but not from the miserable impression that I had received; it haunted me day and night. Only the sea-sickness in the Bay of Bothnia had sufficient elemental power to conquer it for one night. In St. Petersburg I remained for about a month, drove in a Troika on the Neva, and was every second night at parties till three in the morning. I regretted that my heart was not free, so that I might have lost it to one of these Russian ladies.

It was quite natural that before I returned to England I should visit some factories in Germany. In the course of these visits I went to Saxony, and Dresden attracted me irresistibly; I made the excuse that I wanted to look over the "Art School of Industry," and form a connexion with its manager.

On the way I visited Immanuel Hertz in Leipzig. He was married to a brawny Jewess, who had presented him with several children. Into his nature had come something more restless; otherwise he was the same gentle fellow.

Tears came into his eyes when he spoke of his mother, who had lived with him and had died six months before, a fact which he had already written to tell me. She was buried in Dresden by the side of her husband.

" And Minna ? " he asked. " We had a letter from her when mother died, but in that she spoke so little of herself. Have you seen her ? "

" Only in passing ; she did not notice me."

" H'm ! Do you think she is happy ? "

" I suppose she is, that is to say, she has had sorrows— lost a child."

" Yes, at that time she wrote to mother ! Oh yes, it must be dreadful for a mother ! " Then he started speaking of a Liberal newspaper of which he was half-owner, and about the opposition to Bismarck.

CHAPTER IV

IN Dresden I went at once to "Seilergasse." Mrs. Jagemann had long since moved away, and the people in the house did not know where she lived. I looked sorrowfully at the summer-house in the little garden, where everything was unchanged, and I went to "zur Katze" in order to ask whether the widow Jagemann still came there. Here they knew more; Minna's mother had been dead for two years.

I walked round the town, it was to me an indispensable enjoyment to look up our precious spots; not all were untouched by time. On the terrace they had pulled down the dear little Café Torniamenti with its naïve columns, where I had got the idea to go to Rathen, and where we had met Stephensen; the streets, through which we had wandered the last time we walked together, did not exist any longer, and one could hardly find traces of them in the new quarter of pretentious buildings. In Grosser Garten and the Park the buds of the bushes began distinctly to show green—we were at the end of March—and everything looked different; but on the black stems I still read the same names on the labels, which in those days we had studied together, one having a very exotic name, which most likely was easy enough in the mouth of a Maori or Tahitian, but the pronunciation of which had caused Minna to make the most comical grimaces. I remained standing there for a very long time, staring at these dry branches, and twigs, and on this little label as if it was a riddle that had to be solved, but that defied solution. And really I had a feeling of not being able to grasp the whole thing ; I did not understand that this plant still stood here and had the same unpronounceable name, understood still less that I myself was here and, least of all, that Minna was not here, or that I couldn't go to " Seilergasse " and embrace her. I realised nothing at all.

When at last I turned round, I saw some children a few yards away putting their heads together, laughing and running away. Evidently they thought that I was mad. And who knows ? From children one hears the truth !

On my way back I passed the beautiful Renaissance Villa, which Minna and I jokingly had called ours. A new riddle ! In those days it had been a matter of course that we two should build a home together, but it was a wild and ridiculous dream that we should ever be able to do it on such a grand scale. And now there was more possibility of my being able to buy this building than of taking Minna to the most modest home. Incomprehensible ! Was this perhaps already a madness, that I had a feeling of not being able to understand anything, where I suppose in reality there was nothing to understand, where everything for a cool brain was clear as daylight, *had* to be so, and for me it *could* not be. Madness ! Sonnenstein ! And why not ? " If I am lodged there," I thought, " it will always be an advantage that no Napoleon will come to drive one out."

At sunset a signal shot sounded, which announces that the Elbe rises unusually. The next morning, when I still lay in a half-slumber, I was alarmed by a second shot, by which the danger of flood is foretold. I got up at once. As I was staying at the Bellevue Hotel, I was quite close to the river. Since last evening, the porter said, people had been

on the bridge amusing themselves all the night through by
watching the rising of the water, and the parapet was now
quite black with the crowd. But this bridge itself, which
usually was lifted so proudly on its high pillars over the
river, now only showed the arches spanning the muddy mass
that dashed along, not like water but like a torrent of lava,
whirling and grinding, covered with overturned yawls,
beams and timber, barrels and bushes, which tossed, went
under and came up again. I made my way to the bridge.
The whole quay had disappeared and also the little stretch
of meadow in front of Neustadt ; over there the gardens were
under water, and on this side waves foamed and whirled
up against the terrace wall.

"Oh, our poor little Rathen," I thought, " what does it
look like there ? I wonder if the dear house, where we have
experienced so much together, is flooded, perhaps even
washed away."

I could not resist my desire to know what had happened,
and a few hours later the train brought me to Pirna ; in
Saxonian Switzerland itself there was not any possibility
of crossing the Elbe. When I had passed over the bridge,
I turned and glanced at the town : I had not seen it since
that day on the outer journey to Rathen, when it had
shown itself in the frame of the cabin window, shining and
wet from the summer rain, with a promising light over the
gables of Sonnenstein. Now the town and the sombre
fortress inhabited by the feeble-minded, lay in sunlight,
but it was a cold, cheerless light that contained no suggestion of Spring.

I walked over Dorf- and Stadt-Wehlen and up through the
famous Zscherre-Grund, which is passed by all tourists,
but was now deserted. The intimate Saxonian mountain
landscapes, with their baroc and steep shapes, moved me

deeply and at the same time—strange to say—vexed me.
I wished, or anyhow I thought I did so, that one of these
overhanging rocks would fall down and crush me. At
about four o'clock I at last reached the Bastei, stepped out
on the plateau and saw the awful devastation under my feet.

Of Erbgericht's Terrace there were only the tops of the
maples over the water, looking like big shrubs on the edge of
the stream, which had almost entirely swallowed up its
rival the " Rosengarten." Between them the river had
flooded the Rathen valley, which usually discharged its
modest brook into it. The three little houses, which behind
some twigs of the " Rosengarten " were squeezed in between the immovable rock and the tearing stream, presented
a miserable appearance. The first one was half under water ;
the quarry owner's house, which lay a little higher and
besides had a base of about six feet, had still its entrance
door free, but only for one who did not mind a bath ; the
water foamed against the hidden stone steps as against a
reef. The little summer-house, where we had sat so often,
had been torn away. The third house was even more under
water. Thanks to my good travelling-glass I saw all this
quite distinctly. On the flat opposite bank, round which the
river curved, there was nothing to remark, except that it had
receded and that the grass grew out into the water without
any decided border line.

A sad sight, so much the more as it had nothing wild
in it. Seen from this dominating point the unnaturally
broad river seemed, I won't say not to rush, but not even
to hasten ; one only perceived the enormous irresistible
moving mass. Calm and peaceful it had in those days
glided by our idyll, as the moving life, occupied with its
own concerns, streams past the happy existences that
desire nothing from it ; it had broken into this idyll,

destroying and washing it away ; but passionless it had
exercised its work of destruction, and indifferently it
rushed by—like life—like fate !

A cold wind blew, it had clouded over, now it even
began to snow a little. A miserable, depressing outlook,
but I would not have exchanged it for a glance over a
smiling landscape, through which streamed the broad
thoroughfare of a frequented river. In this way I could
bear to see Rathen again. I was also content to have
never been on these heights with Minna.

A prosaic circumstance prevented me, however, from
giving myself up too much to this elegiac mood ; I was
almost ill with hunger. When I had satisfied my appetite,
I thought it was too late to go down to Rathen, and I
postponed it to the next day. I went down towards the
Elbe by a forest path, which branches off from the descent
to Rathen, but is indicated as a " forbidden path." The
rough forester came into my head, and I wished I could
meet him. This footpath would take me to the one
that Minna and I had trodden on the way home from
the stone-quarry. But the penetrating wind, which
splashed the ever-increasing fall of thawing snow into
my face, the farther I came down, soon made me return.
Up on the height it surely was easy enough to find shelter,
but it was disagreeable everywhere, and I myself was less
melancholy than annoyed : this whole expedition seemed
to me to be a folly. As soon as the colourless sun had
set I retired to my room, where there was a horrible
draught, and at last went to sleep lulled by the monotonous
cradle song of soughing pines.

I woke up to find a real spring morning. The view
was not changed, but I was told that the river had begun
to fall. When I was on the point of leaving, a lonely

visitor got up from the table, and said, "I say, is it you, Mr.—Professor! Didn't I think so!" It was the schoolmaster, Mr. Storch. I do not know whether I felt pleased or annoyed to see him, but surely enough I wished him at the bottom of the Elbe when it was evident that he intended to stick to me like a leech and wanted to come with me. He had given a holiday on account of the flood, and had now gone up to Bastei to "get an overlook." There was nothing else to do but to accept his company. I had not time to postpone the trip, unless I had once more stayed the night at Bastei.

"Look, you will get company for dinner, it might even be a whole *table d'hôte*," he exclaimed, while we were going down towards the bridge, and pointed back to a landau, which a couple of steaming horses drew up in front of the hotel. "They have come from Pirna, I know the conveyance; the proprietor of it is a regular shark, he makes the travellers pay a pretty penny."

A lady's hat appeared out of the window and allowed a long black veil to fly to one side.

"I say, there are also ladies. A young one, I bet; that's something for you."

"Now come along," I said irritably, and hurried out to the rock-bridge.

The first part we descended with rapid steps. When we came to more even ground, he began, as I had expected, at once to speak about Minna, pretending not to know that we had been engaged, as indeed perhaps he did not.

"I suppose you remember Minna Jagemann? I am sure you do; I saw myself how you flirted with her on the forest path. . . . Well, and right you were. . . . Now, just imagine, after all, she got married to that painter of whom I told you, your countryman, but 'give a dog

a bad name,' you know.   I suppose you haven't forgotten
that I told you that she had had a sort of——"

"Yes, yes, I remember it quite well."

"And you have not seen her in Denmark ?   The country
is not so very big."

"I have lived all the time in England."

"Oh, I see !   I always thought you had got something
English about you."

I made him talk about the flood and the damage it
caused the poor people, and he told me that in all probability only the two innkeepers and the owners of the
three houses by the river would suffer any loss.

When we came down into Rathen itself, I bade him
good-bye, allowing the " English " side of my nature to
come to the fore, so that the honest German did not feel
inclined to force himself upon me any longer.

The flood of the Elbe had not proceeded so far, but
the brook was very swollen.   The simple planks that
led over it were, however, still undisturbed.   I went over
to the Zedlitz Villa, which, of course, was closed, came
past the little birch avenue, and stood suddenly at my
destination, the grotto " Sophien-Ruhe."   The benches
had been taken in ; I sat down on the stone table.   The
birds twittered gaily round me, the bushes breathed the
soft spring air with their little green gills, and the buds
of the trees showed white in the sunshine against the
blue sky.

Again I had that queer feeling of not being able to understand anything : I neither understood that I was here nor
that she was not here.   Into my head came the remembrance of the little glow-worm, which evening after evening
had sat on the same corner of the stone steps, signalling for
a mate ; and it seemed to me that if I could only sit here,

concentrating all my will-power on my loss, I should be able through the compulsion of nature to enchant Minna to me.

It is said that a dying person is able to review, in a second, his whole life in all its main lines, as if his consciousness was already elevated above the earthly order of time. At this moment my youth died in me, and I reviewed in parting the whole course of my love, all that I have confided to these pages, and still many more half-forgotten incidents. It appeared to me that I saw it all in a flash and from above, just as I had overlooked the whole of its birthplace from the platform of Bastei. And in taking this review, one thing struck me which I had not remarked before, the fact that we had all allowed ourselves to be led and driven almost mechanically by the stream of circumstances, without striking in energetically with a " So it must be ! " Even Stephensen's way of behaving, that had certainly had the appearance of spontaneity, had in its essence the same character ; he had evidently given in to his jealous longing to see Minna before she was irrevocably lost, and had thought : " Let us see what I can manage. Who knows ! Perhaps, after all, she will come with me."

But now ? Could nothing be altered ? Was there not yet time to step in with an " I will " ? A marriage is not any longer an indissoluble tie, hers was an unhappy one. I knew more certainly than any words of hers could have told me that all she had hoped for was irreparably lost, that he was found out, weighed and found wanting ; while he, on his part, had long since tired of her. Besides, he was, as he often enough had boasted, a man who did not share the usual prejudices, and I suppose he, least of all, would insist that an unsuccessful union could not rightly be dissolved, or that it was justifiable to bind a wife who stayed against her will. Surely the theories of liberty are not always

welcome, when they go against the men of liberty themselves. But even if his vanity shrank, *could* he in the end
oppose, when *she* would and when *I* would ?

Would she ? She had made the trial, and it had failed.
Why not give up the impossible to realise the possible ?
That she had guarded her love and confidence in me I felt
with an unswerving certainty.

Would *I* ? Yes, I would ! I said it for the first time in
our relations with one another, said it with triumphant joy.
To-morrow evening I could be in Copenhagen, and the day
after speak with her.

Strange indeed is the dream-nature in human beings !
Never, perhaps, in those days, when I had Minna at my side,
had I felt so happy as in this moment, when I looked back
on our first youthful love and forwards to its consummation
in a tested matrimonial love, and these two parts in my will
united into a single life.

So true are the myths about " Paradise lost " and " Paradise regained " : happiness is a remembrance and a hope.

CHAPTER V

At this moment something happened, that at the time seemed to me supernatural, and does so still when recalling it.

The gravel crunched under light quick steps. I started. The situation reminded me so much of the old days when I had sat there and Minna had come, that I fully and firmly believed it was an hallucination. And really, it sounded exactly as if it was a repetition—a copy I could almost say of those steps. "If this hallucination continues," I thought, "I shall see her, and what will then happen to me ? God help me, am I really on the point of going out of my mind, as I said, half jokingly, but yesterday. . . ?"

I jumped down from the table with a cry, and with a cry Minna stopped in front of the grotto—yes, Minna herself, no vision !

We had not yet controlled ourselves, when Stephensen appeared and bowed with an astonished, but at the same time a little ironical smile, that clearly enough said : " This is really a coincidence, which looks like a plan."

The usual exclamations : " You here, Harald ? That I call a surprise ! " " I thought you were in England, Mr. Fenger." " I imagined you in Copenhagen, Mr. Stephensen," masked for a few moments our painful embarrassment.

After the first nervous rapture, which the sudden sight of one's beloved infallibly produces, had calmed down, I felt a painful disappointment. The lady and her husband on a pleasure-trip together ! How little did it harmonise with the relations that I had imagined between them, with the plan that had inspired me !

"I suppose southward bound, to Italy ? "

"No, we shall limit ourselves to Saxony."

"I imagine you have business in Dresden, Harald ? "

Minna was, strange to say, evidently the first of us to regain her self-control; she only continued to breathe somewhat quickly and irregularly. Her smile and voice—yes, even her movements, expressed the most vivid joy at this meeting.

"Very likely you are going back to Pirna ? That's capital, then you can drive with us."

"There is plenty of room," Stephensen said. "It is not a victoria. And besides, I would willingly sit on the box."

He forced his usual polite smile; the lips obeyed, but not the eyes. He was obviously irritated; but Minna either did not notice it, or did not care.

"Very likely our talk will tire you, we have so much to speak of after so many years," she said.

We started at once on the return journey. In a window of the school-building stood the master. He leaned far out and continued to follow us with his eyes. Minna laughed.

"Well, my cousin still exists ! Do you remember, when he met us on the forest path ? God knows what sort of thoughts he has ! I hope he will not stare his eyes out of his head."

She continued laughing and joking, a little hysterically, it seemed to me.

"There we have the dear old saw-mill, where I came with the little girls in the morning to drink new milk. Why were you never there ? But at that time of course you slept like a log—like you men."

" But you had never told me that you were there at that hour."

" Are you then to have everything given to you with a spoon ? "

" I, for my part, prefer to eat solid food, and with a fork," Stephensen said.

Minna looked astonished, not exactly at him, but in his direction, as if she was surprised that any remarks should come from that quarter. When we began to ascend, the conversation soon ceased. To walk uphill was trying to Minna ; palpitation of the heart and shortness of breath compelled her frequently to stop. Stephensen walked a few paces in front ; she took my arm and leant on it.

At table the conversation was rather halting and in-definite. But when we were in the carriage, Minna seated herself cosily in the corner and said—

" Well, Harald ! Now, you must tell me how life has treated you in these years. Everything, good and bad."

I obeyed her command as well as I could. Minna looked at me constantly, so that at times her eyes stared me out of countenance ; she also smiled continuously, but often as if she was thinking of quite different scenes. Sometimes she laughed—yes, she even teased me a little about the English beauties.

" Oh, pooh," I exclaimed, a little annoyed. " Beauties ! I have not seen any who came up to you."

Minna threw herself back, and laughed with her handker-chief to her mouth.

" Well, there is a feather in your cap," Stephensen remarked.

He sat on the front seat, and looked most of the time out

of the window and lit one cigarette after another. When he threw in a remark or question about art in London or some such thing, Minna regarded him with an astonished and hard look, in the way one looks at a child who has been naughty, and who, without having asked pardon, tries to pretend that nothing has happened and joins in the conversation. It was evident that this treatment annoyed him very much ; each time he grew silent as soon as possible. But it also troubled me ; however painful it would have been to witness a loving confidence between them, it made my heart ache to see their unhappy condition so openly laid bare, and I did not understand how she could behave in such a way, even before me.

True, I would have concealed my meeting with the German musician, but when it came to the point I told it all the same. Minna said nothing, but gazed out of the window.

" Funny how small the world is ! " Stephensen remarked. " One always runs against one another either directly or indirectly."

" And it was then you left ? " Minna suddenly asked, turning her head quickly as a bird, and giving me a penetrating look.

This diversion completely threw me off my guard.

" Yes, then—then I left," I stuttered, and turned crimson.

Stephensen looked at us with an intensely ironical expression, as if he said : " Now I suppose it will soon come to a declaration *in optima forma*. Well, I shan't stand in the way, don't mind me." Minna gave him a short glance, and his smile at once disappeared.

" Do tell me, Harald," she asked, leaning forward on her arm, " why didn't you join us, that evening, in the café ? "

" What café ? "

"Oh, you know very well—à Porta. . . . You thought
I had not seen you ? Yes, indeed I did, but only at the
end ; you remember—when I laughed at Stephensen, and
at all the others too."

Stephensen put on a very dignified face and stroked
himself between the collar and the neck, a pet gesture of
his. Minna turned still more away from him, and looked
at me with a rather teasing smile.

"I did not know any others of the party,—and—
besides——"

"—besides you didn't wish to meet me in that company,
and you were right."

But now Stephensen felt that it was high time to assert
himself.

"I must say it is a very queer way in which you speak
of the company we have associated with."

"*You*—not I. I have been obliged to put up with it."

"It is very regrettable that I could not do better for
you! However, they were almost all people of the most
intellectual set——"

"Anyhow, I did not feel at home in that society, nor,
as a matter of fact, would Harald have done so."

Stephensen compressed his lips and glanced maliciously
at her.

"You yourself know best where you are at home."

Minna shuddered and pressed her hand on her breast,
as if she was suffering acute pain. I suspected that in
these words lay a hidden poison. The idea struck me
that I sat here like a priest who accompanies a condemned
victim to the scaffold, and that it was a police official
who sat opposite to me.

I suffered indescribably, but I felt that the conversation
must be turned into a peaceful channel at any price.

21

Pirna had just come into view, and I asked whether they would stay the night there, or go on to Dresden.

"No, we shall stay the night; perhaps we shall go for a while to Bohemia," Stephensen answered. Minna, who had been leaning almost bodily out of the window, turned directly afterwards towards me; her face was colourless and drawn.

"Do you remain for some days in Dresden?" But this question was accompanied by a look which altered it to a petition.

My answer did not come immediately. Should I not take the opportunity of showing my hand—just a little? If I meant to do it at all, no more time was to be lost.

"As a matter of fact," I began deliberately, "when I was discovered sitting on the stone table in the 'Sophien-Ruhe grotto,' I had just come to the conclusion that I would leave to-night for Copenhagen."

At the last words Stephensen involuntarily made an uneasy movement, then straightened himself up and set his features in a highly disapproving manner. So the shot had gone home. I saw this perfectly though my eyes were riveted upon hers, which had not for a moment left my face; and in their wonderful greenish brown depths, I beheld a brighter and brighter golden light.

"I s—see," she said or rather breathed, scarcely moving her lips.

"But now I certainly shall alter my plans. I have work enough to detain me in Dresden for a week or two; for many weeks, if it comes to that."

"I am glad," said Minna.

Stephensen took refuge in his pet gesture—his finger between neck and collar—and seemed disposed to say something bitter, perhaps to the effect that I ought not to upset my arrangements for *their* sakes ; but he though better of it.

None of us spoke after that.

I had previously mentioned that I was staying at the Bellevue Hotel. So I knew that Minna could communicate with me, whenever she wanted to. That she would, I had now no doubt whatever. I was at rest on this point, but I was very uneasy about this strange journey of theirs. " What have they come here for ? " I thought. " It is evident that they are not going to Bohemia." Why I found it " evident," I do not know. . . .

> " The chariot rolls, the bridge is quaking,
> The stream beneath it flows so sadly,
> Once more the joys am I forsaking
> Of that fond heart I love so madly."

As soon as we had passed the bridge, Stephensen stopped the carriage.

Then I pressed Minna's hand, bowed to Stephensen, and hurried to the railway station.

CHAPTER VI

WHEN I arrived at Dresden, I could not make up my mind to leave the Bohemian station. I had a suspicion that both or one of them would return from Pirna.

The evening train rolled in, and I saw Stephensen's face at a carriage window. He stepped out—alone. I rushed towards him.

"Where is Minna?"

Stephensen regarded me coldly, as if he would beg to be excused from intrusive questions. But he changed his mind.

"You are right, Mr. Fenger, you ought to know it. She is at Sonnenstein."

"Sonnenstein!" I murmured, as if I did not understand. Then I was seized with giddiness, and the commotion of passengers and porters on the half-dark platform made me feel ill. "Sonnenstein! What does it mean?" I caught hold of his overcoat, partly to steady myself, partly to prevent him from getting away. "You don't mean to say that she—that Minna——"

"Well, don't take it so pathetically!" Stephensen said with a semblance of kindness. "She is not exactly weak-minded or really insane, only very melancholy and a little hysterical. You have seen for yourself. In short, it was the best thing to put her under the treatment of a doctor. What is there in that? In our nervous times, it is nothing unusual. . . . She preferred Sonnenstein, because her

324

home-sickness was rather overwhelming, and then, of course, also to avoid talk in Copenhagen. It is now said that she is visiting her people, though, as I have already remarked, it is in our days so usual, all educated people have got over these prejudices——"

My dull incredulity had, during this explanation, given place to an absolutely conscious fury.

" It is you who have done it, *you—you !* "

My voice was stifled. I shook my fist in front of his face ; he tore himself loose, a gendarme stepped towards us. Stephensen whispered a few words to him, shrugged his shoulders, and disappeared in the crowd. I leaned against a pillar ; late-comers were rushing about, the conductors shouted, there was a sound of whistling and puffing.

As soon as I had recovered control of myself, I asked the porter whether there was a train for Pirna ; but I had to wait until the next morning.

By the first train I was in Pirna, reached Sonnenstein breathless, and fortunately at once had an interview with the Professor. I presented myself as a friend of Mrs. Stephensen's and her husband's, the latter of whom I had met last night, and went on to say that I had promised frequently to give information to him about his wife's condition, as I was remaining in Dresden for some time. But as I myself was also very troubled about my friend, and only had been able to speak to Mr. Stephensen for a few minutes, I had at once hurried out, and now wanted earnestly to know the whole truth.

The Professor calmed me for the time being ; there was hardly any cause for immediate fear, it was one of the cases for which in former days one would never have thought of applying to a doctor, and where the asylum essentially served to isolate the patient from mental infection. Further information he could only supply after having her under observation for about a week, but he would then be very pleased to give it.

When, therefore, I called upon him eight days later, he stated that Minna assuredly was suffering mentally, but was not liable to go out of her mind, at any rate not if she was rightly treated and lived under the favourable conditions that an asylum would give her until she recovered her mental balance. She was in a very nervous, excited condition. But the real danger was the heart disease, the seed of which must have been sown several years back. She might grow old with the complaint, but also it might suddenly cause her death. Most of all it was necessary to avoid any agitation of mind, which he thought hitherto had constantly given nourishment to the complaint.

"Do tell me," he suddenly said, "you are a friend of her's and her husband's. Did they live happily together?"

I considered a moment whether I had the right to be candid. "No," I answered, "I almost dare say that they did not."

"There we have got it! Or anyhow the principal cause. It will no doubt be best for her not to return to him. That is to say, if it can be done without too much pain on her part, when the time comes. As far as he is concerned, he seemed to me to be reasonable enough. What do you think?"

"I am quite of your opinion."

My emotion was too strong to escape the notice of an experienced man. He smiled, and looked at me firmly with rather contracted eyes:

"But it will be a long business. . . . I have told her

that you have been here, and am to give you her regards. You will remain for the time being in Dresden ? That's good. Once a week I should like you to call. I think it has a calming effect on her, but a considerable time will have to pass before I shall dare to allow you to speak to her."

I returned with a good heart, and firmly decided to devote my whole life to Minna, married to her or not, in whatever manner it could best serve her welfare and health. I was satisfied to contribute all that I could to make her as little unhappy as possible, if she could not any longer be happy (though, why should she not still be capable of being so ?), without consideration of the harm it might do my career. If it would suit her best to live in her native town, I would try to get a situation in Dresden ; if she needed a southern climate, then I would find a means to live in the south. The latter, however, was not very likely ; yes, it even was most probable that England, being quite new to her, would be the most suitable place. But all this did not trouble me much. What made me shiver was the consciousness of the sword of Damocles that hung over her head. Had it perhaps at this moment already fallen ? And it would remain there constantly, even when the doctor had sanctioned her departure. Yes, even if it was taken away, my fear would still imagine it to be present. . . . But I promised myself that this terror should only make my love stronger, my tenderness more constant. How could I ever leave her in anger or even in a fit of sulkiness after a matrimonial dispute, when an inner voice whispered to me that perhaps when I returned to seize her hand and read love in her eyes, the hand would be cold and the eyes glassy ?

My uncle would have to agree to my absence, at all

events for a year. I hired a modest room as in olden days, and threw myself into a detailed study of pottery, which I hoped would be useful to our factory, and for which, both in a practical and literary respect, Dresden afforded ample opportunities.

CHAPTER VII

THE 3rd of May, in the afternoon, when almost everything was green in the gardens and in the public park, I took my usual walk out to Grosser Garten.

At the beginning of Bürgerwiese, my eye was attracted by a portrait, which hung in the window of a curio-shop. I rushed across : yes, indeed, it was Stephensen's pastel picture of Minna. But how dreadful it looked now ! The pastel powder had fallen away in big patches, especially off the hair, but also on a spot of the forehead and on the cheek ; where the one eye ought to have been, the canvas showed light through. It had been put into a worm-eaten, shabby frame in bad rococo style, and under it was written on a scrap of paper : "Unknown master, middle of the eighteenth century."

I stepped into a dark booth, where one could hardly move for old rubbish. The curio-dealer, a tall thin old man, who surely from my German detected the foreigner, and perhaps even suspected something English, mentioned an exorbitant price ; it was, he explained, one of those genuine pictures, which now grew more and more scarce, very likely a Mengs. I soon disillusioned him, and bought the picture, certainly for a good deal more than it was worth.

In Grosser Garten, I did not care to walk with a big parcel under my arm, but I needed exercise, and strolled about down the Johannes' street. Of course I had not bought the picture in order to possess it, but only because

it was to me an intolerable thought that it should hang there
" in the stocks," and later on in a stranger's house—as a
Mengs !

I thought I would take it home and burn it.

But, as I found myself facing the Albert Bridge, I was
struck suddenly by the thought : " Why not throw it into
the Elbe ? " Then I should avoid opening it, and seeing it
again.

There were only a few people on the bridge. I went out
to the parapet of the middle pillar, towards the stream ;
it was still somewhat high water. Quickly I looked round ;
there was nobody near. Then I let go the picture. It
disappeared under the water, and I heard it crush against
the ice-break of the pillar.

Depressed in spirit, I went home.

On my table lay a letter from the Professor.

Minna had died that morning, quite unexpectedly,
from apoplexy of the heart.

CHAPTER VIII

THE next morning I received a little parcel directed in Minna's handwriting, and with the asylum seal.

At the top lay six sheets of note-paper, closely written; but on the last one the writing stopped at the top of the second page.

"SONNENSTEIN, *April 17th*, 188–.

"DEAREST FRIEND,—The doctor has told me that you have been here, and brought me your regards; he also has promised to give you my love, when you come again. It is an intense consolation to me to know that you are so near.

"I will write to you, only a little now and again, for it always moves me deeply, and the doctor has impressed upon me, most of all, to avoid all agitating thoughts, which, with this one exception, I do. But write I must, because only in that way can I avoid a constant restlessness. For I have the feeling that I might die suddenly; the doctor laughs at me when I say so, but it seems to me that I can see that he himself thinks the same. Still perhaps it is only weakness. At the same time it will be a comfort to me to know that you will get a message from me, if it should happen.

"I have so much resting on my heart that I must tell you. I have collected your letters and some little things that I should not like to fall into other hands; and each time I add to this letter, I will enclose it in the parcel that I have already addressed to you.

331

" Perhaps we shall one day laugh together at this idea. God grant it may be so !

" I cannot very well bear to write any more to-night. Good-night, my Friend."

" April 18th.

" Do you know what made me carry through (by the way, with great difficulty) this trip to Rathen, before the asylum closed its doors behind me, and why I came to the Grotto ? Not only that, which likewise brought you there, but also the idea, that something would happen to me there, something extraordinary. However, not what happened, which was in reality still more wonderful, no, I thought that the agitation of mind in coming there would be too overpowering for me—that it would either kill me or drive me mad, even this I would prefer to the state of mind in which I was.

" But how blessed it was to meet you there, Harald ! I saw that you were the same, and you also felt that I was unaltered—towards you. Towards *him* I surely was changed.

" I know quite well how painful it was to you that my indignation towards him was so apparent, and still I could not help it. So nasty I have already become, so much bitterness—yes, hatred—has risen up in me.

" This you will very likely not understand.

" How is it possible to detest a human being one has loved ? Or perhaps better ask (for very likely, to you, that is what seems incomprehensible) : ' How can one love a being whom one comes to look down upon to such a degree, when by daily intercourse one gets to know his true character ? ' And here we are not speaking about a passing falling in love, for I did know something of him.

" This I have thought of more than anything else, and

in order that you may understand me thoroughly, I must tell you what I think of it.

" A nature like Stephensen's, in which from the beginning, after all, there were some noble seeds (without them I suppose he would not have been an artist, not even the artist he is) ; when such a nature, still young and not quite debased, feels love for a young girl, then he grows higher and nobler, and she comes to know—and to love—a different being from what he was before. Still, this is not a deceit ; on the contrary, she knows and loves just what he will be through their relations to one another, and in her something corresponding takes place, she develops, her character gets stronger and her views broader.

" All this is beautiful and true.

" But then the difference between the different natures appears in the course of time : such men in whom the nobler seeds are strong enough, really develop towards this ideal and gradually strengthen in it, but the others cannot keep themselves on the height to which they have been raised, they even sink below it."

" *April 20th.*

" What I wrote last strained and affected me very much. It was so sad to think of and so difficult to make plain. Yesterday I could not write anything. I will not try to develop this idea any further, though it is of great importance to me that you quite understand, for it is in this point alone that my excuse lies. But surely you have understood. I dare not insist that it answers generally, but in this case it must be so.

" It was about my life in Denmark I wanted to tell you something.

" I wonder if you remember what Sieglinde says about her life with Hunding—

"' Foreign seemed all until now,
Friendless I was and forsaken ;
I counted strange and unknown,
Each and all that came near.'

" Still it was not because of my being ' a foreigner ' in a national sense, though I suppose that has also done something. Besides, you know well that there is a good deal in the German nature and also in our art—apart from the great classics—with which I have never sympathised.

" In the beginning I really found everything lovely : liberty, broadness of mind, education, and all that sort of thing.

" But soon I felt how hollow the kernel was. I had indeed had a quintessence of the whole in Stephensen to observe too closely. After all it was no wonder that I did not blend with this circle, as it consisted of my husband's friends, anyhow by name. Some few, of course, appealed more to me. But none of them resembled you. When I now and again met a person sympathetic to me, it was as a rule one who belonged to another set, and by some chance came in touch with ours, but soon retired. That our circle, however, was the most spiritual in Denmark and represented the highest intellect of the country, I heard almost every time we met. Indeed, it was also the most honourable ; for the others were not only more or less idiots, but also sworn enemies of truth and righteousness. Ah, I could write much about these things, for I have a good memory, and I have heard many brilliant speeches !

" There was a time when I tried to settle down and give in to it ; it was my duty, Stephensen said. I thought that perhaps they were right and I was wrong, possibly I was queer and absurd. I shrugged my shoulders with the others at things that at the bottom of my heart I found noble and elevating, I tried to admire what was repulsive to my inmost self, I pretended to believe that the quality of virtue was hypocrisy and the word itself an absurdity, no, an 'indecency,' as one of Stephensen's intellectual friends said. In short, I tried to howl with the wolves I was among (after all you have wolves in Denmark, haven't you ?—do you remember when you made fun of me ?—but no lions). I did not succeed in getting my stiff neck bent, perhaps the fault is mostly yours, and this is not the least I have to thank you for."

" *April 26th.*

" We lived very sociably, as Stephensen had a real mania for diversion, and this sociability often lasted far into the night. As I had to get up early in the morning—after the German custom I was a rather industrious housewife, and had to be so to make two ends meet—this added considerably to the breaking down of my health.

" Sometimes I tried to excuse myself, which always made Stephensen most irritable. Very likely I should in the end have got my way, had it not been for one thing : my jealousy.

" How I have suffered from jealousy, I can hardly make you understand. I do not believe any man can understand it, though your sex is supposed to have produced Othellos.

" One would think that when a wife has lost so much respect and love for her husband, and when hardly any relationship exists, she would be able almost with indifference to see him run after others. With me it was almost the reverse. The cooler I felt towards him, the more burning was my jealousy. As a painter's wife I had besides a special enemy—the model. I have lowered myself to listening at the door when he had models. No wonder I could fight against sleep at insufferable parties in order to keep an eye on him.

" These efforts, unfortunately, were crowned with a terrible success. I had for a long time suspected the blonde lady you saw at Café à Porta. One day, shortly after that evening, I discovered that he had locked himself up with her in the studio, under pretence of having a model. I was so insistent that he confessed. Once having got into a sort of talkative repentance, he poured forth much more than I had suspected. I heard that his unfaithfulness went as far back as the first years, nay, even to the period when he most of all——

" No, I cannot write about it.

" How I hate him ! "

" *April 30th.*

" When my child died I grieved dreadfully, but a year had not passed before I looked upon it as a blessing. I have told you so much about my father; you see I feared that I might have been a mother of the same kind. For I felt the same process of petrifying beginning in me, like the one the effect of which I had felt as a child, and which later I have understood.

" There was now no duty to prevent me from retiring into myself. My one and only life was to read our great poets and cultivate music—especially Beethoven and Wagner, whose piano scores I possessed. It was a world after my own heart, and so different from all that I was doomed to come in contact with.

" You know how passionately fond of music I am, but also how strongly it affects my nervous system to play much. I once said to you jokingly that if I wanted to kill my reason, it would be through piano-playing. Perhaps I really have tried mentally to take my life through this heavenly poison.

"Had I seen any light, had I known what I am now aware of, surely I should have spared myself more."

"*2nd May.*

"I wish I knew really what you think of death. Do you believe in a reunion? It is difficult to realise, still, I cannot understand that my own self should quite vanish. I often think of old Hertz, whom I have heard talking about the soul and immortality on many different occasions. As it was, in the main, the doctrine of his beloved Kant (or so I understood), it is no great wonder if I, poor unlearned creature as I was and am, should not have mastered it at all. Nevertheless, it struck me deeply at that time, and in later days the mystic lore he was so fond of has recurred to me in many a lonely and desolate hour. One sentence, and I trust, the very one fitted to be the key to this whole train of thought, has stamped itself upon my memory almost word for word, because Hertz used to recapitulate it on every possible occasion, with many variations, to be sure, but it always came to this : ' What we call Self is not Self as it is in reality (only for this he had a queer phrase, ' in itself,' I think), but only as it appears in our sense-consciousness.' Now, over this sentence I have pondered many and many a time in my own stupid way, because I wanted very badly to know what my self in reality was, hoping that it might turn out to be something better than what I did know of myself. And often I have fancied that *that* which I do not know of myself, because it does not appear in the little dim mirror of consciousness, and that

22

which *you*—for the same reason—do not know of yourself, are in reality, if not exactly the same thing, at least two things that are very closely allied to one another, so much so, indeed, that it shall one day seem to us only a bad and mad dream that we could ever have been separated.

" These are odd thoughts, one may say. But they have their comforting side for all that.

" And perhaps you will not find them so very odd, after all, nor of a wholly unfamiliar stamp. For you have told me that your father was an old disciple of Schopenhauer's, and that he used to speak to you of his beliefs and his views. Now, I certainly have read nothing of Schopenhauer myself, but I remember that Hertz often mentioned him as a great thinker of the school of Kant, though rather too mystical for his taste. So, perhaps, what I have said may even have a familiar ring about it.

" But I really am glad that I have a good safe lock to my writing-case, and can shut up these sheets. For I have a shrewd suspicion that if the Professor read these ' odd thoughts ' he would have me removed at once to the other part of this great castle, where the incurables are lodged."

For a long time I sat musing with the sheet in my hand. Alas, but one remained, and only the first page was covered with writing. I had no need to hurry ! It seemed to me that all that was worth reading was there, on the last sheet of note-paper.

So I mused over these " odd thoughts," which touched me deeply. Minna was quite right : they reminded me of my dear father, recalled to my mind many a ramble by his side through our great woods, rambles on which he liked to indulge in metaphysical speculations about the " will in nature," as manifesting itself in the lives of the trees and animals of the forest. How much had I lamented, in the days of my engagement to Minna, that I could not take her to him, who would have been as sure to be a father to her as she to be a daughter to him. Both were deep and original natures and had so much in common. How fond they both were of plants and animals, how responsive to every beauty of nature! Both, too, had a strain of melancholy and a golden touch of humour. And now they had, as it were, already met; they belonged to another world, and I was left alone—oh, so utterly alone!

But in the last lines Minna was so vividly present that I could hardly realise she was no more where I could reach her. That little humorous touch of hers that gushed forth fountain-like amid thoughts of deepest earnestness and sadness, that note of subtle irony at the expense of the worthy professor, whom she had long found out as the up-to-date man of science, with no mystical nonsense whatever about him, was so thoroughly in her own dear manner, that I almost fancied I could see the arch smile on those sweet lips which now . . . alas . . . alas! . . .

And now there remained but the last page of the tiny manuscript!

At last I took heart of grace to read it.

" But why am I speaking of death and of the beyond the grave to-day? It is strange, for I have not for a very long time been in so hopeful spirits as to-day.

" The weather is so lovely. All the forenoon I have been sitting with my sewing in the Professor's garden. He is an excellent man.

" To-morrow I shall tell you more about how time goes here. But to-night I am not writing any more. I will read Schiller. The other day, when I was turning over the last volume, I got such a desire to try if I could grasp *Ueber das Erhabene.* The Professor is afraid that this kind of reading may prove trying to me, and recommends historical works. I also began to read Schiller's *Thirty Years' War,* but it wearied me dreadfully. I cannot help it ; it was already like that in my schooldays, everything historical bored me.

" Good-night, Harald ! "

The reading of this journal had created so deep and solemn an impression upon me that I had been unable to find relief in tears ; I had not yet wept since her death.

But as I finally clutched for the remaining contents of the parcel, and got a strangely crumpled and curled letter in my hand, that letter from me which she had carried on her breast, then I pressed it to my lips and sobbed like a child.

I have read again the first of these leaves. How could I write those foolish words—

" And have I ever regretted it ? Even to this very day, it is now five years ago, I am unable to answer this question."

As if I, for any prize in the world, would give up our love, give up the remembrance of Minna ! As if any happiness could be to me so precious as my grief !

I arbitrarily undertook to look after the funeral. To my joy—yes, it really was a joy to me !—I secured a grave on " Der weite Kirchhof," quite close to the resting-place of Hertz and his wife, under one of the giant poplars.

On the tomb I ordered a broken column of the most beautiful Saxonian Serpentine to be placed, without any other inscription than the name :

MINNA

CPSIA information can be obtained
at www.ICGtesting.com
Printed in the USA
BVHW010817040320
573803BV00022B/117

9 781117 316185